THE NOVEL AND REVOLUTION

The Novel
and Revolution

ALAN SWINGEWOOD

BARNES & NOBLE
BOOKS
10 East 53d St. New York 10022
(a division of Harper & Row Publishers, Inc.)

First published 1975 by
THE MACMILLAN PRESS LTD
London and Basingstoke

Published in the U.S.A. 1975 by
HARPER & ROW PUBLISHERS, INC.
BARNES & NOBLE IMPORT DIVISION

ISBN 0-06-496682-8

Printed in Great Britain

For Hazel, Michael and Peter

Contents

Preface

This book is an attempt to relate revolutionary movements, ideas and practices, or the threat of revolution, real or imagined, to the novel form. Given the great number of novels which in one way or another take revolution as their theme some selection has been inevitable. The choice of novels was ultimately narrowed down by the decision to focus exclusively on European revolution and in particular the 1917 Russian Revolution.

The book is in two parts. Part One discusses and criticises some of the current theories of the novel (Lukács, Goldmann, Ian Watt), especially their deterministic, reductionist character. Gramsci's concept of hegemony is introduced to provide a more genuinely dialectical theory and brief examples are given from English, French and Russian literature. There can be no adequate analysis of the novel, of course, unless it is related to realism and modernism and in Chapters 3 and 4 there is an attempt to explore both the concept and practice of revolution in terms of hegemony and fictional form. Equally important is the necessity to distinguish between Marxism and Stalinism and to emphasise the degeneration of Marxist literary theory after the 1920s. Part Two examines these themes and problems in the novels of Gissing, Conrad, Jack London, Zamyatin, Victor Serge, Koestler and Solzhenitsyn.

Many of the ideas in this book were first developed in the sociology of literature seminar held at the London School of Economics during the years 1970—2. Without that stimulus it is doubtful if this book would ever have been written and I would like to thank those who participated in those most enjoyable meetings.

A.S.

January 1975

The State is not competent in artistic matters.   Courbet

No new values can be created where a free conflict of ideas is impossible. . . . The dictatorship of the proletariat opens a wider scope to human genius the more it ceases to be a dictatorship. The socialist culture will flourish only in proportion to the dying away of the state.   Trotsky

I never read the products of 'socialist realism' . . . They smell of privileged rations and writers' dachas.   Nadezhda Mandelstam

PART ONE

1 Some Problems in the Sociology of the Novel

Two major, interrelated theories dominate sociological discussion of the novel. The first attributes its development to the growth of the *bourgeoisie* and modern capitalism: 'In its moral and psychological focus, in the technology of its production and distribution, in the domestic privacy, leisure and reading habits which it required from its audience, the novel matches precisely the great age of the industrial, mercantile *bourgeoisie*.'[1] The second theory suggests a more complex link between liberal ideology and the novel form:

> This state of mind has as its controlling centre an acknowledgment of the plenitude, diversity and individuality of human beings in society, together with the belief that such characteristics are good as ends in themselves. It delights in the multiplicity of existence and allows for a plurality of beliefs and values. . . . Tolerance, scepticism, respect for the autonomy of others are its watchwords; fanaticism and the monolithic creed its abhorrence.[2]

This and the following chapter will explore these two arguments and attempt to relate them to some recent discussions of the sociology of the novel and to the problems of method and general theory.

I

It is now widely accepted that the history and sociology of the novel are closely bound up with industrialisation. The novel form emerges as a major literary genre in societies characterised by industrial capital, urbanism and a fluid class-system. It is in this very general sense that the novel reflects the world view of the industrial middle class, a class whose patronage has largely sustained the novel's resilient cultural significance. Much has been written on the class origins of the novel, its fate as a cultural artefact linked directly to the ideology of individualism and secular progress of the industrial middle classes. It is argued, for example, that in its realistic historical and specific depiction of time, character and social change, and its emphasis on *detail*, the novel is clearly distinguished from previous prose fiction (epic, the picaresque). The ideology of individualism is organically bound to the novel's portrayal of the hero as an individual freed from the constraining fetters of pre-industrial 'traditional society', a hero who, rather than accept his fate and ascribed social position challenges their basis in the social order; the conflict between the individual and society is thus seen as one of the basic structures of the novel form.

The relationship between social stratification and the novel is highly complex, but it has often been stated in starkly simple terms: industrialism creates a literate middle class in need of fictional entertainment and instruction. In his influential book, *The Rise of the Novel*, Ian Watt has argued for the close social connection between the development of the novel and the English middle classes, suggesting that this class correlate is embodied in what he calls the 'formal realism' of Defoe, Richardson and Fielding. Watt defines formal realism in terms of the narrative techniques necessary for 'a full and authentic report of human experience' in which the novelist satisfies his readers 'with such detail of the story as the individuality of the actors concerned, the particulars of the time and place of their actions . . .'[3] He argues that through the increasing secularisation of culture a realist epistemology, based on *materialist* philosophy (for example John Locke) developed, thus helping to shape the novel form. Materialist philosophy held that the world constituted an objective reality existing independently of men, determining their thoughts and character; through experience and by the faculty of reason, consciousness, self and character were forged while the philosophy of individualism, the middle classes' secular creed, made clear that man's fate was not the product of God's will or divine inspiration, but flowed directly from man's complex relations with the social world:

> The novel could only concentrate on personal relations once most writers and readers believed that individual human beings, and not collectivities such as the church, or

transcendent actors, such as the Persons of the Trinity, were allotted the supreme role on the earthly stage.[4]

Defoe's hero Robinson Crusoe embodies this new secular, individualistic philosophy: his concrete aim is to transform his society, not to accept passively the status quo — making one's way is the ethic of the rising middle class.[5] Thus the role of time becomes increasingly important, for the realist novel is no 'timeless story' but a concrete historical portrait, its plot 'distinguished from previous fiction by its use of past experience as the cause of present action: a causal connection operating through time replaces the reliance of earlier narratives on disguises and co-incidences, and this tends to give the novel a more cohesive structure'.[6] Thus the rise of the urban, middle-class society of eighteenth-century England, with its circulating libraries, independent tradesmen, administrative and clerical workers, groups based on commerce and manufacture, 'may have altered the centre of gravity of the reading public sufficiently to place the middle class as a whole in a dominating position for the first time'.[7] The decline of patronage, which until the eighteenth century had been a major factor in literary production, further facilitated the emergence of the writer as a professional worker closely bound up with the middle class.

This theory of the novel as essentially a middle-class cultural product developed in the eighteenth century and brought to completion in the nineteenth has enjoyed widespread critical support. Arnold Hauser has written, for example, that Richardson's novels exercised their great influence on eighteenth-century European novelists — Goethe, Rousseau, Diderot — simply because 'he was the first to make the new middle class man, with his private life, living within the framework of the home, absorbed by family affairs, unconcerned with fictitious adventures and marvels, the centre of a literary work.' Richardson's 'reduction of the novel to the domestic scene', his portrayal of ordinary people and everyday bourgeois life, constitutes a direct reflection of a specifically middle-class culture. Thus for Hauser the eighteenth-century sentimental novel (*Pamela, La Nouvelle Héloïse*) is pre-eminently an ideological weapon used by the middle class in the struggle with the landed aristocracy; sentimentalism becomes 'the expression of bourgeois class consciousness.'[8]

Likewise, Madame de Staël, in her pioneering survey of
literature written at the beginning of the industrial age, while
arguing that literature depended for its form and content on
'national character' and climate, went on to suggest that its
development hinged on the support of a strong middle class
since only members of this class produce and sustain the
qualities of liberty and virtue without which the novel form was
impossible: 'Happy the country where the writers are gloomy,
the merchants satisfied, the rich melancholy and the masses
content.'[9]

Like Madame de Staël, Hegel linked the novel to the
bourgeoisie embodying the literary reflection of the basic
characteristics of social development, of the historical evolution
of an industrial age. The novel, he wrote, is 'the epic of the
middle class world', a world in which industrialisation,
specialisation of work, individualism and the growth of
bureaucracy condition the forms all art takes. In the modern
age human activities are highly organised, dominated by custom
and law to such an extent that man appears determined and
unfree, the antithesis of art. In epic poetry man is depicted free
and self-determined with the heroes as their own independent
masters. Thus comparing Homer with contemporary novelists,
Hegel praises Homer's 'primitive simplicity of objects' in
contrast to 'the medley of manufactured goods of modern
society'. The novel is 'a specific outlook on the world'
expressing not heroism but the 'prosaic mind', the
commonplace reality of commercial and industrial society. But
precisely because the novel is an art-form it struggles to
transcend the mundane reality of bourgeois life it necessarily
depicts, to turn everyday experience into poetry and recreate
'the banished claims of poetic vision'. As the expresssion of the
modern middle-class world, the novel reflects the fragmentation
and loss of unity implicit in the movement from a society based
on land to one dominated by commerce and industry. The epic,
in contrast, is the expression of an unorganised and heroic age
in which an organic unity of purpose and community
characterises men, nature and society. But modern industry,
with its division of labour, rationality, efficiency in work and
administration, can no longer constitute the social basis of epic
action: the ideology of individualism and the developing

division of labour succeed in tearing men away from a living contact with nature and others. The novel thus becomes the middle-class epic only in the sense that it embodies a striving for unity, for poetry in life. But the striving is negated by the reality it describes, the hero asserts his freedom and self-development within a world which denies it. The novel, concludes Hegel, embodies the contradiction between the artistic 'poetry of the heart' and 'the prose of external conditions antagonistic to it.'[10]

Hegel's discussion of the novel is important for its grasp of the relation between inner *form* and external social conditions expressed in dialectical not mechanical terms, for while the novel constitutes a middle-class cultural product, as an art-form it transcends the limitations that such a nexus imposes. The novelist must transmute material hostile to art into art; the unfreedom of the modern world and its heroes must be transformed into their opposite. Thus if the novel is art, then it cannot be grasped solely as an emanation of 'prosaic' bourgeois consciousness, which by definition is hostile to art itself.

Hegel's concept of the novel as a bourgeois art-form thus differs quite sharply from those critics who followed the environmental determinism of Madame de Staël, such as Taine, whose work strives to develop a more rigorous method for analysing literary forms, a science of literature to specify the causal elements responsible for the appearance of this or that writer, novel, poem. The sociological approach to literature originates with Taine and his sustained attempt to apply the method of the natural sciences to the social sciences, to treat literature as an external fact, the literary work as an object to dissect and analyse. For Taine, literature reflected society and an environment of racial and climatic forces; it could thus be used as a document of its period. Literary creation was transformed into the art of documentation. The novel, he wrote, was a 'portable mirror which can be conveyed everywhere and is most convenient for reflecting all aspects of life and nature.' As the major literary genre of industrial society, Taine argued, the novel depicted what was, the 'facts', and represented no more than 'an accumulation of data which through the operations of scientific laws would fall into inevitable patterns.' In nineteenth-century positivism* the novel is degraded to the status of object, it becomes the private and public record book, the repository of individualistic ideology and *useful* historical information.

This grasp of the novel as documentation became the dominant characteristic of nineteenth-century positivism; literature was analysed and judged for what it contained, quarried for information on the state of society and the moral health of man. This approach was frankly utilitarian: the novel performed the valuable social function of recording information and transmitting it to the reader; literature reflected real life with the artist illustrating its basic social features. Thus when the utilitarian Russian critic, Dobrolyubov, discussed the passive hero in Russian literature, Turgenev's Rudin and Goncharov's Oblomov, he argued that in exposing this particular *type* both writers had performed the valuable function of pointing out the serious social and moral problems of this peculiar Russian trait.[11] This mechanical approach was characteristic too, of nineteenth-century Marxism; George Plekhanov, who first applied Marx's social theory to the analysis of culture, wrote that sociological analysis consisted of searching for the 'sociological equivalents' within literary works, relating literary structures to class structures. Cultural history, he argued, represented no more than 'a reflection of its classes, of their struggle, one with another.'[12] Taine's rigid environmentalism becomes pared down to a question of opposing classes, but the status of literature remains the same: the literary work reflects society and must be analysed as a document.

Thus the sociology of literature during its development in the nineteenth century was essentially deterministic; the writer and his creative activity were reduced to an appendage of geographical or class environment. Literature was causally related to and reflected *whole societies*. And since the novel was pre-eminently produced by and for the literate middle class, it

---

*Nineteenth-century sociology was largely dominated by positivistic methodology. Originating with Comte the term came to mean the treatment of social and human activities and institutions as so many *external things* which could thus be analysed with the same scientific rigour as the objects of the natural sciences. As a result scientific laws of cause and effect could be framed. In literary analysis positivism took the form of reducing literature to a reflection and product of the writer's biography, environment or the prevailing ideology. Literature was thus assimilated completely to another, different order.

necessarily reflected their dominant values, ideology and material existence. The novel was grounded concretely in the basic structure of bourgeois society, its form and content mechanically determined by external forces which it then reflected. Taine's method, like that of Plekhanov, was *to explain away* the work of literature, to see it as a passive and total response to determinate, external conditions. There is little awareness of the complex dialectic between form and content, form and external conditions suggested by Hegel. And whereas Hegel had drawn attention to the dialectical unity of a literary work, the relations between its various parts and the whole, neither Taine not Plekhanov made any attempt to link specific parts of the text with specific external elements or to grasp the text *as a whole*, as an aesthetic unity. Taine could thus write that 'vice and virtue' were simply products like 'vitriol and sugar' and thus subject to the same research methods. Literature was no more than an objective fact, useful for illustrating sociological themes. Taine's reductionist method, therefore, produced simple, mechanical one-to-one relationships: society and literature condition one another causally and passively. Literature is produced by a series of external forces acting on a talented but passive writer: all mediations between the writer and society have been eliminated.

This mechanical and external definition of literature is clearly bound up with the positivist conception of man as an animal totally determined by the external environment, by ineluctable objective laws of social existence which condition and dominate him.* In sharp contrast, Marx, working in a wholly different direction from positivistic sociology, developed a dialectical theory of society which stressed the role of consciousness and man's activity in producing *his* world. No positivist, for example, could have written that

> At the end of every labour process, we get a result that already existed in the imagination of the labourer at its commencement. He not only effects a change in form in the material on which he works, but he also realises a purpose of

---

*The fatalism and resignation implicit in positivism were well expressed by Comte: '... the positive spirit tends to consolidate order, by the rational development of a wise resignation to incurable political evils. A true resignation ... can proceed from a deep sense of the connection of all kinds of natural phenomena with invariable natural laws.'

his own that gives the law to his modus operandi, and to which he must subordinate his will. And this subordination is no mere momentary act. Besides the exertion of the bodily organs, the process demands that, during the whole operation, the workman's will be steadily in consonance with his purpose.

or:

By thus acting on the external world and changing it, he at the same time changes his own nature. He develops his slumbering powers and compels them to act in obedience to his sway . . .[13]

This is Marx's concept of *praxis*, human purposes and human activity, the ways whereby man ascribes significance and meaning to the social world. But to write of *praxis* is at once to raise the problem of Marxist determinism. Marx's remarks in such writings as *The German Ideology* and *A Contribution to the Critique of Political Economy* on the dependent relation of the 'superstructure' of society (its culture) to its 'base' (the economic infrastructure) have moved many critics to condemn attempts to derive a theory of literature from Marx as one-dimensional and reductionist*. But such interpretations ignore what is perhaps the more significant emphasis in Marx's writings on the life and movement of social phenomena, the complex richness of economic, technological, and cultural structures; they transform him from a dialectical to a mechanical materialist, a standpoint his whole work rejects. To be sure, the physical environment which comprises geography and climate is independent of man in the strictly mechanical sense implied by Madame de Staël and Taine; but an entirely different relationship subsists between the objects of the social world, such as tools and machinery, and man himself. In his *Grundrisse* (1857—8), for example, Marx wrote that locomotives and the electric telegraph are not the products of nature but of human

---

*'In the social production which men carry on they enter into definite relations that are indispensable and independent of their will; these relations of production correspond to a definite stage of development of their material forces of production. The sum total of these relations of production constitutes the economic structure of society — the real foundation, on which rises a legal and political superstructure and to which correspond definite forms of social consciousness. The mode of production in material life determines the social, political and intellectual life processes in general. It is not the consciousness of men that determines their being, but, on the contrary, their social being that determines their consciousness.' Marx, *A Contribution to the Critique of Political Economy* (Moscow, 1971) pp. 20—1.

activity, 'natural material transformed into organs of the human will to dominate nature or to realize itself therein . . . organs of the human brain, created by human hands.'[14] The relationship of man to society is thus far from the mechanical, but is complex and dialectical, for as man changes his environment through the inventions and applications of science and technology, so he changes himself, his nature.

Such observations are clearly relevant for a theory of literature: the written and the spoken word embodied in printed books and oral tradition do not merely describe and imitate the social world in a mechanical and passive manner, rather they function as man's cultural technology for his understanding and mastering of the historical and social world. Literature and human purpose are inextricably intertwined; the values by which man in society lives are rendered through definite literary and artistic structures and in this sense reflect his desire to reshape the world. For although Marx argued for the crucial role of class conflict in shaping economic, political and social structures, he continually emphasised that society was made by men — but not men living in isolation from others. Marx's analysis of capitalism showed that the isolated individual of classical political economy was simply an illusion: each individual belonged concretely to a social class, a social group, his experiences within this group conditioning his total response to society. But this is not to suggest that every single act flows irresistibly from an external cause; the argument that Marx minimised (or even eliminated) the role of the individual in favour of socio-economic determinism ignores the very basis of his social theory, that the social world is made by men, modified and changed by human *praxis*.

Marx wrote little on literature that compares with his analysis of economics, politics and philosophy, but two important points can be made:

1. Marx saw writers who directly expressed class interests in their work as mediocre artists, for the *immediate* transposition of economic and political interests into literature transforms it into ideology and thus bad art.*

*Marx's analysis of the petty bourgeois poet supporters of the 1848 bourgeois revolution, whose art served openly to defend the interests of private property and the capitalist state, together with his discussion of Eugene Sue's celebrated novel, *Les Mystères de Paris*, leave no doubt that when political interests are transposed directly into literature it becomes ideology, useful only as a document, nothing more than an epiphenomenon.

2. It is only when the writer transcends his own class standpoint — and all writers are bound historically and sociologically to a specific social group and class — that he reflects truthfully the nature of society and man's relations within it. That is, the creative writer becomes a critic of society precisely because of the dialectical relation of artistic activity to social values, individuals, institutions, society.

Thus, for Marx, Balzac's accurate historical depiction of French society was possible only because he transcended his narrow ideological sympathy with the French nobility (historically doomed as a class) to express artistically the triumph of the bourgeois class. And Shakespeare, in his portrayal of the dominating power of money over human relationships (in *Timon of Athens*), grasped the fact of alienation which the very structure of bourgeois society necessarily produced.[15] The trans-individual element thus cuts across Plekhanov's notion of 'class equivalents' and for the genuine creative writer there cannot be a direct transposition of class interests into literature. This theme was taken up by Marx's collaborator, Engels. Writing to Mary Harkness, whose novel *A City Girl* was published in 1888, Engels urged that she adopt a less militant and obvious political standpoint. A socialist novel, he wrote, achieved its purpose not through a direct political commitment, but by depicting the bourgeois world realistically, that is, 'by breaking down conventional illusions' and inducing doubt on 'the eternal character of the existing order, although the author does not offer any definite solution or . . . line up openly on any particular side.' This, and other writings of Engels, no more than mere *suggestions*, have tended to become the basis of a Marxist literary theory. Here Engels discussed realism and the relation between realistic portrayal of period and character in terms which make it absolutely clear that a Marxist theory of literature must reject the view that literature reflects class and economic interests *mechanically*. Thus his analysis of Balzac's *Human Comedy* is built around the negation within Balzac's art of his private and reactionary support for the French nobility:

> Well, Balzac was politically a legitimist . . . his sympathies are with the class that is doomed to extinction. But for all that, his satire is never keener, his irony never more bitter, than

when he sets in motion the very men and women with whom
he sympathises most deeply — the nobles. And the only men
of whom he speaks with undisguised admiration are his
bitterest political antagonists, the republican heroes . . . the
men who at that time [1830—6] were indeed representatives
of the popular masses.

Marx, too, in his comments on Diderot's ironical novel *Rameau's
Nephew* opposed any mechanical relation between artistic
activity and economic structure. For Marx, Diderot's anti-hero,
the cynical, worldly sponger living off the charity of others can
be understood only in terms of alienation. Marx echoes Hegel's
analysis of the novel in his *Phenomenology of Spirit* (1807)
when he writes of the sponger's 'scornful laughter' at existence,
his 'imperious' character and describes him as 'the self
expressing pessimism of the self consciousness'. For Marx,
Diderot's novel is explicable in terms of the 'negative' aspect of
historical progress, of the alienation of man within bourgeois
society, and not simply a reflection of the bourgeois class's
struggle with the French aristocracy in the late eighteenth
century.[16]

This concept of alienation is crucial for Marx's general social
theory and particularly for the relation between literature and
society. Marx analysed capitalism as a system of production,
which, through its extended division of work including that
between mental and manual labour, had the effect of creating a
society in which man's sense of *wholeness*, his potential
manysidedness, becomes reduced to a mere fragment — his
sensual, emotional, creative potential turned into one
specialised activity, a limiting work function. Capitalism, its
system of private property and the domination of one class over
another, creates the social conditions in which man's labour, *his
creative potential*, becomes an external, oppressive activity,
something which, rather than fulfilling him, 'denies him'. Man
within capitalist production is a thing, an object, his labour a
commodity to be bought and used by *others*, the capitalists, the
State, bureaucracy. Man's labour becomes 'forced labour' and
the world an alien and hostile place.

The problem of alienation raises the question of the writer's
position in alienated society and the fact of alienation within
the creative act itself. For the writer who works within a society

dominated by the values of the capitalist market in which social relations are increasingly mediated through money and things, the creative act becomes in itself an important aspect of the struggle against alienation. It is in this sense that man creates his social world, moulding and changing himself as he changes society and nature; man is not simply an appendage of an external economic process going on *outside* him *in* society, the prisoner of external laws and tendencies over which he has no control. Man is the agent whose activity is the social world, but it is a social world of alienated relations, in which he finds himself an object of others. Creativity is the direct antithesis of such alienated relations.

Thus there is no direct, one-to-one relation between literature and society, rather a complex structure of mediations. Literature is not a passive reflection of determinate interests — class, race environment — or merely the personal biography of the writer; rather, literature emerges as both an interrogation and a questioning of reality, the complex response of specific men, who live out their lives within specific social groups, to the dominating human, social and political problems of their time. It is such questions as the degree of autonomy which literature and the writer enjoys, the dialectical relation between the inner world of a literary work and its external existence as cultural artefact, which constitute perhaps the essential problem of the sociology of the novel.

II

In Marx's writings there are hints, suggestions but no theory of literature. Clearly Marx opposed the reductionist tendency of positivism, striving to see literature as more than a mere document and passive reflection of historical processes and social facts. However, a Marxist literary theory cannot be built from fragments of letters and occasional asides; it must be based on the basic elements of Marx's social theory. Of course, this involves explaining a literary work in class terms, but not mechanically. Above all, the explanation will be *genetic*, that is, seek to understand literature as a living, creative *praxis*. The text under analysis should not bear the status of object, as with positivism, not be *used* simply to illustrate social, economic and political history in which the different parts are ripped out of their context to serve as illustrative material; rather the parts must be grasped in terms of the *whole*. The major weakness of the sociology of literature as it developed from the work of Taine lies precisely in its failure both to generate a distinctive method of analysis and in its strictly utilitarian concept of literature. The failure of method is bound up with this functional, non-creative definition of literature, and in the refusal to treat separate literary texts as wholes, as totalities in their own right within which the separate parts function and acquire their meaning in relation to the whole.

Such an approach, explicit within Hegel's aesthetics, emerges only in twentieth-century sociology and literary theory largely as a reaction against nineteenth-century positivism. Russian Formalism, modern structuralism and semiology, the American New Criticism and in England the work of F. R. Leavis reject the positivistic concept of literature as an epiphenomenon of economics, geography, psychology or biography. Literature is defined not in terms of an extra-literary environment but as a self-enclosed structure having its own laws, conventions, traditions. In his essay 'Literary Environment' the Russian Formalist, Boris Eichenbaum, raised 'the problem of the interrelationship between the facts of literary evolution and those of literary environment.' He accepted that changes in the writer's social and economic position must influence literary production, but remained adamant that 'literature, like any other specific order of things, is not generated from facts belonging to other orders and therefore cannot be reduced to such facts . . . the facts of the literary order and facts extrinsic to it cannot simply be causal relations but can only be the relations of correspondence, interaction, dependency, or conditionality.' Since literature is not reducible to, or simply derivative of, another order 'there is no reason to believe that all its constituent elements can be genetically conditioned'.[17] The extrinsic can be only mere background and literature becomes a *praxis* in itself, generating from within itself its own momentum, development, innovation. Thus the emphasis on literary culture, the literary traditions as the most important external factors shaping literary evolution. It is in this spirit that F. R. Leavis criticises what he calls the 'contextual approach', and the whole of his work, although it differs sharply from formalism and structuralism, can be read as a sustained attack on a method which binds literature deterministically to extra-

literary forces: 'The serious critic's concern with literature of
the past is with its life in the present . . . informed by a kind of
perception that can distinguish intelligently and sensitively the
significantly new life in contemporary literature.'[1][8]

These formulations of Eichenbaum and Leavis are directed as
much against positivism as the cruder forms of Marxism which
dominated the Marxist movement at the turn of the century.
The anti-positivist schools of thought identified and rejected as
Marxism the naive and mechanical theories of 'base' and
'superstructure': when Leavis writes, for example, that 'the
dogma of the priority of economic conditions' constitutes
everything which his magazine *Scrutiny* opposes for while
culture is closely bound up with the means of production the
cultural tradition survives irrespective of economic change, this
is not a criticism of Marx (although Leavis believes this to be
so).[19] The profound weakness of Marxist literary theory in the
face of these criticisms can best be illustrated by turning to the
work of Lukács* widely regarded as the most significant
Marxist literary theorist of the twentieth century, generously
described by George Steiner as 'the one major talent to have
emerged from the grey servitiude of the Marxist world.'[20]

Lukács's 'talent', however, has less to do with a developed
Marxist theory of literature than with the social function of
literature and its value for education. His aesthetic is frankly
utilitarian and his frequent praise for the nineteenth-century
Russian materialists — Chernyshevsky, Dobrolyubov, Pisarev —
is clearly related to their pragmatic concept of literature as
useful or harmful documentary material for developing or
retarding social consciousness.[21] Thus for Lukács the great
realist writers — Balzac, Tolstoy, Mann — are to be read for
their *example*, acknowledged for their moral power over the
reader. Lukács sees Tolstoy's art as a 'means' of communicating
a specific content, a 'sermon' to humanity for the renewal of
positive ideals; the nineteenth-century Swiss novelist, Gottfried

---

*The literary work of Georg Lukács (1885—1971) falls into two distinct phases. The
first is the pre-Marxist writings of the period 1908—19 which inlude *The Soul and
the Form,* and *The Theory of the Novel,* the latter forming part of an unfinished
Aesthetic. The second phase, beginning with his membership of the Hungarian
Communist Party in 1919, corresponds with the triumph of Stalinism in the Soviet
Union and the defeat of the European revolution. Living in Russia during the 1930s
Lukács wrote many of the studies on which his present reputation rests: *Studies in
European Realism, The Historical Novel, Essays on Thomas Mann.*

Keller, is praised for achieving 'the unity of the poetic and the needs of popular education', while Thomas Mann became, through his novels, 'the educator of his people'.[22]

This documentary, ethical function of the novel is close to Taine's positivism, which is frequently criticised by Lukács as reductionist. Lukács formal argument is that great literature mirrors its age through the artist's active participation and involvement with 'progressive' social trends. But, like Taine, Lukács uses literary texts to furnish evidence for the 'progressive' elements of the text itself, that is, the literary features are compared with real *social* tendencies and not set in their own specific literary context; their meaning is fixed wholly *outside* the text. Literature comes to reflect society as a whole in much the same way as it does in the work of Taine and Plekhanov, and the only mediation between the text and society becomes the individual writer himself. Lukács is concerned with great realist literature, especially the novel, which he links in its development directly with the 'progressive' bourgeois class. His argument is that realism embodies an objective approach to the social world and thus realist fiction provides a convincing picture of historical and social change. But objectivity is not created spontaneously: the ways in which a novel mirrors society are not direct but intentional, for objective reflection, Lukács argues, depends on the writer's attitude towards social development. His depiction of society will be objective only if he makes the right choice of material, a choice made possible in two ways.

(a) If the writer lives in a society characterised by 'progressive' social tendencies such as an economically expanding bourgeois class engaged in developing capitalism (for example, Goethe, Balzac, Stendhal, Tolstoy);

(b) or, living in a politically reactionary period when the bourgeois class has become parasitic and a fetter on the further development of society (in Western Europe, post 1848) he actively fights against decadence (Keller, Mann).

Thus genuine realism, true objectivity, is entrusted to the personal honesty of the writer, to the individual. Yet it is this same individual who, according to Lukács's sociological analysis, must become increasingly alienated in bourgeois society:

> The really honest and gifted bourgeois writers who lived and wrote in the period following the great upheavals of 1848 naturally could not experience and share the development of their class with the same true devotion and intensity of feeling as their predecessors . . . And because in the society of their time they found nothing to support wholeheartedly . . . they remained mere spectators of the social process.[23]

The high point of the realist novel is thus coeval with the social domination of the bourgeois class as a whole; with the advent of socialism and the working-class movement bourgeois society is condemned by the very historical forces its own activities had brought into being. The writer becomes an *onlooker*, an impartial spectator of society. Yet this formulation is inconsistent with one of the main elements of Marx's social theory, that society is not defined in terms of a heap of individuals, i.e. atomised, but consists of definite social formations — classes and groups within classes. Marx had defined class broadly, in terms of the systems of economic production, but he had also argued that class consciousness resulted from one class opposing another, a conflict nexus which generates class identification and solidarity; the different groups within the class are thus bound together and become one. Thus the writer's relation to his class is clearly important: in his social origins the nineteenth-century realist writer was part of the middle class and in general remained within this class although not always in sympathy with it. It is precisely this mediation which is missing in Lukács's analysis: at no point does he relate the specific writer to a concrete social group and the literary works to the specific social structure of this group. For Lukács the writer does not transpose a world view of a class on a literary level, but rather reflects in his work the 'progressive' forces at work in the economic heart of society, always providing he possesses the necessary moral qualities or the good fortune to be writing when such 'progressive' trends characterise society as a whole.

The lack of a concrete analysis of the specific groups within which writers function as social animals and the definition of society as an undifferentiated whole, lead Lukács into a basic dilemma: how is it possible to distinguish different writers of the same generation? Lukács's failure of method is nowhere more blatant than his attempts to claim Turgenev, Tolstoy and Dostoevsky as realists, and Stendhal and Balzac as identical in their *form*. Thus while he can write of Stendhal's 'romanticism' and Balzac's 'fantastic' elements — the character of Vautrin, for example, — both are subsumed under the generic concept of realism; these elements are not *explained*, rather isolated from the text and not grasped as part of the overall structure of Balzac's and Stendhal's world view.

These problems are further highlighted in Lukács's discussion of Russian nineteenth-century realism. In his analysis of Tolstoy he follows Engels, arguing that the late development of Russian capitalism created a bourgeois class and ideology less apologetic than that existing in Western Europe: 'The social conditions [in Russia] which favoured realism and which determined the development of European literature from Swift to Stendhal were still in existence . . . though in a different form and in greatly changed circumstances.'[24] Unlike Western Europe, Lukács argues, Russia was not riven by class conflict; the battle between the proletariat and the bourgeoisie had not yet become 'the central issue of every social problem' for the slow growth of capitalism 'delayed' the appearance of this conflict in literature. Tolstoy could thus become 'the poetic mirror' of Russian social development at a time when European realism was declining into the 'naturalism' of Flaubert and Zola. For Tolstoy's realism was closely bound up with the awakening of revolutionary possibilities, and unlike Flaubert and Zola he was no mere spectator but a writer passionately involved with life, with the problems of the masses. He could thus present a more accurate picture of society than his contemporary Dostoevsky who was not so closely involved with the life of the Russian people. Yet Lukács claims that Dostoevsky was just as realistic as Tolstoy, notwithstanding the 'irrational' elements in his fiction (the 'underground man', for example). Lukács sees Dostoevsky, as much as Tolstoy, reflecting the dynamics of late Russian capitalist development, and therefore both writers must be broadly similar in their artistic method; both are realists.

Lukács argues that Dostoevsky's work expressed a deep crisis

in Russian society. In contrast to Tolstoy's sympathetic
portrayal of the Russian peasant, Dostoevsky's fiction embraced
the city and its 'urban misery', depicting 'the same process of
dissolution of the old Russia and the germs of its rebirth . . . in
the misery of the cities.' The apparent chaos of the
Dostoevskian world, writes Lukács, is no more than 'a powerful
protest against everything false and distorting in modern
bourgeois society.' In short, Dostoevsky was *on the side* of the
underdog, 'the insulted and the injured', and it is this which
constitutes the 'progressive' element, a beacon shining 'in the
darkness of Petersburg misery, a light that illuminates the road
to the future of mankind.'[25] Dostoevsky — with his deep
religiosity, his hatred of Western Europe, industrialisation and
science, his essential mysticism, all important elements of his
fiction — was simply 'lucky' to live at a time when external
social and economic processes were broadly 'progressive' (the
industrialisation of Russia) and so mitigated the irrational
components of his 'realism'.

Thomas Mann was not so fortunate, for he wrote at the time
when imperialism and capitalism had reached a state of
profound crisis. Unlike Dostoevsky, Mann's realism was more
the result of personal decision. *The Magic Mountain*, for
example, is characterised by Lukács as 'progressive' because it
accurately reflects bourgeois society and its basic problems,
presenting 'a complete picture of bourgeois life'. Yet how is
such genuine realism *possible* in the imperialist period? The
answer is simple: Mann was personally associated with broad
progressive political currents; after 1918 he grasped the essential
fact that without democracy 'a truly German culture' was
impossible and thus the struggle for democracy became for him
a struggle against German decadence — that is, irrationalism in
art and pessimism about the future. Thus Mann developed
individually beyond his bourgeois vision given by a bourgeois
birth and social position to a position which acknowledged
socialism as inevitable.[26] Mann was able to create realistic
fiction because he transcended alienation *personally*, as an
individual: his honesty is thus the most important dimension
for Lukács — a curious analysis from a follower of Marx.

Thus for Lukács the novel reflects the economic and
political fortunes of the bourgeois class and *society as a
whole*. Clearly, the general historical development of bourgeois

society is important for understanding the evolution of the
realist novel, but to argue that such a general history is the
sufficient condition for grasping the meaning of specific literary
texts is wholly unscientific. Such a history cannot adequately
explain cultural contradictions — Sterne and Fielding, Balzac
and Stendhal, Tolstoy and Dostoevsky, Mann and Kafka — for
Lukács's 'method' is not designed to explain the complex,
dialectical relations between literature and society. Like Taine,
he establishes a system of rigidly deterministic connections,
and the specific differences between writers are explained
away as a result of background, education and personal
ideology. Lukács at no point relates the specific text to
the writer's own specific mode of existence: there are no
mediations, only a simple reflex of politics and economy. The
text is sliced up to illustrate a predetermined social theme: that
capitalism was 'progressive' but is no longer. For Georg Lukács
a work of literature is never grasped as a coherent whole, only
as the embodiment of 'progressive' or 'non-progressive' social
forces.

This brief discussion of Lukács highlights the obvious but
important point that writers are not socially isolated but live
their lives within definite social groups and through the
processes of socialisation — in the institutions of education,
family, politics — articulate values and a specific view of reality,
a *praxis* which finds a complex expression within their work.
The revolutionary Marxist, Leon Trotsky, once wrote that
'artistic creativity . . . is a very complex web which is not
woven automatically . . . but comes into being through complex
interrelations . . .'[27] It is this grasp of the specific mediations
involved in the writer—society nexus which constitutes the
hallmark of a genuine sociology of the novel.

III

In general the Marxist theory of literature has remained firmly
positivistic in orientation, grounded in a highly deterministic
theory of history in which the writer becomes the medium
through which significant social—historical trends find literary
expression. Lukács is perhaps the best representative of this
tendency which attributes to capitalism the power both to
create great literature and, in its inexorable decline, an

alienated, dehumanised art. In *Illusion and Reality* (1937)
Caudwell writes:

> The novel was bound to develop . . . under capitalism, whose
> increase in the productive forces brought about by the
> division of labour not only vastly increased the
> differentiation of society but also, by continually
> revolutionising its own basis, produced an endless flux and
> change in life. Equally, as capitalism decayed, the novel was
> bound to voice the experience of men that economic
> differentation had changed from a means of freedom to a
> rubber-stamp crushing individuality . . . . Necessarily
> therefore in such a period the decay of the novel occurs
> together with a general revolutionary turmoil.[28]

And Ernst Fischer argues quite simply that to attain a genuine
objectivity the modern writer must take 'sides with the working
class' and adopt 'the viewpoint of an undogmatic Marxist.[29] In
the face of such crude formulations it is hard to resist the
argument of the American critic Northrop Frye who, with
Marxism in mind, writes that 'instead of fitting literature
deterministically into a pre-fabricated scheme of history, the
critic should see literature as . . . a unified, coherent and
autonomously created form, historically conditioned but
shaping its own history, not determined by any external
historical process.'[30] Dogmatic Marxist theories are easy targets
for such criticism, and the strength of critics such as Frye, as
well as contemporary structuralists, lies in their grasp of the
literary work as a whole and the importance of specific literary
conventions and traditions for analysis. However, the weakness
of these critics lies in their dogmatic assertion that the literary
can never be explained in terms of the non-literary, that a
sociological explanation must automatically assimilate literature
to history and the social context. Of course no one would deny
the importance of literature as an influence on literature, but
the significant point about such formulations is that literature
itself does not select the elements of the existing tradition to
develop or reject. Such selection is carried out by the writer
himself; his selection and the ways in which he transforms
particular structures within the literary culture are not
explicable except by reference to the extrinsic, to the writer's
social values and his group affiliations. Thus while many

structuralist critics acknowledge the importance of social factors in the production of literature, they often give the impression that they would rather society and history did not exist at all. Too often structuralist analysis of literature comes close to denying its essential character as part of a human as well as social context serving man's ends and purposes; for without such purposes there would be no literature of any kind. Lucien Goldmann's 'genetic structuralism' is one recent attempt, working within a broad Marxist framework, to combine a grasp of literature as a partly autonomous whole with the specific historical context without reducing it to epiphenomena.* However, as will be argued, while Goldmann's work represents a clear advance beyond the dogmatic Marxism of Lukács, he ultimately fails to develop a genuinely dialectical theory.

Goldmann's approach centres on the concept of 'collective consciousness'. He writes, 'A literary work is not the simple reflection of a real and actual collective consciousness, but the outcome, at the level of a highly developed coherence, of the tendencies proper to the consciousness of this or that group, a consciousness which must be conceived as a dynamic reality . . .[31] The relationship between individual literary works and the collective consciousness which they express lies in what Goldmann calls an 'homology of structures', that is, the internal structure of a literary work bears a close parallel relation to a specific social structure. The internal coherence of a novel, for example, is made to depend on homology; literature, which embodies the collective consciousness, is thus based on an external relation but one which does not imply an identity of content. Thus the social character of literature flows from the fact that an individual *by himself* is incapable of establishing 'a coherent mental structure', 'a world vision'. Goldmann's concept of world vision refers to 'the whole complex of ideas, aspirations and feelings which links together the members of a social group' who thus attain a coherent consciousness of the world. A world vision — total complexes of thought such as rationalism , empiricism, Marxism — is expressed only by

*Goldmann's most important writings in the sociology of literature are the study of the 'Tragic Vision' in the philosophy of Pascal and the theatre of Racine, *The Hidden God* (1956), and the short programmatic essays on Malraux, Robbe-Grillet and the new novel, *Pour une Sociologie du Roman* (1964). While Goldmann's work is silent on the Marxist writings of Lukács, it is strongly influenced by the pre-Marxist essays on the novel and tragedy as well as the later *History and Class Consciousness* (1923).

'exceptional individuals', writers and philosophers, in whose work the vision takes a 'complete and integrated form'. A world vision expresses 'the whole of life' and constitutes 'the maximum possible awareness' of a specific social group and class.[32] The talented individual transposes this vision on to the level of creative thought developing it to the highest possible coherence.

Goldmann, then, approaches literature not as a passive mimesis of the writer's class position, nor is the writer *as an individual* asked to transcend alienation for, *as an individual*, he expresses the aspirations, values, feelings of a particular social group. Of course the collective consciousness of a social group develops as the result of the individual's own activity within the social world, from his active involvement in political, economic and social life. There is therefore a *praxis*, and literary works emerge out of the writer's and the group's social activity. Goldmann's method recognises that literary structures are made and remade by men through human *praxis* and are not simply *given facts*. Class is significant in this respect, for social classes are made up of particular social groups and it is through membership of specific groups — occupational, legal, familial — that the individual is linked with major social and political change. Thus the individual's group affiliations sharpen his awareness of the social world, driving him to express, however obliquely, the significant social tendencies of his period in a literary or philosophical form.

Goldmann calls his method genetic structuralism: genetic for its stress on literature as a creative process, each literary work developing historically and organically from the conjunction of the writer's social position and the values of his group and class (Goldmann's 'collective subject'). The writer extrapolates the significant structures of his group through a literary work. Goldmann's premise here is that all human activity strives to be significant. All men aim to make a coherent and significant structure of their thought and as a specific form of activity literary creation achieves coherence and significance to the extent that it approximates to the social, political, and ideological aspirations of the group. Genetic structuralism seeks to identify the significant structures within each literary work and those external to it in the group, and is in essence a continual movement, a shuttling forwards and backwards from the text to the social structure of the writer's group. The literary work is analysed continually in terms of parts and the whole — with each part related to the whole of the text from which its ultimate literary meaning derives. In this methodology Goldmann clearly follows Marx, for whom the isolated fact was simply meaningless, acquiring significance only by reference to the whole from which it had initially been abstracted for analysis. This shuttling between the whole and the part constitutes the essence of dialectical analysis.

In brief this is Goldmann's *method*, a sociology of literature concerned with cultural creation not simply production for the market. Its deterministic aspects are obvious: the writer expresses the consciousness of his social group at a particular historical moment and although Goldmann emphasises the complex, dialectical relation of the individual to the group, and the group to the class, there is implicit within the method a mechanistic nexus of social group and social development. Perhaps this point can be made clearer by turning to his discussion of the novel *Pour une Sociologie du Roman* in which Goldmann suggests a theory wholly different from those theories discussed earlier which anchored the novel's origin and structure deterministically to the bourgeois class. He begins with a discussion of Georg Lukács's pre-Marxist essay, *The Theory of the Novel*, which, unlike the work of Taine and Plekhanov, attempts to develop a genuine theory of the novel *form*. The debt to Hegel is obvious: the novel, Lukács writes, constitutes an attempt by modern man to reconcile life (existence) with true self (his essence) through a form of epic narration. But the novel must remain a pale shadow of the true epic for the historical conditions which made the epic possible, the organic community with its unquestioned value system, have disappeared in the Western world. Lukács describes the epic as an 'extensive totality', a closed art form in which the hero is never an individual for the epic must describe not his destiny but that of the community: the epic hero never questions the values of the community and is never lonely, connected as he is 'by indissoluble threads to the community whose fate is crystallised in his own.' In contrast, the hero of the novel is the product of man's alienation from the world, a world in which values are no longer universally binding and where the individual is no longer bound to a closed community. Unlike the hero of the epic, the hero of the novel develops an inner life; he becomes solitary and subjective, forever brooding on life's meaning. No longer part of a meaningful organic world, the hero of the novel must seek meaning to his life through individual action: the novel is therefore an unfinished art-form forever fluctuating between 'being' and 'becoming', the novelist striving to impose a sense of wholeness on an irrevocably fragmented world. Thus the novel 'is the epic of an age in which the extensive totality of life is no longer directly given, in which the immanence of meaning in life has become a problem, yet which still thinks in terms of totality.' The hero is therefore 'problematical', he must stand in opposition to nature and society, and because for Lukács the novel seeks to 'uncover and construct the concealed totality of life' the hero must seek the goals and meaning of life within a mundane world which denies and frustrates him. Thus the 'structural instability' inherent in the novel form flows directly from the necessary tensions between the 'problematic hero' and the contingent world, the conflict between the universal values sought by the hero and the brute fact that in a mundane, commonplace world they are impossible to realise. For to realise such values would be to destroy the novel form itself and recreate epic wholeness.[33] The essence of Lukács's early theory of the novel is thus the antagonism between the external world, 'a stranger to ideals and an enemy of interiority', and man's inner 'soul': 'The novel tells of the adventure of interiority; the content of the novel is the story of the soul that goes to find itself, that seeks adventures in order to be proved and tested by them, and, by proving itself, to find its own essence.'[34]

Having thus defined the novel in idealist Hegelian terms, Lukács elaborates a typology of forms which in Goldmann's sociological discussion are related to specific social structure. Goldmann argues that the concept of a problematic hero characterised the novel as it developed during the nineteenth century, for the essence of middle-class liberal ideology lay in its strict code of individualism and its appeal to the formal, universal values of liberty, equality and tolerance, values which underpin *individual* development. It is from these values that 'the category of individual biography as the constitutive element of the novel' emerges, but a category in which the hero 'will take the form of the problematic individual'. In bourgeois literature the tension generated between idealistic values and the mundane world creates different types of novel: the novel of 'abstract idealism' in which the hero struggles hopelessly to find a rapport between his own ideal values and those of a world which he sees as outmoded and traditional (Cervantes' *Don Quixote*; Stendhal's *Scarlet and Black*); the psychological novel built around the subjective state and passivity of the hero whose values are too generous for the world (Goncharov's *Oblomov*, Flaubert's *Sentimental Education*); and finally, the novel of education (Goethe's *Wilhelm Meister* and the novels of the Swiss writer, Keller).

These different forms of the novel develop not as the products of exceptional individuals, but from the complex interrelations between the writer's social group and society. Goldmann, unlike the young Lukács, stresses the sociological mediations: society is not atomised but composed of definite social strata, social classes engaged in capitalist production with a similarity of economic rewards and life-style. Each social class is not homogeneous but made up of definite strata, some of which can be analysed as distinct groups — although the groups themselves are united in as far as they share a broadly similar social and economic relation to society as a whole. Writers in the main are born into and remain within the upper and middle classes of society, since writing as a distinct activity requires both education and leisure and thus a degree of culture denied to the mass of the population. Goldmann's argument is that a writer's text reflects this privileged status on the one hand and yet through his activity as a creative worker a transcendent critical element on the other. The novel of the problematic hero is the novel of bourgeois society, but a novel which refuses to accept bourgeois values. In short, while the bourgeois class develops the social conditions and an ideology which makes the novel form possible, its practical involvement in transforming society into capitalism drives its writers into some form of critical opposition.

Goldmann suggests that the novel of the problematic hero, that is, of bourgeois realism, is closely related to the concept of 'exchange value' within capitalist society. Capitalism, he argues, defines the relations between men strictly in terms of their labour power, which then comes to be regarded solely as a commodity. In the capitalist market, commodities are the sole

mediation between the individual and society as a whole; the
value of human labour and thus of humanity is equivalent to
the 'exchange values' determined by the economic market-
place. The relations between men, therefore, are 'debased',
'inauthentic', mediated through a *thing*, a commodity. It is for
this reason that the realist novel finds the depiction of genuine
human values increasingly problematical. For creative writers
are essentially guided not by 'exchange values' but by 'use
values' and thus exist more and more on the fringes of society,
becoming themselves problematic individuals. In short, the
novel form in its development embodies a struggle between the
genuine values of humanism and the 'degraded' values of
capitalist civilisation.

The novel, then, becomes 'a form of critical opposition', a
creative act of resistance 'to the ongoing development of
bourgeois society'. But this opposition is within the novel form
itself. Thus 'the novel of the problematic hero' constitutes a
literary form closely related 'to the history and development of
the bourgeoisie, but not expressing either the actual or possible
consciousness of that class.'[35]

Given this dialectical nexus of the novel form, the writer's
group and class structure, Goldmann's conclusion is less than
satisfactory In discussing the historical development of the
novel he asserts a dogmatic, mechanical relation between the
economic structure of capitalism and literary forms; economic
forces are transposed directly into cultural activity: 'In market
geared societies the collective consciousness progressively loses
all sense of active reality and tends to become a simple
reflection of economic life.' Goldmann, in short, argues for a
causal link between the novel and *society as a whole*. He
describes three broad historical periods; the first, corresponding
to the growth of cartels and monopolies and colonial expansion
(1880–1914), is reflected in the decline of the hero within the
novel; between 1918 and 1939, the period of 'crisis capitalism',
the hero more or less disappears from the novel, a process which
'consumer capitalism', 1945 onwards, completes.

We have here, in Goldmann's sociological expansion of
Lukács's idealist theory of the novel, a reversion to the positivism
of Taine and the reductionist theories of Plekhanov and the
later Lukács. The novel becomes an unmediated vision of an

increasingly alienated society, the writer passively responding to broad socio-economic change. The dialectical relation of writers to social group, culture, society is eliminated in favour of a fatalistic theory of history; paradoxically Goldmann's sociological theory of the novel has embraced the very position his method had set out to attack. On the one hand there remains a *dialectical* emphasis on the internal criticism of bourgeois society from within the novel form itself, while on the other hand a *mechanical* argument that attributes the decline of the hero to the growth of a collectivist society. The novel accurately reflects the total movement from liberal capitalism to 'organised' capitalism; the hero is replaced by a fictional structure dominated by objects and things (Kafka, Sartre, Camus). Goldmann's sociological theory of the novel seems remarkably close to those critics for whom the novel, by definition, portrays the complex diversity of human experience through a broadly individualistic and liberal outlook and is thus anathema to collectivist ideology and practice. Of course, Goldmann stresses that the literary structures his method seeks to analyse are created by men but his main problem lies in the relation between the writer—group nexus and the wider society. As we have seen, Goldmann's method seeks to explain and comprehend a literary text by relating its internal structures to the external structures of the writer's social group. But in the absence of a dialectical *theory* of the novel and society, one in which the complex mediations of writer, group, class, text, culture, society, are retained, there emerges a dogmatic historicism, the total penetration of economic values into literary forms. Literature has no autonomy, but has been accommodated to a rigid deterministic theory of economic, social and political development.

The value of Goldmann's emphasis on literature as *praxis* is thus contradicted by his sociological theory of the novel. There is here no adequate theory of the 'superstructure' and little real difference between Lukács's mechanical formulations and Goldmann's superficially more subtle theory. It is in this failure to develop a dialectical theory of the 'superstructure' that the fundamental weakness of contemporary Marxism, as well as English cultural theory, structuralism, semiology lies. For without it a sociology of the novel must degenerate into either positivism or/and historicism, and the elimination of the concrete and complex mediations between the novel, its form, its creators and society. The next chapter will explore the problems involved in such a theory.

2 Hegemony and Literature

As we have seen, the sociological study of literature has been characterised by two related theories of reflection — the search for the 'sociological equivalent' in which the literary text is defined primarily as historical document (as with positivism) or the reflection of class ideology (Lukács's concept of the writer as a medium through which large socio-historical trends find artistic expression); Goldmann's version of the theory was to link specific economic structures directly with the rise of literary modernism. The point at issue is the denial of *praxis* and the problem of mediation.

Goldmann's earlier work had resolved these questions by defining the writer as 'an exceptional individual' who, belonging to a certain social group, gave coherent expression, through his work, to the significant problems both of the group and the wider society. But to invoke the mediation of the group (or groups) as a bridge between the individual writer and society as a whole, while accounting for the specific nature of the writer's existence, tends to eliminate the broader societal forces: the result can lead to a mechanical, not dialectical relationship of writer to group and society, a standpoint which seems implicit in Goldmann's methodology, and explicit in his theory of the novel. In contrast, a genuinely dialectical theory of literature is one in which the writer's vision is mediated both by the specific and the general, by the social structure of the group (or groups) and literary culture, social and political institutions. The great value of the concept of hegemony is that it allows the literary work to remain an autonomous whole with its specific nature influenced but not determined by the socio-historical context.

I

Raymond Williams has written of 'the notion of hegemony' as 'fundamental' for cultural analysis through its central ideas of

31

society as a union of man's own activity and practice in shaping
the social world and the domination of economic and political
forces in that world. A dialectic of man's actions and the 'facts
of domination' are thus grasped within the concept in a way
impossible with the crude 'base' and 'superstructure' thesis with
its notion of a static, reciprocal relation of forces.[1] Although
Marx had argued that the major ideas of an epoch are those of
the dominant class and for the stabilising influence of ideology
as mediator of class consciousness and action, it was the Italian
Marxist Gramsci who enriched and deepened these insights. A
'rising class', he once wrote, will strive to establish its authority
over all other social strata both by the straightforward
domination of economic, political and military power and
through 'intellectual and moral leadership'. Writing in 1916, he
argued that all revolutions are preceded by 'an intense work of
cultural penetration' as the rising class strives to subjugate allied
and subordinate strata to its ideas. A dominant class is thus
defined as one which has saturated society with the spirit of its
morality, customs, religious and political practices: 'The
founding of a ruling class is equivalent to the creation of a
Weltansauung.'[2] In capitalist and socialist societies hegemonic
values are thus disseminated by those institutions which have
commonly been subsumed under the heading of the
'superstructure' — religious, educational, etc. — and it is through
them that individuals are socialised into accepting the
legitimacy of the dominant ideology. Other 'superstructural'
institutions — the literary for example — refract and transmute
these values more broadly into artistic works. The importance
of Gramsci's analysis lies in the clear distinction he draws
between hegemony — associated with equilibrium and
consent — and domination — associated with coercion and state
power. Hegemony is thus identified with the institutions of
'civil society' (the family, church, education) and not those of
the state or 'political society' (army, government bureaucracy
etc.) through which governments may be forced to exercise
'direct domination'.

The significance which Gramsci attributes to the autonomy
of the 'superstructure' cannot be exaggerated. Arguing that man
is not the mere recipient of external, empirical facts 'which he
must store in his brain as in the columns of a dictionary . . .
responding passively to stimuli . . .' Gramsci suggests that the

superstructure constitutes 'an effective operating reality', one which commands the obedience of subordinate strata. And while clearly corresponding to the interests of the dominant class the institutions which maintain hegemony cannot be reduced simply to the economic structure: a dominant class exercises hegemony by diffusing through society not merely a unity of political and economic aims but an intellectual and moral unity. Its specific interests become the interests of the whole society. When a ruling class resorts to force it does so from a position of weakness; the aim is always an hegemonic equilibrium, a balance between the elements of force and consent.

Writers, of course, live and work within the institutions of 'civil society', and usually there is no coincidence of state interests and literary production. Since the end of the eighteenth century the novel has been practised largely by social groups whose economic and social existence has been shaped by the development of the capitalist division of labour, with writers emerging as a distinct professional stratum increasingly living off their earnings in the public media. And in the nineteenth century, English writers were largely drawn from a professional stratum (for example the English clergy) while others lived off profits drawn from capitalist or landed enterprises.[3] The point is not simply that the novelist is socialised into the values of the dominant culture but rather through his specific existence within definite groups his work refracts such values dialectically. Between the writer and the dominant culture subsists an uneven and contradictory relation: thus while the novel refracts bourgeois individualism and liberal ideology, its affirmation of man's freedom occurs within a fictionalised world that seems to deny it. The concept of man as simultaneously the creator of the social and historical world through his practices, and yet an object apparently determined by those very forces he has brought into being, the dialectic between man's freedom and autonomy and the arbitrary compulsions of an external world, constitute the dominant structure of the novel form. It is in this sense that the novel was born with and nurtured by the bourgeoisie but emerging only as secular history in conflict with the bourgeoisie, a class whose practices deny the values its ideology originally enshrined. Thus the novel, in its origins, is broadly conservative: through the category of individual biography and more directly through an omniscient narrator, it translates bourgeois values into art, setting the individual hero organically into a changing social structure, his fate bound to society as a whole, as much dependent on external history as his own individual will.

But while the novel expresses this conflict between the hero and society, the individual and the collectivity, the novelist does not seek to change those conditions obstructing the affirmation of man's autonomy. Writers such as Balzac, Stendhal, Flaubert and Dickens might have agreed with Marx's remark that 'capitalist production is hostile to certain branches of spiritual production, such as art and poetry',[4] but novelists, bound to liberal ideology and bourgeois values, critical of but not rejecting bourgeois society, remained uncommitted to the social forces which Marx identified as the harbingers of man's future. Here, therefore, is the structural dimension missing from Goldmann's analysis: the novelist resonates the fact of hegemony (or direct domination) through the novel of bourgeois realism and the problematic hero. It remains now to clarify the concept through a brief discussion of the novel form.

II

It was pointed out in the first chapter that the rise of the eighteenth-century novel does not correlate directly with the emergence of a bourgeois class; the *economic* expansion of the English bourgeoisie occurred twenty years *after* the writings of Defoe, Fielding and Richardson. In the previous century the English civil war had exercised one profound effect on the development of bourgeois culture: by creating an alliance between capitalist democracy and the aristocracy it assured the survival of aristocracy within a society increasingly geared towards profit, capital accumulation and rational accountability. At the same time, however, the bourgeoisie itself remained constrained within a political framework strongly influenced by the aristocracy. It is this compromise, embodied in the 'Glorious Revolution' of 1689, which provided the main impetus for cultural development in the eighteenth century. Prominent members of the bourgeois class were socially absorbed into the aristocracy through marriage or political promotion with the result that the 'rising class' of bourgeoisie never constituted an independent dominant social

class until the nineteenth century and their assumption to
political power through the 1832 Reform Act. But as a class
they dominated 'civil society' long before, and in the cultural
sphere challenged aristocratic values. Thus the eighteenth-
century novelists, especially Defoe, Richardson and
Fielding, explore the social world with remarkable precision;
problems of social status and snobbery (Richardson) honour
(Fielding), commerce (Defoe) are meticulously delineated, and
within the novel a specifically bourgeois 'mentality' emerges.
The English bourgeoisie's claims as a 'universal class' capable of
generating commercial and industrial expansion could be met
only in terms of its challenge to the dominant culture. As a
rising class the English bourgeoisie strove to negate the values of
the class it was seeking to displace politically. Thus the
emphasis within literary culture on the norms of classicism is
directly challenged by the middle-class emphasis on reportage,
on brute facts and details of low life (Defoe), the virtues of
family life (Richardson) and the replacement of wit and heroic
display by sentimentalism (the novels of Henry MacKenzie). In
the fiction of Richardson, middle-class manners and an acute
sensitivity to problems of social status embody artistically the
bourgeois class's struggle for hegemony. The realism
characteristic of these eighteenth-century writers, varied and
complex as it is, can be understood as a response to the
developing but far from dominant power of the bourgeois class.

   In France, on the other hand, a largely backward economy
still dominated by feudal land rights and political structure
could yet produce a philosophy and literature to rival the
English. A paradox in the sociology of culture? Trotsky
observed that backward nations can sometimes reflect 'in their
ideology the achievements of the advanced countries more
brilliantly and strongly' but only, it must be added, if the rising
class enjoys genuine aspirations for hegemony.[5] In 1789 French
culture had long been subjugated by the bourgeoisie. Similarly
German culture at the end of the eighteenth century (Goethe,
Hegel, Kant) reflected the *political* achievements of France,
breathing, as Engels wrote, 'a spirit of defiance and rebellion
against the whole of German society', while in Scandinavia the
same contradictory process took place during the latter years of
the nineteenth century (Ibsen, Strindberg).[6] The novel form
shares this uneven and contradictory relation with society and

enjoys a problematic history. And the fact, presence and
practice of revolution plays an important part in shaping the
relation of the novel to a hegemonic class. Nineteenth-century
French realism, for example, developed within a rapidly
expanding capitalist society but one with the heritage of 1789.
In the novels of Stendhal and Balzac the antithesis between the
hero and society is more sharply delineated than in previous
fiction. Thus Fielding's picaresque novel *Tom Jones* (1749)
portrays a hero who passively accepts his low status and bastard
origins with good-humoured resignation. Tom Jones is neither
socially ambitious nor does he possess much personal initiative.
He accepts the social world *as it is* and his actual intentions are
never concretely realised through himself. Seduced by Mrs
Waters he becomes the paid lover of the corrupt Lady Bellaston
and is finally reunited with his upper-class love, Sophie, not
through his own efforts, but as the result of other people
discovering his genuine social origin. Unlike the heroes of
nineteenth-century fiction Tom Jones has no concrete aim:
Rastignac and Julien Sorel are characters endowed with a
thrustful ambition, their personalities are wholly positive and
their fictional lives embody actual social aims: they are heroes
by will, not by birth. The French Revolution had the effect of
liberating fiction from the picaresque mode on the one hand,
and the rather narrow provincialism of writers such as Rousseau
and Richardson on the other. Thus although a society more
agrarian and economically undeveloped than England, France
generated a novel form which revolutionised the genre: 'In
contrast to the metropolitan and cosmopolitan qualities of the
French realists the Victorians seem insular and provincial.'[7] The
ideas of liberty and equality combined with the rapid
capitalisation of French society in the 1830s produced a form
of realism radically different from that of any other culture.
English nineteenth-century realism had no counterparts for the
Sorels and Rastignacs, the uncompromising and brutal honesty
of Balzac.

    In Russia the novel emerges as a distinctive genre only during
the 1840s and 1850s, practised by writers largely drawn from
the Russian gentry (Turgenev and Tolstoy) or the small
professional stratum (Dostoevsky), rarely from the nascent
bourgeoisie. The relation of writer to bourgeois class is highly
problematical, for as Gramsci observed the bourgeoisie in its

development cannot train its own intellectuals, and therefore draws them from professional and landed strata. In Russia, the bourgeois class, merchant manufacturers drawn from peasant serfs, shackled by strongly entrenched feudal elements and a powerful Tsarist bureaucracy, was weakened not strengthened by the slow development of nineteenth-century Russian capitalism. Moreover, capitalist development was largely European, rigidly and bureaucratically controlled by the Tsarist government. The Russian bourgeoisie was never allowed to emerge as an independent class; an oppressive bureaucratic state controlled that realm of 'civil society' in which the Western bourgeoisie had organised cultural opposition to aristocratic semi-feudal domination. In an important sense, therefore, the Russian bourgeoisie never constituted a 'rising class', its hegemonic pretensions were partial and fragmented, incapable of infusing the social structure with its ideology and rallying behind it the numerous anti-Tsarist forces: the 1825 Decembrist Revolt and the political agitation of the 1840s were largely the work of 'Westernised intelligentsia and disenchanted nobility'. The history of the Populist and Socialist movements, the government's frequent use of force against opposition, illustrates the lack of hegemony within Russian society. The novel develops as a bourgeois art-form under the influence of French realism but within a society in which hegemony is made impossible by the politically impotent bourgeoisie. The conflict between the individual and society is thus sharply drawn and the problematic hero achieves its highest expression in the figure of the 'superfluous' man in the novels of Goncharov, Turgenev and Dostoevsky.

But the transformation of culture is a lengthy, complex, and contradictory process. The French Revolution revolutionises the genre of the novel thirty years later, at a time when the ideas of the revolutionary bourgeoisie fail to work out in practical social life. The period 1815—1848 sees the assumption of the bourgeoisie to economic and political authority; the aristocracy survive only as a 'declining' class (even during the Restoration period, 1815—30, the bourgeoisie continued to develop), their political power challenged by the alliance of bourgeoisie and nascent working-class movement. The growth of the bourgeoisie as a hegemonic class is paralleled by the emergence of the proletariat, potentially a new hegemonic class in opposition to the capitalists, but too weak to act as an independent power. It is a time, therefore, of class alliance, the interests of the bourgeoisie and proletariat coincide in their defence of liberal democracy. After 1830 the proletariat cannot be ignored even though French capitalism lagged behind the English. As a leading Saint-Simonist noted: 'It is no longer a question of priests and nobility as it was in 1789 . . . but rather an opposition between the people and the bourgeoisie, or better between working people and the leisure class.'[8] The official organ of the Saint-Simonists commented that 'the fundamental character of the period is marked by the triumph of the bourgeoisie . . . [who] produces nothing, teaches nothing and has no other care for himself . . . a slothful class living in the midst of a hardworking society.' The triumph of the French bourgeoisie between 1830 and 1848, while spectacular was not totally dominant: the big bourgeoisie — the *haute bourgeoisie* — merged with the landed aristocracy to form a new governing class, while other bourgeois strata fought desperately to maintain and improve their social status. The ideals which had generated the 1789 Revolution had been gradually eroded, the values of liberty, equality and fraternity subverted by bourgeois practice. Stendhal complained, 'far be it for me to conclude that industrialists are not honourable. All I mean is that they are not heroic.' And he wrote bitterly of 'this so moral, so hypocritical and consequently so boring century.'[9]

The revolutionary ideals of a revolutionary bourgeois class were now translated quite cynically into a crude materialism; progress came to mean the commercialisation of culture. Balzac's miser Gobseck proclaimed that 'everywhere the struggle between rich and poor has set in, everywhere it is inevitable', while for Rastignac and Lucien de Rubempre ambition is realisable only through deception and fraud. Balzac's problematic heroes have no answer to the arguments of the master criminal Vautrin who understands French society without their illusions. His first meeting with Lucien saves the latter from suicide through the power of Vautrin's rhetoric:

> . . . society is forced, for its own sake, to make distinctions; that is what I want you to do for your own sake. The great point is to measure up to the whole of society. Napoleon, Richelieu and the Medicis measured up to their century.

Present day society no longer worships the true God, but the Golden Calf. . . . What then must you get into that handsome head of yours? Just this simple idea: set yourself a splendid goal, but don't let anyone see what means you adopt and the steps you take to reach it. You have been acting like a child: be a man. Do what the hunter does. Lie in wait, lie in ambush in the world of Paris.[10]

When Stendhal turned to write a novel of the French aristocracy he found impossible the task of creating a hero at once energetic and heroic. In the marginal notes to his novel, *Lucien Leuwen*, he wrote: 'What is L's character like? Certainly not Julien's energy and originality. That is impossible. To suppose so is clearly unrealistic . . . The rich young Frenchman does not think of matters of love; lacks the courage to love.'[11]

Balzac's heroes, unlike Stendhal's, are consciously making their world within the framework of capitalism. For them there is no problem of identity, their character is important only as it relates to membership of definite social groups. The sense of community in his fiction is predominantly bourgeois: for the fictional hero is not fragmented and isolated from others but genuinely seeks the meaning to his life not in an anachronistic sense of honour (as in Stendhal) or in the transcendental beyond (as in Romantic fiction) but concretely within the palpable capitalist world. It is in this sense that individualism is the key element in Balzac, for his characters work out their fate only in direct conflict and competition with others, as members of an egoistic community in which money functions as the sole measure of human value. In *Old Goriot*, Vautrin convinces Rastignac that there is no difference between legal violence as practised by the rich and the overt violence practised by Vautrin. Rastignac succumbs to Vautrin's logic simply because it is *realistic*: for him to conquer Paris money, not honour, is needed, and if some innocent person is killed as part of this necessity then the end justifies the means. For capitalist civilisation is the transvaluation of values. Stendhal echoed a generation of French writers in his disgust and hatred of bourgeois society. Industrialists, he once wrote, had created a strong France; as a class they could only be despised. Flaubert, too, when he finished his novel *Salammbô* wrote: 'It will: 1) annoy the bourgeois; 2) unnerve and shock sensitive people;

3) anger the archeologists; 4) be unintelligible to the ladies;
5) earn me a reputation as a pederast and a cannibal. Let us
hope so.'[12]

Here, then, was the artistic problem for the nineteenth-
century realist. Both the novel and French society
had been revolutionised in 1789 but after 1830 it became
increasingly obvious that further revolutionary development
was bound up with the emerging proletariat and nascent
socialist movement. Particularly after 1848, when the fragile
alliance of bourgeoisie and proleteriat was dissolved in blood,
the French realists were faced with the problem of integrating
these new social forces into the novel. In Russia there was no
such problem: the working class as a potentially hegemonic
class did not exist and the state firmly controlled a weak
bourgeoisie. But for the nineteenth-century French and English
novel the 'social problem' associated with the conflictive claims
of capital and labour became increasingly important.
In France, moreover, hegemonic equilibrium was more unstable
than in England. The bourgeoisie experienced far greater
difficulty in imposing its hegemony on a weakened aristocracy
and weak proletariat, a crisis of authority exemplified in the
1848 Revolution, the Paris uprising of 1871 and the frequent
resort to 'direct domination' especially in the immediate
post-1848 period. Paradoxical as it may seem, the more
powerful English proletariat threatened but never challenged
the bourgeoisie. The 1832 Reform Act had peacefully concluded
the union of bourgeoisie and proletariat against the aristocracy:
subsequent anti-labour legislation and practice — the 1834 Poor
Law, the imprisonment and deportation of striking trade
unionists — emphasised the break between the bourgeoisie and
proletariat. Yet neither militant trade unionism nor the Chartist
movement of the late 1830s and 1840s seriously threatened
bourgeois rule. As a movement, Chartism lacked cohesion of
purpose and organisation, its ideology a contradictory mixture
of reformist illusions and revolutionary rhetoric. Bourgeois
society survived without recourse to 'direct domination'. But in
France bourgeois values and culture seemed more problematical
and the novel comes increasingly to depict a social world
dominated by the power of money, a world in which man is no
longer capable of fulfilling his genuine self through the need to
compromise with the forces of authority or to withdraw from

social life itself. In contrast, the English novel continues to sustain and define as non-problematical those values underpinning bourgeois hegemony. It is in this sense that the nineteenth-century novel criticises obvious social abuses yet gives expression to some of the basic assumptions of the dominant class, a contradictory structure especially brought out in those novels written during the 1840s which take as their basic theme the 'condition of England' problem: Disraeli's *Sybil* (1845), Mrs Gaskell's *Mary Barton* (1848) and Kingsley's *Alton Locke* (1850). Many critics have noted the 'fear of violence' and the concept of the working class as an irrational 'mob' which runs through these novels (also in Dickens's two historical novels, *Barnaby Rudge* and *A Tale of Two Cities*), and the ways in which a highly melodramatic plot and action resolves fundamental problems of capital and labour.[13] Alton Locke, for example, is depicted as a Chartist tailor, a poet who, as the novel progresses, transforms himself into a spokesman for the middle class. When a demonstration of labourers turns into a bloody riot, the hero accepts the necessity for moderate middle-class leadership: 'Not from without, from Charters and Republics, but from within, from the spirit working in each.' The conflict between the hero and society is thus flattened and rendered non-problematical: Sybil is portrayed by Disraeli as a working-class girl speaking perfect middle-class English, whose marriage to an aristocrat is finally facilitated by the discovery that she is, after all, the heir to a considerable estate. Mrs Gaskell's *Mary Barton* remains the best of these novels for its greater feeling for working-class life, language, mores: the characters are set organically within the working-class environment and the way in which the details of the culture are rendered gives the novel its great significance.

The novel's hero, Mary's father, John Barton, a Chartist and trade unionist, is driven to a desperate act of murder by unemployment, poverty and class callousness. There is nothing in previous fiction which compares with Mrs Gaskell's detailed and sympathetic portrait of the physical and moral depredations of working-class life, the constant anxieties over the basic needs of food and shelter brought about by periodic and lengthy bouts of unemployment and compounded by the ever-present threat of premature death. Such was Mrs Gaskell's power that one contemporary reviewer wrote that the novel embodied 'the dominant feeling of our times — that the ignorance, destitution and vice which pervade and corrupt our society must be got rid of', while another suggested that here lay the explanation of 'why working men turn Chartists and Communists'.[14] Unlike Disraeli (and Dickens in *Hard Times*, 1854) Mrs Gaskell lived in the north of England and experienced the realities her novel portrays: the dense, personalised web of working-class culture emerges organically and the individuals are set firmly within it. John Barton's visit to the dying Davenport is not documented simply to show the horrors of working-class life, but forms an integral part of Barton's radicalisation. But Mrs Gaskell cannot allow all her material (the content) such autonomy: the social conditions which drive men to socialism are realistically depicted, yet they are not allowed 'to speak for themselves'. The writer must intrude and mediate between the facts and her middle-class readers and encourage them to believe that given goodwill then a 'natural' harmony between employers and employees is possible. Thus Mrs Gaskell portrays trade unions and socialism as 'unnatural' consequences of temporary economic forces and fails to grasp their necessary relation to working-class life. Barton's political activities are seen as *external* to his domestic life and when Mrs Gaskell describes trade unionists as 'desperate' men, she must add, 'The actions of the uneducated seem to me typified in those of Frankenstein, that monster of many human qualities, ungifted with a soul, a knowledge of the difference between good and evil.'[15] Trade unions are portrayed as 'secret societies' given to terrorism and 'those fierce terrible oaths which bind members of Trades' Unions to any given purpose', including assasination.[16] In these descriptions, and the subsequent murder, the organic nature of *Mary Barton* collapses; the conflict between labour and capital, which dominates the first part of the novel, recedes in structural importance in the second, melodramatic part: Barton confesses and dies symbolically in the arms of the employer whose son he has murdered:

> The eyes of John Barton grew dim with tears. Rich and poor, masters and men, were then brothers in the deep suffering of the heart . . . now he knew that he had killed a man, and a

brother, — now he knew that no good thing could come out of this evil, even to the sufferers whose cause he had so blindly espoused.[17]

Thus the structural conflict between antagonistic classes is ultimately dissipated by Mrs Gaskell's assimilation of the potentially 'negative' values of the working class to the 'positive', humanist, and reformist values of the bourgeoisie. George Eliot's *Felix Holt* (1866) written, like *Mary Barton*, against a background of working-class agitation (for the 1867 Reform Act) portrays a similar, non-problematic social world in which the working-class 'hero', spurning the idea of becoming middle class. ('Why should I want to get into the middle class because I have some learning? The most of the middle class are as ignorant as the working people . . .'),[18] nonetheless accepts the necessity for middle-class leadership over the labour movement. Involved in a bloody and senseless riot, Felix Holt concludes that the road to working-class power is neither through class struggle nor even the extension of voting rights to manual workers, but rather through an enlightened public opinion, 'the ruling belief in society about what is right and what is wrong, what is honourable and what is shameful.'[19] The significant point about George Eliot's 'hero' is his non-problematic status: Sorel, Rastignac and, in a slightly different sense, Dostoevsky's Raskolnikov, are heroes in conflict with their society, their sense of ambition and egoism driven by the equalitarian and commercial ideals of bourgeois democracy and its ideology. But Felix Holt's plebeian origins and incorruptible honesty and frankness, his acceptance of the basic character of capitalist society, are explicable only in terms of a society and stratum of writers which remained largely impervious to the revolutionary ideals of 1789. The sustaining vision behind *Felix Holt*, as well as other nineteenth-century 'social problem' novels is of a society purged of problematic elements, a resiliently immobile, fairly stable 'rank' or class structure. There is class inequality, class conflict and corruption but society can be improved only through education, reform and goodwill, not by working-class 'mob' violence and terrorism. In both *Mary Barton* and *Felix Holt* the basic tendency is towards stasis, to *reunite* the hero or heroine with

society; Barton's and Holt's values are not compromised by
reconciliation for they and the enlightened bourgeoisie share
the same humanist assumptions.

III

Not all nineteenth-century English fiction can be so easily
accommodated to the above arguments. George Eliot's
Middlemarch (1872) and Dickens's *Bleak House* (1853) are far
more complex in their analysis of English society than any of
the novels written in the 1840s. Nonetheless, the fact of
bourgeois hegemony is refracted through their structures; the
difference is that in these novels Dickens and George Eliot were
able to rise above bourgeois ideology and thus provide a more
profound and problematic vision of nineteenth-century
bourgeois society. Yet it remains true that the English novel has
no real problematic hero, no superfluous men such as
Turgenev's Rudin, Insarov and Bazarov who find the resolution
of their conflict with society in futile death.[20]

The next chapter will attempt to explore the themes of
hegemony and *praxis* in relation to realism and modernism.

3 Realism, Modernism and Revolution

The last chapter suggested a broad relation between the hegemonic values of a dominant class and the novel form. The novel is a bourgeois art-form but its evolution is not to be identified mechanically with the bourgeois class. For the bourgeoisie does not create its own intellectuals, and novelists are drawn largely from non-bourgeois strata. And as these intellectuals transform the novel form into nineteenth-century realism the bourgeoisie's hegemonic status is threatened by the emerging proletariat. The result is a highly complex dialectic between the form and content of the realist novel and bourgeois values. It is not that bourgeois realism represented a passive cultural support to bourgeois order, but rather a revolutionary *and* a conservative art-form, created by an independent stratum of intellectuals, resonating yet criticising the values of modern capitalist culture. It is this contradictory character of bourgeois realism which is important. This chapter will explore the concept, theory and development of bourgeois realism in its relation to the theory and practice of revolution, and to the novel itself.

I

The European novel emerges as a major literary genre in the nineteenth century: the rise of the bourgeoisie, the rapid development of industry and growth of a reading public all contributed to a new concept of the novel form — realism. This is not to argue that the eighteenth-century novel was not realistic, only that the historical, social and political environment through which personal relations find expression were conceived statically. The nineteenth-century realist novel is pre-eminently concerned with the present, the contemporary as history: man is firmly structured within a totality of political, economic and social forces. The relatively immobile social background of the epistolary novel (Richardson's *Clarissa*,

Rousseau's *La Nouvelle Héloïse,* Choderlos de Laclos's *Les Liaisons Dangereuses*), the memoir novel (Prevost's *Manon Lescaut*), the mock epic and picaresque form (Fielding) as well as the complex and private world of Jane Austen, contrasts sharply with the more dynamic, fluid reality portrayed in the novels of Stendhal, Balzac, Flaubert, Turgenev, Dostoevsky and Tolstoy.[1] The nineteenth-century realist novel depicts not simply 'low life' and the mundane triviality of everyday experience at the expense of heroic values, but conceives the individual and his fate as indissolubly bound to a constantly evolving society. Thus although Jane Austen's fictional milieu is similar to that of Turgenev the latter's characters, their values and inner conflicts cannot be understood except in terms of contemporary political and social history.

The realist novelist, then, accepted, however critically and grudgingly, the fact of bourgeois society and necessary historical change. Thus Balzac, with all his admiration for the anti-Enlightenment philosophers, de Maistre, Chateaubriand and Bonald, and overt political sympathies for the Royalists knew that the social change initiated by the 1789 Revolution was irreversible. He grasped its significance not as a mere episode but as a world-making event: society would never return to the traditional, hierarchical, immobile social structures of pre-capitalism. Balzac's artistic understanding of historical necessity, his grasp of revolution in its entirety is one measure of the realist method. Balzac, writes Arnold Hauser, is the most bourgeois of writers and by far 'the most successful apologist of the bourgeoisie',[2] while for Goldmann, Balzac's fiction may well constitute 'the sole significant expression of a universe structured according to the conscious hunger for power, wealth and eroticism . . . '[3] The Balzacian metropolis and the urban culture which he sketches so densely and enthusiastically is a wholly different world to that portrayed by Richardson, Laclos and Jane Austen: Rastignac's and Balzac's France is a social world dominated by an overpowering *egoism* and his realism depicts with sober detail the capitalist city culture.

These interpretations of Balzac are clearly linked with the more general Marxist theory of 'critical realism' which attributes to the nineteenth-century novelist the power to transcend his own limited class position and political sympathies through a 'negative' critique of capitalism. Engels's formula, 'the triumph of realism', has become the touchstone of

Marxist orthodoxy. Thus Lukács, defining realism as 'a correct dialectical conception of the relationship between being and consciousness,'[4] concludes that only those writers who portray the 'typical' in opposition to the eccentric, pathological and average, are genuine realists:

> The central category and criterion of realist literature is the type, a peculiar synthesis which organically binds together the general and the particular both in characters and situations. What makes a type a type . . . is that in it all the humanly and socially essential determinants are present on their highest level of development, in the ultimate unfolding of the possibilities latent in them, in extreme presentation of their extremes, rendering concrete the peaks and limits of men and epochs.[5]

For Lukács the typical merges the public and private worlds, personal ambition and historical significance. The private conflicts of Balzac's Rastignac are 'those of the entire younger generation in the post Napoleonic period', while through the character of Old Goriot, Balzac exposes the contradictions inherent in bourgeois society.[6] Realism, Lukács argues, depicts 'the essential determinants' of social progress through a positive affirmation of historical inevitability — the triumph of the capitalist class in Balzac's fiction. But after the 1848 Revolutions, writers turned to the average and the pathological rather than the typical (except as was noted in Chapter 1, for the 'lucky' Russians and rare 'exceptions' such as Thomas Mann), losing confidence in the bourgeoisie and rejecting the claims of the proletariat. Lukács rejects Flaubert and Zola precisely for their portrayal of mere 'everyday' life through average, pathological, and eccentric characters. It might be asked, of course, if 'positive' characters are always essential for the artistic understanding of a 'decaying' capitalist society? Would 'negative' characters in 'decadent' situations perform the same critical function as the 'typical'"?

Engels's brief remarks on realism have been transformed into inviolable dogma in Lukács's mechanical formulations. The 'typical' enables the writer to reflect not a mere 'slice of life' (as in Zola's 'naturalism') but a *totality*:

> The true artistic totality of a literary work depends on the completeness of the picture it presents of the essential social

factors that determine the world depicted. . . . The hallmark
of the great realist masterpiece is precisely that its intensive
totality of *essential* social factors does not require . . . a
meticulously accurate or pedantically encyclopaedic
inclusion of all the threads making up the social
tangle . . . the exact copying of reality by a mere onlooker
offers no principle of grouping inherent in the subject matter
itself.[7]

Totality is defined by Lukács as the organising principle
allowing the writer to select essential from inessential material,
that is, those historically progressive elements which point the
way to the future. Totality is quite simply the 'correct'
reflection of external history; the novel's 'usefulness' is
therefore obvious, as a source of information on the critical
nature of bourgeois society and ideology. Literature becomes
bound to the economic and political fate of a particular social
class *broadly defined*, an appendage to the waxing and waning
of realism, to the rise, decline and ultimate collapse of
capitalism.

Lukács's defence of the nineteenth-century realist novel as
exemplar of revolutionary literature, his uncompromising
hostility to all forms of 'modernism' (Proust, Joyce, Musil) has
led many critics to endorse Robbe-Grillet's argument that
revolutionary literature is mistrusted by the socialist revolution
which prefers the old realist art forms of the age of the steam
engine and the three-decker novel.[8] Although Robbe-Grillet is
criticising the doctrine of socialist realism in the name of
modernism it is true that Marxists such as Trotsky, Lenin,
Bukharin and Lunacharsky preferred realism to any other
literary form although as will be argued in the following chapter
their defence of realism was neither homogeneous nor of the
same crude character as that of Georg Lukács: for it is neither
adequate critically nor historically correct to define realism in
historicist terms or counterpose a 'conservative' realism with a
'subversive', 'revolutionary' modernism.

II

The revolutionary nature of nineteenth-century realism is
contained in its central precept that the social world is
explicable in social not divine or metaphysical terms. In his

idealist *Theory of the Novel*, Lukács expressed this materialist conception by defining the novel as 'the epic of a world foresaken by God', in which man, through his own actions, wills and creates the ends towards which his ideals impel him. A similar idea informs Marx's early writings on Hegel: 'The outstanding thing in Hegel's *Phenomenology* . . . is that Hegel grasps the self-creation of man as a process . . . and conceives objective man . . . as the result of his own labour.'[9] For Marx, therefore, history is the struggle of men to create their own freedom in societies characterised by class and ideological conflict. And it is a human history, a history of *labour*, of human activity:

> History does nothing; it does not possess immense riches . . . does not fight battles. It is *men*, real living men, who do all this, who possess things and fight battles. It is not 'history' which uses men as a means of achieving . . . its own ends. History is *nothing* but the activity of men in pursuit of their ends.[10]

Marx's writings on revolution revolve around this theme, that the social world is knowable and can be changed by human action and initiative. Revolution becomes the means whereby an old, declining social order is swept away by the irresistible force of the new, no mere act of rebellion against existing political and social order but a total break with the existing society, a transformation of the entire social and political structure. In his *Critique of Hegel's Philosophy of Right* (1844) Marx had dismissed the idea of revolution as a *political* act for 'a partial, merely political revolution . . . leaves the pillars of the building standing', while for Engels 'every real revolution is a social one, in that it brings a new class to power and allows it to remodel society in its own image.'[11] For both Marx and Engels revolutionary activity was human activity, *praxis*, through which the individual changed both his world and himself. In *The German Ideology* (1846) they wrote that 'in revolutionary activity change of self coincides with change of circumstances', and it is this theme which dominates Marx's early and later writings.

Marxist social theory and the nineteenth-century realist novel, then, share this one assumption: both celebrate man's potential freedom from an arbitrary world — Marxism to

remake it through revolutionary *praxis*, the novel to
contemplate those struggles and conflicts which define man's
social and historical being, yet which obstruct their complete
fulfilment. It is in these senses that the realist novel and
Marxism are linked to the 1789 French Revolution.

1789 marks the beginning of the modern era and the word
revolution unquestionably derives its modern usage from this
single event. For here was a practical demonstration of the
Enlightenment belief in the workings of social, not divine order.
It was 1789, too, which was to become the model for all
subsequent European revolutions. In the writings of Marx,
Lenin and Trotsky clear historical parallels are drawn between
the events of 1789, the unsuccessful European revolutions of
1848, and the successful Russian revolution of 1917. Thus for
Trotsky, Stalin's assumption of power in the 1920s followed
the historical pattern established by the victory of the
Thermidorians over the Jacobins in that both flowed from 'the
weariness of the masses and the demoralisation of the leading
cadres'.[12] In both revolutions the ideals are systematically
destroyed by the growth of conservative social strata dedicated
not to revolution but to evolution and order, the virtues of
nationalism and self-interest.

But direct parallels between events separated by over one
hundred years of European industrial and social history can never
be more than superficial. Between 1789 and 1917 the concept
of revolution acquired a new meaning, one which corresponded
to the great changes brought about by the rapid growth of
European capitalism. In the 1789 Revolution the working
classes had played an insignificant role in an action largely
inspired and carried through by the bourgeois class. But during
the course of the nineteenth century the industrial, urban
proletariat emerges as a distinctive social class, separated from
the bourgeoisie by its own trade union organisations, uprooted
from the land and settled in the rapidly expanding cities,
regimented and disciplined by the factory system, forming a
broad, almost homogeneous mass increasingly given to
anti-bourgeois collective action. In the course of the nineteenth
century the mass politics and action initiated by 1789 serves as
the dominant model for working-class agitation and revolution;
the political terrorism associated with secret societies and
brotherhoods becomes increasingly rare, and by 1848 both the

French and the English working class formed a potential threat to bourgeois society through the ideals of Utopian Socialism (Robert Owen, Charles Fourier) and European Communism.

Marx was not the only observer who understood the significance of these developments. The conservative historian and sociologist, Alexis de Tocqueville writing as an observer of the 1848 Revolution, noted that it 'seemed to be made entirely outside the bourgeoisie and against it'. The philosophical impetus behind the Paris revolution, he went on, emphasised that oppression and misery did not flow from political constitutions but from 'the unalterable laws that constitute society itself'. Tocqueville grasped that socialism meant the abolition of private property and the total overthrow of bourgeois society. Of course, in 1848 there was not one socialism but many forms often in conflict with each other, but to Tocqueville they seemed unanimous in their concept of revolution as the transformation of *social* not *political* structures. It is in this sense that revolution ceases to be bound up with the fate of the bourgeois class but becomes the necessary task of the working masses. The 1848 European revolutions and the English Chartist movement had clearly disclosed that modern bourgeois society was compounded of class conflict and contradiction. Had not the French bourgeoisie in its battle with the nobility been forced to ally themselves tactically with the working class? It was the masses who mounted and defended the barricades:

> Having secured it arms in hand, the proletariat impressed its stamp upon it and proclaimed it to be a *social republic*. There was thus indicated the general content of modern revolution, a content which was in most singular contradiction to everything that, with the material available, with the degree of education attained by the masses, under the given circumstances and relations, could be immediately realised in practice.[13]

The French bourgeoisie, having conquered state power, clearly understood the threat posed by the armed and class-conscious masses. It now turned *its* power won *with* the workers against them: the resulting massacre and transportation of working-class leaders was merely the normalisation of politics by the bourgeois republican government. The 1848 June uprising of the Paris workers, described by Marx as 'the most colossal event in the history of European civil wars', is the dividing line between two wholly different conceptions of revolution — bourgeois and socialist. By 1848, revolution had become identified with socialism and the struggle for individual liberty became increasingly the collective, ideological struggle between two conflictive social classes.

But although revolution may be 'the locomotive of history' and while men *make* revolution there are definite social conditions which help to obstruct or enhance revolutionary possibility. In his preface to *A Contribution to the Critique of Political Economy*, Marx wrote:

> No social order ever perishes before all the productive forces for which there is no room in it have developed; and new, higher relations of production never appear before the material conditions of their existence have matured in the womb of the old society itself. Therefore mankind always sets itself only such tasks as it can solve; since, looking at the matter more closely it will always be found that the task itself arises only when the material conditions for its solution already exist or are at least in the process of formation.[14]

After 1848, revolutionary *praxis*, ideology and organisation become increasingly identified with the proletariat: the contradictory nature of capitalist society is nowhere better shown than in the fact that it creates the conditions for its own downfall through the exploitation of labour and the social and organisational consciousness forged in trades unions and the Socialist and Communist parties all of which arise organically on the basis of bourgeois property relations.

In his early writings the young Marx had written that the task of the modern proletariat was human emancipation. All history is the history of class struggle and social development is attained only by a social class whose economic function lies in revolutionising society as a whole. It is in this sense that Marx refers to the bourgeoisie as a 'universal class' in that its specific economic interest coincides with the *general* interest of the whole society. But the bourgeoisie is progressive only within a definite period of capitalist development. Once capital has been established as the dominant economic force of modern society then the ideals which inspired the bourgeois revolution become empty slogans with no real, positive content. Equality and liberty come to mean the freedom of the capitalist to exploit the worker, to use his own privileged position to augment bourgeois hegemony over the proletariat. Bourgeois values must remain abstract and formal: a new, proletarian revolution becomes necessary to complete the task which the bourgeoisie had begun. The French Revolution had proclaimed freedom and justice for all men; its programme was general social and political emancipation. But this ideology was impossible to *practise* precisely because the bourgeoisie's economic interests opposed its own ideals once power had been assumed:

> It is in the interest of the ruling section of society to sanction the existing order as law and to perpetuate its habitually and traditionally fixed limits as legal ones . . . this comes about of itself in proportion as the continuous reproduction of the foundation of the existing order of the regulations corresponding to it gradually assumes a regulated and orderly form. And such regulation and order are themselves indispensable elements of any mode of production, provided that it is to assume social firmness and an independence from mere accident and arbitrariness.[15]

The values of the bourgeois revolution, Marx concluded, can be realised only by the working class, for proletarian revolution means the abolition of class society and the establishment of genuine equality and freedom.

In the *Paris Manuscripts* (1843—4) Marx makes explicit this theory of revolution. The proletarian revolution releases man's creative potential, the sense of wholeness fragmented by the capitalist division of labour. In a striking passage Marx argues that the bourgeois revolution had transformed man into an abstract, rational being in terms of public life and an egoistic being in his private life. And this was necessarily so, for in bourgeois society the selfish individual is regarded as the *real* man while the citizen, the public man, is seen only in abstract terms. The 1789 Revolution had 'shattered everything — estates, corporations, guilds, privileges — which expressed the separation of the people from community life.'
As an expression of bourgeois values, the ideal of the Revolution lay in the rigid divorce made between man's political and social character. Unlike the Greek *polis*, Marx

argued, bourgeois society, its revolution and ideology, divide
man into separate and distinct parts; the unity of public and
private life, the political and the social is broken precisely
because the essence of bourgeois values lies in their radical
individualism and egoism:

> Man as a member of civil society — non-political
> man — necessarily appears as the natural man. The rights of
> man appear as natural rights because conscious activity is
> concentrated upon political action. Egoistic man is the
> passive, given result of a dissolution of a society, the object
> of direct apprehension and consequently a natural object.
> The political revolution dissolves civil society into its
> elements, without revolutionising these elements themselves
> or subjecting them to criticism. The revolution regards civil
> society, the sphere of human needs, labour, private interests
> and civil law, as the basis of its own existence, as a
> self-subsistent pre-condition, and thus as its natural basis. . . .
> Thus man as he really is, is seen only in the form of egoistic
> man, and man in his true nature only in the form of the
> abstract citizen.

For Marx 'human emancipation' becomes possible only 'when
the real, individual man has absorbed into himself the abstract
citizen', that is, when political and social life form an organic
unity. And this is possible only through socialist values, when a
genuine community replaces class domination. Such is the task
of the proletarian revolution.[16]

Bourgeois revolution thus affirms a radical individualism and
egoism. Surveying the state of contemporary fiction at the
beginning of the nineteenth century Madame de Staël
anticipated Marx as she argued that the contemporary novel
could now free itself from outmoded romanticism and
concentrate on the real, emerging world, a world dominated by
pride, avarice, ambition and vanity.[17] In the figures of Julien
Sorel and Lucien de Rubempre, Stendhal and Balzac grasped
the essential significance of 1789: egoism was now free from
traditional restraints (Church, Family, Community) and private
ambitions lauded in a society which formally claimed equality
for all but which, through the institutions of private property,
denied it in practice.

The ideology implicit in the bourgeois revolution can thus be

seen as exalting the individual over the collectivity, of raising
the individual against community. For bourgeois revolution and
bourgeois values demand that 'the only bond between men is
natural necessity, need and private interest, the preservation of
their property and their egoistic persons.'[18] Socialism is not,
therefore, an extension or a mere improvement of bourgeois
values but their real supersession. The bourgeois value of
equality, for example, means only that some must forever
remain unequal in societies characterised by differential access
to privileged positions. Socialist equality in contrast demands
that individual achievement is not gained at the expense of
others and to the detriment of community. The development of
all is the necessary condition for the development of the
individual. Thus Marx wrote of the Commune as 'the glorious
harbinger of a new society' for demonstrating the ability of the
working class to organise itself as a community of equals and
effectively challenge bourgeois property and authority.

The year 1871 represents both a continuation and
development of 1848; and while Marx criticised the
Communards for not going far enough, he praised their
egalitarian legislation, the substitution of an armed people's
militia for the professional standing army and police force and
their demand that the political representatives of the masses be
subject to recall.[19] Revolutionary theory and doctrine now
became identified with these spontaneous working-class
organisations and the workers councils which had first appeared
during the 1848 Revolutions reappeared in 1871, in the two
Russian revolutions, the 1919 German and Hungarian
revolutions and in Hungary during 1956. Workers councils, the
Russian Soviets, constitute the embryo of socialist community
out of which springs the revolutionary potential, the
transformation of the entire society. As chairman of the
short-lived St Petersburg Council of Workman's Deputies in
1905 Trotsky described it as 'in reality *an embryo of a
revolutionary government* . . . a true, unadulterated democracy,
without a two chamber system, without a professional
bureaucracy, and with the right of the voters to recall their
deputy any moment and to substitute another for him.' 'The
Soviet', he wrote 'was an organised expression of the will of the
proletariat as a class.'[20] In 1917 Lenin, too, grasped the
significance of the Soviets, arguing in his *April Theses* that the

goal of the Russian Revolution was to establish 'a republic of
Soviets of Workers', Poor Peasants' and Peasants' Deputies
throughout the country, growing from below upwards.' Unlike
some Bolsheviks and Marxist theorists, Lenin understood the
historic significance of the Soviets, seeing in them an entirely
'new type of state', one 'closely bound up with the people', free
of 'bureaucratic formalities [and] far more democratic than any
previous apparatus.'

The revolutionary *praxis* embodied in the Soviet, in its direct
confrontation with bourgeois state power, must be seen as a
total negation of bourgeois values and ideology: the essence of
bourgeois revolution and institutions lies in the emphasis on the
formally free and equal individual who, if left to himself will
egoistically work both for himself and the whole society.
Socialist revolution and *praxis* challenge the passive role
accorded to the masses politically, the divorce between man as
citizen and man as private individual. Revolutionary socialism is
thus not merely a theory of changing both the circumstances
and the individual, but an attempt to re-integrate the individual
into society as both a political and social being. It is in these
senses that revolutionary socialism and literary realism meet:
Marx and Balzac portray a social and historical world
dominated by money and egoism, but a world in which man
through his own free actions transforms both himself and
society.

III

The revolutionary dynamic of realism lies in its attack on
modern society, the alienation and dehumanisation inherent
within it. Its conservative side is the necessity to stabilise
potentially 'negative' elements. The point at issue is not the
realists' depiction of the social world in terms of the 'typical' as
opposed to the 'average' and 'eccentric' — the Greek word for
type, *tupos*, implies eccentricity rather than the emblematic or
symbolic — but rather the way in which they portrayed the
dialectic of freedom and constraint, alienation and knowledge,
praxis and passivity through the problematic hero's quest for
'ultimate' values. Balzac's Rastignac, Turgenev's Rudin,
Dostoevsky's Raskolnikov are not typical in Lukács's sense:
these egoistic individuals are eccentrics whose values place them
in conflict with their society. There is thus no simple

assimilation of realism to the social structure of the bourgeois class: and neither is modernism to be equated with a 'disintegration' of realism at the end of the nineteenth century for modernism is not merely implied in realism but was always present. The inner life of the problematic hero, the revolutionary aspect of bourgeois realism which affirms the autonomy of the individual, is precisely what is meant by modernism.

The broad relation of culture to economics is therefore complex and dialectical. In his brief comments on Greek art Marx noted that the epic, as a major literary genre, emerges at a low level of economic organisation and 'undeveloped stage of artistic development'.[21] Of course, Marx does not argue that art is free of social and economic determinations. Writing of the great Italian artist, Raphael, he stressed that like other painters Raphael was 'determined by the technical advances in art made before him, by the organisation of society and the division of labour', and suggested that the development of artistic talent itself hinges 'on demand, which in turn depends on the division of labour and the conditions of human culture resulting from it.' The economic organisation of cultural work is as important for understanding art as is the aesthetic dimension. Alienation is a key term here. The capitalist division of labour has the effect of concentrating artistic ability disproportionately through the population, a situation remedied only by a Communist society in which 'there are no painters but at most people who engage in painting among other activities'.[22] There is thus a conflict between the economic organisation of culture (the cultural needs of the dominant class) and the internal aesthetic demands of art itself. It is in this sense that art might be said to necessitate alienation thus promoting a critical and potentially subversive structure.

Thus nineteenth-century realism, while inspired by bourgeois philosophy, was unashamedly anti-bourgeois (Balzac, Stendhal, Flaubert, and to a lesser extent, Dickens, Mrs Gaskell). The capitalist organisation of industry alienated the worker and produced what Marx called 'fetishism', a belief that the existing society, its institutions and ideology were natural and unending. Class domination, wrote Marx, is legitimised by 'commodity fetishism'. In art and literature a similar process occurs: if a literary work is dominated by ideology then its social function is one of support to the dominant class; genuine, creative literature, while not escaping ideological influences, will strive to criticise the existing order, to transcend its immediately given forms. Literature which is completely ideological must be perpetually brought up to date, to legitimise and fetishise the changing situation. Such literature cannot survive, except as historical documents; there is no problem here of 'artistic autonomy'.

The 'alienation effect', the complex dialectic between the writer and the society which makes his writing possible, between the demands of the creative imagination and the dominant class ideology is central to Marx's sociological method — yet it remains rarely discussed by Marxist writers for whom literature is a reflection of an historically 'progressive' social movement (for example Plekhanov, Lukács). Trotsky, however, clearly follows Marx's inspiration when he writes that artistic activity 'by its very nature, lags behind the other modes of expression of a man's spirit, and still more of the spirit of a class.'[23] And as was argued in the previous chapter the development of nineteenth-century bourgeois society had the effect of progressively alienating the writer from the values of the dominant class, a process which was neither uniform within particular societies nor between them: the unstable French bourgeois hegemony and the stable English bourgeois hegemony contrast with the absence of an effectively operating hegemonic structure in Russia and Germany.[24] The 1848 Revolutions and the development of working-class political movements further compounded the complex nexus of writer, class and society.

To be sure, failure to depict genuine revolutionary aspirations of the working class does not invalidate the realist novel. But it does suggest the limits of nineteenth-century realism. Flaubert had written that the contemporary novelist must confine himself 'to relating the facts', a sentiment echoed in Zola's admiration for science and his desire to push the novel 'towards the exact study of facts and things'.[25] Realists therefore turned to the study of 'low life', the dispossessed in society, to the workers, prostitutes, servants and peasants. In the preface to their 'proletarian novel' *Germinie Lacerteux* (1864) Edmund and Jules Goncourt put the case for the proletariat:

Living in the nineteenth century, in a time of universal suffrage, democracy, liberalism, we asked ourselves whether

what one calls 'the lower classes' have no right to the
Novel . . . We asked ourselves whether there should still exist,
be it for writer or reader in these times of equality, classes too
unworthy, sufferings too low, tragedies too foulmouthed,
catastrophes whose terror is not sufficiently noble. We began
to wonder whether . . . in a country without caste or legal
aristocracy the sufferings of the poor and humble could
touch our interest, our pity, our emotions, as sharply as the
sufferings of the rich and mighty. . .[26]

Thus although the realist writer accepted the need to depict
accurately and fully the complex ramifications of capitalist class
structure, and while committed to the values of honesty, truth,
and above all to sincerity,[27] the problem persisted. In bourgeois
societies lacking a proletarian hegemony the working class,
while not idealised, remained either unknown or portrayed
externally; and as the potential revolutionary force described by
Marx the nineteenth-century proletariat are found only in
minor, forgotten works, not in the mainstream of fiction. The
Goncourt brothers have well described their own estrangement
from society and their attempts to understand it from the
outside. In their hands the novel became a report on its state:
the contemporary novel, they wrote, 'is made with documents
narrated or selected from nature, just as history is based on
written documents.' Thus working-class men and women

can be captured only through an immense storing up of
observation, by inmumerable notes . . . by the amassment of
a collection of *human documents*, like those heaps of pocket
sketches which, assembled at a painter's death, represent his
life-time of work . . . human documents make good books:
books in which there are real human beings on two legs.[28]

The Goncourts' prescription for a democratic literature,
although never fully realised in their own work (the
working-class characters are not drawn from industry and the
trade union movement), illustrate forcefully the bourgeois
writer's increasing concern with working-class organisation:
after 1848 bourgeois hegemony was conterminous with the
development of socialism, Marxism and anarchism, the growth
of trade union and Social Democratic parties, and there can be
no doubt that many bourgeois ideologists and writers defined
these tendencies negatively, as threats to bourgeois culture.

That the bourgeois novelist had little genuine experience or understanding of working class political culture is evident in the frequent assimilation of revolutionary politics to terrorism and anarchism (for instance James's *The Princess Casamassima*).

But perhaps the most significant aspect of the Goncourts' prescription for a science of fiction was not that it produced a democratic art, but, in Zola's novels especially, a deterministic and fatalistic literature which circumscribes man's actual and potential freedom. In Flaubert's *Sentimental Education* (1869) and Dostoevsky's *The Devils* (1872) the problematic hero — Frederic Moreau, Ivan Stavrogin — remains an autonomous individual, bound by environmental and external forces but not crushed by them: Zola's heroes are non-problematical precisely because their fate has already been decided by the novel form itself. Naturalism differs from realism through the fateful workings of an invincible heredity combined with an oppressive external milieu; the subtle dialectic conjoining socio-historical forces and the problematic individual has been eliminated within a broadly non-problematical although critical structure. The dialectical balance between self and the external world, freedom and necessity, the dominant characteristic of the nineteenth-century realist novel, has been transformed not into democratic but a totalitarian art. It is but one step from Zola's naturalism to Gorky's *Mother* (1907) and socialist realism and a literature in which the deeply problematical and revolutionary elements of bourgeois realism are transmuted into a didactic realism amenable to political control. This is the link between the decline of nineteenth-century realism and the rise of naturalism and a politically committed literature which originates with *Mother*.

Gorky wrote *Mother* after the failure of the 1905 Revolution as a conscious attempt 'to sustain the failing spirit of opposition to the dark and threatining forces in life', to keep alive the hopes of revolution and socialism. The novel greatly impressed Lenin: *Mother*, he told Gorky, is 'useful for the Russian working man . . . summon[ing] him to battle against the autocracy.' Later, in the1920s, Gorky rather more critically described the novel as 'a really bad book, written under the spell of bad temper and irritation after the events of 1905 . . .'[29] Written in a straightforward realist vein, the novel depicts a group of idealist revolutionaries led by Pavel Vlasov who stoically endure prison, exile and the largely apathetic responses of the working class to their ideas. The revolutionaries are portrayed as wholly good, the representatives of the Russian autocracy as degenerate and evil. The novel describes the gradual transformation of Pavel Vlasov's illiterate and religious mother from a blind allegiance to the Tsarist government to rejection and rebellion. From a lifetime of abject misery and oppression a revolutionary consciousness is gradually forged and the novel closes with Pavel exiled and his mother taking up the battle:

> Someone struck her in the breast and she fell down on the bench. The arms of the gendarmes flashed over the heads of the crowd, clutching at collars and shoulders, pushing people aside, snatching off caps and tossing them to the other end of the room. Everything swam before the mother's eyes, but she conquered her weakness to cry out with what was left of her voice, 'Band together, good people, into one strong force!'[30]

This, then, is Gorky's prescription for 'elevating life' through literature, of recharging the nineteenth-century realist tradition: but the work is insipid and unreal: the characters have no interior life or subjective development, their personalities are presented as simple properties of political ideology. The tension between the hero and the world, the deeply problematical nature of this relationship which had largely sustained nineteenth-century realism, is replaced by a simplistic psychology which reduces interiority to a question of progressive political consciousness. Even the potential conflict between religion and scientific socialism is rendered non-problematical as the mother easily reconciles her growing socialist convictions with her ingrained religious beliefs: socialism will inaugurate the kingdom of God on earth.

There is thus a paradox: the apparent contradiction between the novel's political commitment to freedom and the unfreedom within it. Character and political ideology are one, the novel form is non-problematical, a political pamphlet which affirms unanimously the justice of socialism, the wickedness of capitalism. And within this structure there can be neither complex character nor motivation, only a uniform pattern of cause and effect. The 'positive hero' emerges, an active and passionate advocate of the future; there is no room for problematic heroes and 'superfluous' men. And it is this kind of structure which is criticised for its ultimate conservatism, sustaining the charge that socialist revolution distrusts revolutionary art. The point is, of course, that Gorky's novel does not form an organic part of nineteenth-century realism but departs from it on the important question of freedom. The connection between Zola and Gorky and the decline of nineteenth-century realism is thus obvious.

But what of modernism and its relation with realism? The Yugoslavian critic, Mihajlo Mihajlov, has written that 'the twentieth century was born in mid-nineteenth century Russia', that the origins of modernism can be traced to Dostoevsky's 'underground man', the anti-hero of the short novel *Notes from Underground* who loudly proclaims his envy and hatred of science, rational thought, progress, man.[31] It is this irrational, highly subjective element which characterises one strand of modernism: J. K. Huysmans' hero, Des Esseintes, in the novel *Against Nature* (1884) is a typical anti-hero, a neurotic nobleman who strives to insulate himself totally from the outside world through the cultivation of esoteric and bizarre sensations and whose *rejection* of society represents the inward turning, highly subjective romanticism associated with the decline of bourgeois realism. In Huysmans' novel, plot in the traditional sense has disappeared, for nothing happens apart from the steady heightening of Des Esseintes' sensibilities; the pulsating social world of Balzac and Dickens has been transformed into a wholly private subjectivism.

In the novel this new sensibility could take many forms, from the crude naturalism of Henri Barbusse (*L'Enfer*, 1908), which unsuccessfully strives to eliminate authorial presence and traditional plot in favour of minutely observed scenes of ordinary, prosaic life, to the highly complex structure of Proust's *A la recherche du temps perdu* (1914—26) in which the social world is rendered and communicated to the reader through the subjective consciousness of the 'I', Marcel. In James Joyce's *Portrait of the Artist as a Young Man* (1916) the reader is introduced to the social world through the introspection of young Stephen Dedalus. The novel opens with the mental experience of the main character:

Once upon a time and a very good time it was there was a
moocow coming down along the road and this moocow that
was down along the road met a nicens little boy named baby
tuckoo . . .

His father told him that story: his father looked at him
through a glass: he had a hairy face.

He was baby tuckoo. The moocow came down the road
where Betty Byrne lived; she sold lemon platt.

The author has been successfully effaced; reality is conceived
subjectively, no longer rendered narratively, but through the
mind and the memories of the characters. The 'interior
monologue', the elimination of the author and the steady
erosion of plot, hero and structure while constituting the basic
elements in the trend towards modernism, were already present
in the realist novel through the heightened subjectivity of the
problematic hero. The realists' depiction of society as
contemporary history and man as an organic part of a prosaic,
frequently monotonous life (Flaubert's *Madame Bovary*,
Dickens's *Bleak House*) imply a consciously subjective approach
by the novelist: both George Eliot and Proust display a
profound grasp of human subjectivity without losing the
specific sense of society as uniquely historical.

It would be a mistake, therefore, to set up modernism as the
direct antithesis of realism. The Symbolist movement of the late
nineteenth century has often been cited as forming one of the
foundations for modernist literature (Joyce, Proust, Svevo) but
the relation of realism to symbolism is far more complex than
this suggests. Russian symbolism, for example, was a movement
which exercised a deep influence on early Soviet writing and in
the work of the philosopher Vyachevlav Ivanov and the poets
Andrey Bely and Alexander Blok was defended as a more
legitimate mode of expressing reality than nineteenth-century
realism. Symbolism, it was argued, went far beyond the realists'
descriptions of an external, objective world in portraying not
the mundane surface of events but 'the phenomena of the
human spirit'. For many this higher reality was synonymous
with religion and mysticism; but it was also defined as the
subjective element in human experience, the 'inner life' of
feeling, dream, hallucination and unreason: 'From the point of

view of contemporary psychology, *reality is the sum total of all
possible experience* (inward and outward . . . the visible world is
but a small part of reality.'[3][2] Bely's statement is close to the
ideas of Joyce and the stream of consciousness writers. Like
them, the symbolists grasped the truth of life as inward
experience, not as something 'out there' in the external world.
Unlike Joyce, however, they defined the task of art in activist
terms, as the embellishment of prosaic reality: art, wrote Bely,
acts as 'a *creative* revelation and *transformation* of the forms of
life',[33] sentiments echoed in Maxim Gorky's argument that it is
'absolutely essential that contemporary literature should begin
to embellish life, and as soon as it does so life will embellish
itself, that is, people will begin to live at a greater pace, more
brilliantly.' Often described with some justice as the father of
socialist realism, Gorky saw himself as a realist and his novels,
stories and plays in terms of the nineteenth-century realist
tradition which he defended tirelessly against the practitioners
of modernism: 'We have quite enough in life itself of things
shadowy, dim, distorted, and depressing . . . Life demands more
light and clarity, but has no need for obscure repulsive paintings
or nervously morbid verse, devoid of all benefit to human
beings and infinitely removed from genuine art.'[34]

Marxist critics such as Lunacharsky followed Gorky in
rejecting what they termed 'the morbid, pathological' features
of modernism, but accepted the dictum that art does not
function as a passive mirror of reality but rather as a partially
autonomous activity which transforms it. 'It is a question not
simply of engendering life at one's own level', wrote
Lunacharsky in 1904, 'but of creating it higher than oneself. If
the essence of all life is self-preservation, then beautiful, good,
true life is self-perfection. Neither, of course, can be confined
within the narrow frame of individual life, but must be set in its
relation to life in general. The only good, the only beauty, is the
most perfect form of life.'[35] For the mistaken assumption is
that modernism, as a whole, must be opposed to socialism,
realism and human *praxis*. This is simply not the case: Russian
symbolism, as Alexander Blok observed, was clearly
distinguished by a tendency towards realism but the dichotomy
was too deep and ingrained for any kind of genuine
reconciliation by Marxist critics. In the 1920s the debate over
realism and modernism continued in much the same vein with

the two tendencies remaining firmly estranged. The leading
Russian writers — Zamyatin, Pilnyak, Pasternak,
Olesha — experimented with modernist ideas, their work
strongly influenced by the pre-revolutionary symbolists. In
contrast, the realists produced few enduring literary works,
perhaps only Sholokhov's *Quiet Don* which appeared in 1928,
and in many cases 'proletarian writers' were strongly attracted
to and influenced by 'decadent' modernist prose and ideas. The
view that literature must be politically committed, forms the
basis of socialist realism, and while Russian modernism did not
reject artistic commitment to truth it firmly repudiated the
principle of political ideology as the crux of creative literature.

The great schism between realism and modernism was finally
settled by bureaucratic fiat in 1934, but the conflict between
the two tendencies had been strikingly illustrated in two
pre-revolutionary novels, Gorky's *Mother* and Bely's *Petersburg*
(1913), the former acclaimed by Soviet critics as a masterpiece
of socialist realism, the 'first proletarian novel', while the latter
was contemptuously dismissed as an example of degenerate
modernism. Based on the 1905 revolution, Bely's *Petersburg*
depicts a group of revolutionaries as they strive to assassinate a
highly placed government official. But with this description all
similarity between *Petersburg* and *Mother* ends. For Bely's
novel is the culmination of Russian symbolism in literature
which, in a manner reminiscent of Joyce but independent of
him, makes use of newspaper reports, interior monologue and a
complex juxtapositioning of events within a shifting time scale.
Described variously as 'a turning point in the Russian novel',
'one of the most arresting Russian novels of the twentieth
century',[36] *Petersburg* communicates a profound sense of
disorder, of impending doom, the highly charged, feverish
atmosphere of a city on the verge of revolution. Bely, like
Joyce, has dispensed with the traditional trappings of
nineteenth-century realism: *Petersburg* has no identifiable hero
but a number of anti-heroes whose feelings, thoughts and
dreams dominate the twenty-four hour span of the 'plot'. A
parody on Dostoevsky's *The Devils*, the novel vividly portrays
the conflict between the reactionary, bureaucratic Senator
Apollon Ableukhov and his son Nikolai, an indolent, spoiled
student who has become involved with a group of
revolutionaries, agreeing to help them kill his father: they now

demand he honour his pledge. A terrorist called Dudkin hands him the bomb hidden in a sardine tin. Nikolai has other problems however, for, attracted by the bohemian wife of an army officer, Sofya Likhutin, whose salon is a rendez-vous for the revolutionaries, he masquerades as a red domino, terrorising the city and alerting both the newspapers and police to his activities. Appalled by the bomb, his revolutionary associates and a general sense of incompetence and lack of purpose in his life, Nikolai passes through a series of nightmares and hallucinations which culminate in an accidental and abortive explosion in Ableukhov's study.[37]

Bely's novel, unlike *Mother*, is not 'future oriented'; it has no identifiable 'positive hero', its structure being built around a subjective, chaotic sense of reality, a nightmare vision of an alienated, fragmented and hostile world. But while Bely captures the revolutionary atmosphere of 1905, the novel's subjective form has the effect of eliminating the profoundly historical dimension of the nineteenth-century realist novel: Bely's characters are no longer organically embedded within a concrete political, social and economic totality — contemporary reality has become non-historical — and thus revolution is depicted episodically, as chaos.

Gorky's *Mother* and Bely's *Petersburg* stand at the crossroads of the modern novel. Gorky builds on the degeneration and weaknesses of realism to produce a utilitarian, propagandistic and unfree novel form; Bely builds on the strengths of realism, its subjective and problematic character, but by excluding a socio-historical perspective the novel affirms an *absolute*, unconditional freedom. This is not true of all modernism — Proust's great novel for example — but during the 1920s, Soviet literary theory, and later Stalinist orthodoxy, identified modernism with cultural degeneration and realism with cultural vitality. Gorky's realism transforms literature into an unmediated, direct reflection of class interests; the result is the erosion of the complex nature of individuals, ideas and events. The theory associated with Marxist critics such as Walter Benjamin and Bertolt Brecht, which attributes to the realist writer the political—sociological task of 'discovering the causal complexes of society/unmasking the prevailing view of things as the view of those who rule it/writing from the standpoint of the class which offers the broadest solutions for the pressing

difficulties in which human society is caught', is equally false.
The author is not primarily a producer for a specific class: as
this chapter has argued, a complex, dialectical relation subsists
between the realist novel, bourgeois class and proletarian
revolution, bourgeois hegemony and the novel form, and at no
point can it be argued that genuine literature walks hand in
hand with class interests and ideology. Brecht's injunction that
'a living and combative literature which is fully engaged with
reality and fully grasps reality . . . must keep step with the rapid
development of reality'[38] denies that necessary mediation
without which no critical literature can exist at all.

   It will be argued in the following chapter that if the rising
proletarian class lacks hegemony, then its literature can
be little more than a substitute for its own revolutionary
praxis. For the novel form is pre-eminently a meditation on the
problematic nature of human life and social existence; it neither
fights battles nor wins wars; it is neither a call to action nor
mere passive entertainment but a telling of the complex moral,
political and social fate of man in modern society as he strives
to affirm his freedom and autonomy in a world of apparent
necessity, to shape that world to his purposes and will.

4 Bureaucracy, Socialism and Literature

In her reminiscences, the German Socialist Clara Zetkin wrote of Lenin that he had little sympathy with the artistic *avant-garde*, and like Marx, Engels, Plekhanov and Trotsky he much preferred realism in art and literature. For Lenin the greatest pinnacles of literary acheivement were the works of Dante, Shakespeare, Pushkin, Balzac, Dickens and Tolstoy. As for the *avant-garde* he declared himself 'a barbarian', unable 'to consider the products of Expressionism, Futurism, Cubism and other 'isms' the highest manifestation of artistic genius. I do not understand them. I experience no joy from them.' When Lunacharsky, the first Bolshevik Commissar of Education, allowed Futurist and Cubist artists to decorate Moscow for the 1918 revolutionary festivals Lenin described their efforts caustically as 'straightout mockery and distortion.' Of Mayakovsky's poem, *150,000,000*, he commented: 'You know, this is very interesting literature. It is a special type of communism. It's hooligan-communism.'[1] Unlike Lenin, Trotsky's tastes were more sophisticated and Futurism, Formalism and Constructivism were not as easily rejected; but throughout his literary criticism he, too, maintained an ambivalent attitude towards modernism in favour of critical realism. As for Lukács all forms of modernism are identified with decadence, psychopathology, morbid eccentricity and artistic incoherence. Writing in his most dogmatic vein. Lukács argues that the realist novel poetically reflected reality through depicting 'the essential pattern which the relationships of human beings to each other to society and to nature form in real life,' by rejecting all surface phenomena and the 'everyday' world. The 'average' is mediocre, 'diluting and deadening', 'unpoetic': it lacks that necessary 'perspective' which determines the form and content' of literature for, drawing together 'the threads of the narration, it enables the artist to choose between

the important and the superficial, the crucial and the episodic.'
The 'ideology of modernism' is thus found in its underlying
naturalistic character, its absence of hierarchical structure and
failure to comprehend the inherently 'meaningful' character of
each human act. Thus Symbolism, with 'its impressionist
methods and its cultivation of the exotic', and 'the
fragmentation of objective reality in Futurism and
Constructivism', reflects a crisis in capitalist culture: only those
writers endowed with a socialist vision, or at least not hostile to
socialism, can create an enduring, realistic literature.[2] In effect,
therefore, Lukács asserts the necessity for modern writers to
take sides *politically* in order that they may safeguard a
bourgeois art-form, nineteenth-century realism: as will be
argued later, this rejection of modernism means only the
assumption of a profoundly conservative aesthetic, not the
development of a genuinely revolutionary realism.

The rejection of modernism is clearly linked with a somewhat
mehanical equation of materialism in Marxism and realism in
art, combined with a highly deterministic theory of
'superstructure' and infrastructure'. Plekhanov, for example, as
the most erudite and authoritative literary Marxist after Marx,
linked realism with the economically progressive features of the
bourgeois class and modernism with its decline. Surveying
nineteenth-century French literature, he concluded that since
the 1848 revolution French literature had degenerated from the
objective powerful realism of Balzac into a subjective
withdrawal from social life, exemplified in the 'art for art's
sake' movement and the work of Flaubert, Baudelaire and
Huysmans in particular.[3] This dogmatic, mechanical theory was
widely accepted as the basis of a Marxist literary theory and,
when socialist realism was officially designated as the artistic
mode of the proletarian future at the 1934 Soviet Writers
Congress, it seemed to many a logical result of the basic Marxist
tenets. Such a view, however, would be dangerously misleading,
for the fact that Lenin objected *personally* to artistic
modernism did not prevent Lunacharsky from encouraging all
forms of artistic expression not openly antagonistic to the 1917
revolution, nor did it inhibit the development of the most
creative period of Soviet literature and art. 'There had never
been so many theatres (and incidentally, at that time theatres
were free); never had so many books — particularly volumes of

poetry — appeared. Never had there been so much experiment in the theatre and in painting.'[4] The Bolshevik revolution ushered in an epoch of modernism and internationalism in art, a cultural movement which contrasts starkly with the overtly nationalist and conservative art of the post-1930 years. In the film the contributions of Eisenstein (*Potemkin, Strike*), Pudovkin (*Mother, The End of St Petersburg*), Dovzhenko, Kuleshov and Vertov changed the course of world cinema; modern painting and architecture were pioneered by Tatlin, Malevitch, Lissitsky, Kandinsky, Rodchenko; and in prose fiction and poetry, Pasternak, Babel, Olesha, Fedin, Zamyatin, Mandelstam, Mayakovsky, Leonov, and Sholokhov made the 1920s the golden age of Soviet letters. But by the 1930s a dogmatic conservative orthodoxy pervaded every facet of Soviet culture, and artistic experiment was rewarded by isolation or death. The artistic innovations pioneered by these artists and writers now came directly into conflict with the ultra-conventional assumptions of socialist realism. The triumph of socialist realism was not simply the result of an inherent aesthetic logic in Marxism itself: tensions between modernist art and literature and Marxism were always present and never more so than during the 1920s. This chapter will explore these tensions as they crystallised during the bitter debates between the left and right in both literature and politics, conflicts finally resolved in the complete bureaucratisation of all art and literature.

I

In the February 1917 Revolution a bourgeois democratic government led by Alexander Kerensky came to power. The Tsar abdicated but Kerensky's government, committed to supporting the Allied War aims, quickly lost the support of the masses and its own authority. In October, the industrial working class rallying behind the Bolsheviks dispatched the unfortunate Kerensky to the 'dustbin of history'. And at once the new government found the most unlikely supporters: Alexander Blok and Andrey Bely, Futurist and Symbolist poets, welcomed the revolution rapturously as the Russian apocalypse. Blok wrote:

A revolution, like a violent whirlwind or snowstorm, always brings new and unexpected things and cruelly disappoints many people. Its whirlpools devour the good and save the worthless, but that is in the nature of revolutions and changes neither the total direction of the current nor the terrible deafening tumult which accompanies it. The roaring noise is an expression of its sublimity.[5]

Other Russian writers were less enthusiastic. By 1922 a mass exodus of Russian writers to Western Europe indicated the widespread hostile feelings of the intelligentsia towards Bolshevism: Ivan Bunin, Leonid Andreyev, Alexei Remizov left for good; Alexei Tolstoy, Gorky and Ehrenburg became temporary exiles while other pre-revolutionary writers who remained in Russia found adjustment too difficult and wrote little of significance. Hopes that the revolution might regenerate the realist genre and create a socialist literature were soon dispelled for the immediate post-revolutionary years brought to prominence a new generation of writers influenced not by the nineteenth-century masters but by the *avant-garde*, Symbolism and Futurism. Modernism, far from being crushed, developed energetically, the revolution finding its highest artistic expression in those writers who, while critically accepting the revolution, remained aloof and sceptical, the literary 'fellow-travellers' as Trotsky called them — Pilnyak, Zamyatin, Fedin, Olesha, Leonov. The modernism which Lenin found difficult to understand was never effectively challenged by a new committed realism, and during the 1920s a cultural policy amounting almost to *laissez-faire* characterised the Russian cultural scene. But by the 1930s dogmatic, rigid orthodoxy had replaced variety and experiment: the doctrine of socialist realism, first expounded at the 1934 Soviet Writers Congress, became the political touchstone of literary validity. And as Stalin's cultural 'reforms' began to shackle Soviet literature, Western writers, attracted by the revolutionary promise, found themselves in the middle of a literary—political debate which effectively decided the fate of the modern socialist novel. Malraux, Dos Passos, Hemingway, Koestler, Romain Rolland, Gide, Barbusse, the Danish author Martin Andersson Nexö, Isherwood, Leon Feuchtwanger and Heinrich Mann: all were involved directly or indirectly in the debate on realism. Many gave an unstable allegiance to the Soviet Union and what they took for socialism and Marxism. Thus some of the most important and serious writers in Western Europe became

attracted and influenced by Communism *after* it had passed its
revolutionary phase: nationalism and the domination of society
by a bureaucratic caste replaced the 1917 ideals of
internationalism and democratic socialism; when disillusion
inevitably set in, especially after the Nazi — Soviet pact of
1939, it was not simply Stalinism which was rejected, but
socialism, Marxism and in some cased democracy itself. The
political novels of Orwell, Koestler, Camus, Sartre and Doris
Lessing exemplify this tendency, while those of Pasternak and
Solzhenitsyn remain haunted by the tragic events of the 1920s.

The development of Stalinism destroyed all vestiges of
modernism; many writers died anonymously in the labour
camps, while others were forced into exile and silence
(Zamyatin, Olesha, Bulgakov), suicide (Mayakovsky) or survived
through a mixture of luck, dishonesty and a willing propensity
for corruption (Sholokhov, Alexey Tolstoy, Fedin, Leonov).
The concept of commitment in general to the revolution
became transformed into a dogmatic commitment to Stalin's
version of history. In Stalin's phrase, the writer, and more
especially the novelist, must become the 'engineer of the human
soul', practically moulding his art for the good of the cause. A
committed, socialist realist literature thus negated modernism as
it rejected an honest, faithful depiction of the social world:
social optimism, a positive hero, heroic workers and sincere
party men embodied the 'activist' literature announced at the
1934 Writers Congress.

This bureaucratic shackling of literature, the regimentation
and political administration of writers with the corollary of an
'activist' literary stance, is sometimes represented as a logical,
historical continuation and summation of Bolshevik ideology
and particularly of Lenin's ideas on the relation of party,
literature and politics. In the one-party state there is no room
for the uncommitted writer. The relative freedom given to
writers and literary groups in the 1920s is therefore interpreted
as an essentially unstable period, an interregnum when the
Communist Party had yet to acquire the total authority and
power to dominate the artistic field. Such an argument,
however, tends to eliminate the most significant feature of these
years, the political struggle of two rival factions, between those
who argued for a socially responsible, utilitarian standpoint in
literature and those who understood that art is not created by

administrative fiat and social conformism but must remain free
of political pressure. By the 1930s the latter tendency had been
effectively destroyed, and Maxim Gorky returning to the Soviet
Union from exile in 1928 could proclaim that the basic
difference dividing 'critical' realism from 'socialist' realism lay
in the former's inability to show man 'a way out of his bondage'
to his freedom. Socialist realism, he argued, should not merely
reveal the 'vices of society' but positively reflect the facts of
'socialist creativity' and its achievements. Socialist realist
writers, Gorky urged, must transcend critical realism's emphasis
on the 'negative' and pessimistic features of social life and
instead 'stir the proletariat of all countries and stimulate its
revolutionary awareness of its rights'. The writer's task as an
'engineer of the soul' must be to create class consciousness, to
show 'how a consciousness of unity of purpose has appeared in
the multinational Soviet Union.' Literature is thus
future-oriented, committed to an inevitable, progressive
transformation of society; the writer's duty is less to such
subjective dictates of art as sincerity, rather to an immanent
purpose in history laid down authoritatively by the state and its
bureaucrats and reinforced by a vast apparatus of police
repression. In Gorky's authoritative prescription literature
functions socially and artistically as ideology; the writer is
merely an appendage to class activity and political organisation,
part of the process to overthrow capitalism and build socialism.
In essence socialist realism embodies the idea of literature
consciously reshaping the world, and it is but one step from this
to the view that only the Communist Party, with its scientific
understanding of history and its clear knowledge of present and
future tasks, has the means and the right to determine the
character and content of literature. Under the guidance of the
Party the writer becomes the 'artist in uniform' and, as a recent
Soviet critic has put it, taught 'to portray what is positive in our
life . . . to reveal and condemn the imperfections that hinder the
forward march of society.' The 'positive' hero triumphs at the
expense of the 'negative'. Given 'friendly advice', the writer
successfully eliminates the 'anarchical tendencies' implicit in
creative work and thus affirms communist ideals: 'Party
guidance is the most important precondition for the successful
development of Soviet literature and the arts.'[6]
In defence of this prescription for totalitarianism, Soviet

publicists invoke the work of Lenin, which they argue
constitutes the source and basis of socialist realist ideological
commitment. Some critics of Marxism, on the other hand, have
seen in Lenin's writings 'the most sweeping statement of the
contempt for literature inherent in Soviet Marxism.'[7] Such
positions are barely reconcilable, but for both the critical text is
Lenin's 'Party Organisation and Party Literature'. Written in
1905, this short article was largely ignored in the debates on
Soviet literature during the early twenties, but since 1932
Lenin's text has acquired the status of inviolable validity, the
theoretical criterion for 'honest' socialist literature. For in this
article Lenin clearly stated the class basis of literature — the
need for the writer to adopt a progressive outlook, postulating
the concept of *'partiinost'*, variously translated as party
mindedness, or partisanship, but unmistakably conjuring up
ideas of strict political commitment which, as Soviet critics
tirelessly suggest, means active, conscious allegiance to the
Communist Party: 'The distinctive feature of partisanship is the
conscious, committed service of the author to his class,
assuming the independent political participation of this class in
the social struggle.' Lenin himself wrote that literature 'must
become party literature' for 'it cannot . . . be an individual
undertaking, independent of the common cause of the
proletariat', it must be 'a cog and a screw of one single great
Social-Democratic mechanism set in motion by the entire
politically-conscious vanguard of the entire working class.
Literature must become a component of organised, planned and
integrated Social-Democratic Party work.'

The meaning of Lenin's article, however, can be grasped only
by relating it to the specific historical situation in which the
Bolshevik party found itself in 1905. Following the revolution
of that year, the Tsarist government had been forced to
introduce a series of reforms into Russian social and political
life, one being the legalisation of opposition parties: the
Bolshevik Party was now able to advertise itself openly and in
this context Lenin's article was directed specifically to the
influx of new recruits: under no circumstance would anti-Party
literature and anti-Party views be tolerated within the Bolshevik
Party. It must be borne in mind that Lenin was writing only of
Party literature, of literature created by Bolshevik members,
published by the Party press and distributed through Party

newspapers and bookshops. Party activity, Lenin argued, must be under strict Party control. But did Lenin also imply a similar control over *all* literature, over problems of aesthetics and criticism, over philosophical matters? 'Calm yourselves, gentlemen,' he wrote, 'for we are discussing party literature and its subordination to party control. Everyone is free to write and say whatever he likes, without any restrictions. But every voluntary association (including the party) is also free to expel members who use the name of the party to advocate anti-party views.' The essential point is that Lenin was not advocating Party control over all literary production, only advancing the principle of partisanship to refer to these writers directly committed to the Bolshevik Party. That this is the correct interpretation is supported by Lenin's notes for the article, which clearly state that he is referring only to '*litterateurs* such as Akselrod, Martov, Parvus, Trotsky . . . and Plekhanov.'[8] After all, in 1905 few novelists, poets and artists were actively involved in Party work and Lenin's words were hardly aimed at them. And when, in the completely different circumstances of 1920, Lenin wrote that although 'every artist . . . has the right to create freely, according to his own ideals, independently of everything else . . . we cannot stand idly by and allow chaos to develop', he did not imply totalitarian control over literature. In this context the Party's decision in 1921, approved personally by Lenin, to publish a predominantly literary journal — *Red Virgin Soil* (*RVS*) — edited by Alexander Voronsky, in which the contributors were modernist, émigré and proletarian, becomes significant. There was no attempt to dictate the 'right' politics, and writers who were largely unsympathetic to the Bolsheviks were published; equally important there was no attempt to dictate policy dogmatically to Voronsky. Pilnyak and Zamyatin were published frequently in *RVS* and Lenin followed the magazine's fortunes and development closely.[9] Of course, the Bolsheviks hoped for a renaissance of realism from the rising generation of Soviet artists: as Lunacharsky wrote, 'realism in literature, the theatre, painting, music, poster design and graphics . . . but of course sharper, more demonstrative, more monumental, shading lightly into pathos on the one hand and into farce on the other.'[10] But Lenin, Trotsky and Lunacharsky were fully aware that literature and art were not so many commodities to produce by political fiat. However opposed Lenin was to modernism the fact remains that his understanding of the relationship of literature to society was dialectical not mechanical: his four short articles on Tolstoy, for example, written before the Revolution are directed against Plekhanov's mechanical theory which reduced the literary work to a mere reflection of class background: for Plekhanov, Tolstoy's artistic achievement flowed directly from his class position as a member of the landed nobility, as a Russian count. These articles, like the earlier one on party literature, are frequently cited by Soviet literary hacks as laying the foundations for a Marxist aesthetic and, with their meaning distorted, as constituting the basis of socialist realism. The truth is that they are neither: Lenin treated Tolstoy's literature as a document of the times, but he did so dialectically, thus emphasising the contradictions within Tolstoy's art, between his ideology and social class position. Lenin's basic point was that Tolstoy's fiction reflected the contradictory development of nineteenth-century Russian society with its fusion of capitalist and feudal elements. The bitter criticism Tolstoy levelled at the Russian ruling classes, the Church, law, militarism, bourgeois marriage, as well as his false prophecies on the future development of Russia, reflect not a working-class and socialist standpoint but rather his position as the spokesman for a peasant bourgeois revolution. Tolstoy, Lenin argued, understood rural peasant Russia, and his critique of the existing institutions 'was that of the patriarchal, naive peasant, whose psychology Tolstoy introduced into his criticism and his doctrine.' Expressing the changes occurring in the peasantry, Tolstoy 'mirrored their sentiments so faithfully that he imported their naivete into his own doctrine, their alienation from political life, their mysticism, their desire to keep aloof from the world, "non-resistance to evil", their impotent imprecations against capitalism and the "power of money".' Lenin, therefore, rejected the theory that the creative writer must 'mirror' his own class background. More significantly, he went on to argue that for Tolstoy to produce great literature it was unnecessary for him to grasp and understand that Russia's future lay with the urban proletariat and revolutionary socialism and not with the peasantry and pacifism. Yet with a false historical view Tolstoy, like Balzac, transcended his utopian philosophy and politics through art — 'the triumph of realism' — in his honest, sincere picture of Russian society. Tolstoy was not politically committed in the sense of supporting a political concept of art: he hated injustice, but renounced politics in favour of moralising and non-resistance to evil. His reactionary utopianism, his belief in moral regeneration as the solution to the evils of the world, his idealist philosophy, all these did not prevent him from creating great literature.[11]

It becomes impossible, therefore, to argue either from Lenin's short texts or his political actions that here lies the source and inspiration for later Stalinist practice, or that socialist realism and the shackling of writers to state ideology were inherent properties within Marxism itself. Such distortions are possible only through a profoundly unhistorical view of the struggle for socialism in the Soviet Union, of the conflict between left and right factions in the Bolshevik Party during the 1920s in which the claims of literature as an activity independent of political power were counterposed to the bureaucratic arguments that literature must be 'socially responsible'. In the 1920s a fierce struggle was waged on these questions, between those who supported a broad latitude in literary expression (Voronsky, Trotsky) and the doctrinaire, bureaucratic tendencies associated with the old Proletkult, themselves the literary expression of the growing power of rule by undemocratic, administrative fiat. The bureaucratisation of Soviet society and the emergence of a nationalist, non-revolutionary socialism were embodied in the figure of Stalin and his slogan, 'socialism in one country', while for Trotsky and his supporters (the 'Left Opposition') the threat to the revolutionary ideals of 1917 crystallised in the very notion of bureaucracy. The historical processes which finally eventuated in Stalin's total usurpation of power in the 1930s are complex, but a brief sketch and analysis is essential for a proper understanding of the doctrine of socialist realism and the tragic fate of those writers associated with Communism.

II

On the eve of the 1917 Revolution, Russian literature was largely dominated by the symbolism of Blok, Bely and Sologub and the 'impressionistic realism' associated with Chekhov, Bunin, Kuprin and Korolenko. The dominant literary influence

was Symbolism and the young pre-war writers like Remizov,
Zamyatin and Alexei Tolstoy attempted to fuse the old
traditions of Russian realism with the Symbolists' rhythmic and
linguistic innovations, in which fantastic and realistic elements
were subtly combined at the expense of objective detail. Of the
literary and artistic tendencies which greeted the October
revolution favourably the most extravagent in their praise and
hope were the Futurists,* who saw in the revolution a
complete break with the bourgeois past. Led by Mayakovsky,
the Futurists declared the art of the future to be proletarian and
in their magazine, *Art of the Commune*, called for the final
reckoning with the 'dead citadel' of bourgeois art and the
creation of 'the living factory of the human spirit'. Classical
art-forms were derided as reflecting the values of the aristocratic
and bourgeois classes: Mayakovsky's 'Orders to the Army of
Art' demanded:

> Enough tuppenny truths!
> Sweep the rubbish out of your heads!
> The streets are our paint-brushes,
> The squares are our palettes!

Other literary groups were more guarded in their response to
the revolution, becoming increasingly demoralised and
frightened by the civil war, famine and the rigours of war
communism. In Andrey Bely's Symbolist magazine, *Dreamers
Notes*, the great poet Alexander Blok gave, in his 'Russian
Dandy', artistic expression to the widespread feelings of
pessimism held by the middle-class intellectuals. 'I am much too
cultured', the Dandy remarked, 'to fail to understand that it
cannot possibly continue along these lines; the bourgeoisie will
be destroyed. But if Socialism should prevail, then all that is left
for us is to die.'[12] Gorky too, voiced his unease with the

---

*The Futurists, a pre-1917 artistic tendency, identified completely with
industrialisation and saw the 1917 revolution as laying the foundations of a new,
dynamic and integrated society. 'Let us seize [the world] from the hands of nature
and build a new world belonging to [man] himself', the great painter Malevich
declared, 'Cubism and Futurism were the revolutionary forms in art foreshadowing
the revolution in political and economic life of 1917.' Another Futurist artist
declared that 'the proletariat will create new houses, new streets, new objects of
everyday life . . . Art of the proletariat is not a holy shrine where things are lazily
regarded, but work, a factory which produces new artistic things.' C. Gray, *The
Russian Experiment in Art 1863—1922* (London, 1971) pp. 219—20.

Bolshevik's assumption of power: a life-long socialist who for many years had been closely associated with the pre-war Russian revolutionary movement, he characterised the new government as totalitarian yet anarchical, instituting a regime in which mob rule and bestiality had replaced the socialist vision of a just society. Lenin, he wrote, lacked moral fibre, his 'utterly pitiless' attitude towards the ordinary worker being 'worthy of a nobleman': 'Lenin, Trotsky, and their companions have already become poisoned with the filthy venom of power, and this is evidenced by their shameful attitude towards freedom of speech, the individual, and the sum total of those rights for the triumph of which democracy struggled.' The Bolsheviks, Gorky concluded, had roused the atavistic instincts of the Russian masses and the only hope of removing the 'inbred slavery' and 'stupidity' was 'by the slow flame of culture'. There was 'too much of politics'; culture could not develop.[13] Gorky's opposition to the Bolshevik government, however, was shortlived and, after working tirelessly to help those intellectuals hostile to the new regime, he accepted a temporary position in Lunacharsky's Commissariat.

Gorky now argued, albeit briefly since he left the Soviet Union shortly afterwards, that the Bolsheviks were striving to create a socialist culture. In this way they made no attempt to establish a cultural dictatorship, and the Futurists, who had arrogantly defined themselves as the only revolutionary artists in Soviet Russia, were soon fiercely criticised by Lunacharsky for their assumption to speak in the name of the government on artistic questions. The Futurists, Lunacharsky argued, were merely one artistic tendency among many and 'it would be a misfortune if artists of the new school were to establish themselves as the final expression of the State school of art, the exponents of the official revolutionary art.[14]

Thus, at the birth of the Soviet State, the leading government spokesman on cultural matters was unequivocal in his opposition to any presumption that revolutionary socialist art and literature must flow from one single doctrine and school. As it happened Futurism was shortlived although its influence persisted through the Left Front in Art (LEF) formed in 1923, which claimed to represent the voice of true revolution; other 'revolutionary' groups soon emerged amidst the deprivations and hardships of war communism, the most important being the

Proletkultists with their vision of a pure proletarian culture. Others included the Constructivists whose poetic vocabulary incorporated the latest scientific and technical terms and innovations, demanding that art must be social and responsible, replacing 'speculative activity' with 'socially directed art-work'; the Ego and Cubo-Futurists, offshoots of Futurism; the Organisation of Peasant Writers; and the 'nihilists' who created nothing at all.

As commissar of the Commissariat for the Peoples Education Lunacharsky played an important role in the development of official Party attitudes to the organisation of art and culture. Although he rejected the extravagant claims of the Futurists, Lunacharsky remained extremely sympathetic to the Proletkult concept, as well as the organisation it had set up in September 1917. This theory of a 'pure proletarian' culture, a culture which would sever drastically all connections with the previous bourgeois culture, was one of the major themes in the early Soviet literary debate. The chief theorist of the Proletkult was A. A. Bogdanov (1873–1928), an old Bolshevik whose ideas on philosophy and literature had met stern opposition from Lenin before the revolution. In 1908 Lenin devoted a large section of his book, *Materialism and Empiro-Criticism*, to a spirited polemic against what he called 'God builders' in the Party, idealists who, in the wake of the failure of the 1905 revolution, strove to accommodate Marxist materialism with religion and philosophical idealism. Both Bogdanov, Gorky and Lunacharsky were members of the Proletkult group, and Bogdanov's espousal of a peculiarly proletarian culture dates from this time.

As a theory, Proletkult was clearly based on a serious misunderstanding of Marxism, for as a social theory Marxism did not separate itself from all antecedent ideas, but both built upon and revolutionised bourgeois theory itself (philosophy, economics) by developing its scientific and critical elements (Ricardo's theory of value, Hegel's concept of dialectic). But perhaps more significant than the Proletkult's mechanical definition of Marxism was its implicit totalitarian assumption that only proletarian writers and artists organised by the Communist Party had the ability and the right to represent and speak for the working class and socialism. Writing in 1910 Bogdanov had argued that the proper function of art was 'to organise, not only the ideas of men, their thought and knowledge, but also their feelings and moods.' Proletarian art, he went on, is art which organised men's minds towards the ideals of collective labour, solidarity and brotherhood, while bourgeois art organised the mind in terms of individualism and egoism: 'Art is part of the ideology of a class, an element of its class-consciousness, hence an organised form of class life, a means of uniting and welding together class forces.' Art is a 'weapon' in the class struggle and each writer reflects a distinctive class ideology; a poet, for example, grasps the world through the eyes, thoughts and feelings of 'a definite class', for 'under the writer's personality is hidden the collective author and poetry is part of this collective author's self-consciousness.'[15] Bogdanov's theoretical position thus implied complete rejection of bourgeois art since this reflected class psychology unhelpful to the proletariat.

In a similar vein Lunacharsky defined art as 'the organisation of the emotions in individual persons or groups, classes and whole nations.' Proletarian art was merely 'the expression of the process of organisation of its soul life.' In Proletkult theory art is ideology, its social function to mobilise and educate the masses, 'a means for the socialisation of emotion' as Bukharin,* another leading Bolshevik theoretician sympathetic to Proletkult, phrased it. As editor of the influential party newspaper, *Pravda*, Bukharin expressed sympathy with the aims of the Proletkult, and in his review of the first number of their journal in 1918 commented on its 'extraordinary favourable impression', arguing, with some reservations, that Proletkult constituted 'a laboratory of pure proletarian ideology'.[16] While Bogdanov, Lunacharsky and Bukharin supported the idea of a politically independent Proletkult the tendency of the argument was unmistakably towards some form of centralised control and cultural dictatorship. The theoreticians of the Proletkult held firmly to the principle of *organisation*: all social classes, they argued, possess some form of culture, however rudimentary, but because of the proletariat's dominant concern with basic

---

*N. I. Bukharin (1888–1938) was widely regarded as the leading Bolshevik thinker superior even to Lenin and Trotsky. During the early stages of the Revolution he adopted a political position to the left of the party ('Left Communism'), advocating the waging of revolutionary war in Western Europe. In the 1920s he moved to the right, becoming the advocate of the N.E.P. policy and supporting Stalin against Trotsky and the left. In the late 1920s he was effectively isolated politically and finally executed as a 'counter-revolutionary' in 1938.

economic questions and the political struggle its leading
intellectuals are seriously disadvantaged, caught up in the
day-to-day tasks and not, like the bourgeois intelligentsia,
involved with the more universal problems of culture. Bourgeois
culture is thus more powerful than proletarian culture, but its
representatives are ideologically incapable of organising the
needs of the proletariat. The Proletarian, Cultural and
Educational Organisation was thus set up to develop and
organise a distinctive proletarian culture. At the Second
Congress of the Third (Communist) International a bureau of
the International Proletkult was established and by 1920 the
organisation claimed 400,000 members, 80,000 active in the
Proletkult studios set up all over Russia.[17]

Proletkult was the most influential of the early literary
groups and many of its ideas found expression in other
organisations. 'Ultra-leftist' art and literature became a
prominent feature of early Soviet culture. Writing in *Pravda* in
1919 on the fledgling Soviet theatre Bukharin had criticised
what he called the 'slavish respect for aristocratic culture . . . of
some of our ideologists' who, by persisting with bourgeois
drama (Chekhov for example) help in corrupting the proletariat.
Advocating the abolition of traditional theatres and drama in
favour of Proletkult studios and militant plays, he concluded:
'We must smash the old theatre. The person who does not
understand that understands nothing.' Many groups and
individuals did understand: within Lunacharsky's Commissariat
the 'Main Committee for National Education' presided over by
no less a person than Lenin's wife, Krupskaya, urged that public
libraries remove from their shelves work inimical to proletarian
ideology: Kant, Plato, Spencer and Schopenhauer were among
the ninety-four authors whose work was judged harmful for the
proletarian cause; Krupskaya provided a circular. *A Guide to
the Removal of Anti-Artistic and Counter-Revolutionary
Literature from Libraries serving the Mass Reader*, and as late as
1920 instructed the political police 'to intervene to see to it
that the task of purging was begun'.[18] In architecture it was
decided that wood was a bourgeois and 'counter-revolutionary
material' fundamentally opposed to proletarian 'revolutionary
building materials', the 'future-oriented' metals of concrete and
glass. Left-wing artists demanded the suppression of the Society
of Easel Painters and the destruction of traditional forms of

painting. Mayakovsky urged the complete destruction of all past art in the name of a purified proletarian future:

> A White Army Officer
> when you catch him
> you beat him
> and what about Raphael
> it's time to make museum
> walls a target
> let the mouths of big guns
> shoot the old rags of the past!

For Mayakovsky art as art was mere illusion: all art was propaganda (ideology) useful in the conduct of everyday affairs. Setting up a 'word workshop' he aimed to supply the revolution 'promptly and on easy terms' with any amount of useful, agitational poetry. In music it was argued that orchestral conductors were merely remnants of bourgeois individualism and in Moscow a 'conductorless orchestra' was formed based on a free discussion of music by the players: thus liberated, however, the orchestra, in the absence of revolutionary proletarian composers, was forced to play 'bourgeois music'. Other leftist experiments with music involved the principle of taking music to the people: streets and factories replaced the traditional concert-hall settings. And, like wood, traditional musical instruments were characterised as bourgeois and replaced by a genuine proletarian instrument — the factory whistle. In 1918 factory whistle symphonies were performed in Petersburg, Baku and Moscow with conductors raised on high towers using flags as batons for the players within the factories: unfortunately the music was barely understood, and like the other *avant-garde* leftist experiments, it lasted only for a brief period, although the theoretical assumptions on which it was based remained influential through the 1920s.[19]

In 1919 a number of dissatisfied proletarian writers detached themselves from the Proletkult; the group's members, who called themselves the Smithy, were critical of the Proletkult's attempts to organise the masses, which they saw as harmful to creative effort. Based on the factories of urban Russia, the Smithy claimed the title of a genuine proletarian writers' organisation, wholly committed to revolution, arguing that 'proletarian art is the prism in which the personality of a class is concentrated, a mirror in which the working masses can see themselves.' Like the Proletkultists they defined art as a weapon in the class struggle but called for a greater degree of commitment to industrialisation and collectivisation by the Communist artist. For the Smithy poets, the factory and the machine thus became the objects of poetic imagination and literature must reflect 'the cosmic sweep' of revolution with poetry transcending mundane existence to encompass sun, moon and planets in the celebration of revolutionary earthly success, ideas soon reflected in the first major organisation of writers in the Soviet Union. In 1920 the Smithy called a congress of proletarian writers and formed the All Russian Association of Proletarian Writers (VAPP) an organisation which in due course became RAPP and one of the most powerful instruments in the Stalin faction's drive towards and final consummation of power in the late 1920s. But as early as 1920 VAPP played a similar role, attempting to organise proletarian literature nationally and striving to establish total control over Soviet writers. The important point here is the tangible connection that exists between the later totalitarian politics of RAPP and the ideas and organisational norms of the early Proletkult as they were reflected in VAPP. But in 1920 VAPP was unsuccessful, and by 1921 when the New Economic Policy (N.E.P.) introduced a limited measure of private capitalism into Russian agriculture and industry, voices were raised claiming the betrayal of the October Revolution. A group split away from the Smithy section within VAPP to form the *October* group. The novelist Yuri Libedinsky and the future overlord of Russian literature, Leopold Averbakh (1903–38), were its leading intellectuals, and their literary principles reflected Smithy and Proletkult ideology:

> In a class society, literature . . . serves the interest of a particular class and only through that class does it serve all humanity; therefore proletarian literature is such a literature as organised the psyche and the consciousness of the working class in the direction of the final tasks of the proletariat as the creator of a communist society.[20]

There was, however, a significant difference of emphasis between the Smithy and *October* groups on the nature of the revolution: while the former stressed the grandeur of revolution, *October* was 'to cultivate a literature which will help the reader see the close connection between the most trifling workday fact . . . and our mighty tasks . . . *October* will attempt not only to show forth "living people" but to show them in their proper perspective.'[21] Already implicit in *October's* formulations was the tendency, later to dominate Soviet literature, to treat the 1917 Revolution as a purely Russian, domestic affair: the emphasis on the day-to-day tasks of the working class embodies a clear retreat from the perspective of world revolution.

The *October* group quickly became the prevailing orthodoxy of VAPP. In 1923 it published its own magazine, *Na Postu* (On Guard), affirming a dogmatic utilitarian conception of literature and arguing for the necessity to create a new proletarian culture. Its aim was to 'Bolshevise' literature: echoing Bukharin's arguments cited above it urged that literature must be judged socially, for 'only that literature can be useful from a social point of view in our time which organises the mind and consciousness of the reader, especially of the proletarian reader in the direction of the final aims of the proletariat as the creator of communist society — namely proletarian literature.'[22] At the first VAPP conference these arguments of *Na Postu* were dominant, and the conference accepted its theses on the ideological militant class basis of literature: the conclusion followed that all other literary influences were dangerous and should be extirpated. This task of liberating proletarian literature from bourgeois ideology devolved on the Communist Party: all culture, economics and politics must become dominated by proletarian organisation and ideology. It thus followed that bourgeois writers and artist were enemies of proletarian culture — even those whom Trotsky had called 'fellow travellers', that is, writers accepting the Revolution but not the Communist Party and Marxism. These writers, the most gifted and creative in Russia, must be forced to renounce their harmful bourgeois ideas by grouping themselves round genuine proletarian writers.

By 1924, then, the fundamental issues were clear: within those organisations dedicated to the idea of proletarian culture an incipient tendency towards totalitarianism was increasingly evident; the writer, art and literature must become 'organised', that is, 'bureaucratised'. In the ideas of Proletkult and *Na Postu* the fundamental basis of socialist realism is clearly anticipated. It becomes a matter of importance, therefore, to grasp the attitudes of the Bolshevik leaders, especially Lenin and Trotsky, to these dogmatic formulations.

Of those in the Bolshevik leadership, it was Lunacharsky and Bukharin who were the most sympathetic to the concept of art and literature as ideology and to the idea that the proletariat must build its own distinctive culture. Lenin and Trotsky, on the other hand, opposed the very concept of proletarian culture which they saw as inimical to Marxism. 'In reality', wrote Lenin in 1910, 'all the phraseology about "proletarian culture" is just a screen for the *struggle against Marxism.*' Lenin's point was quite simple: Marxism had absorbed the scientifically progressive features of bourgeois thought and culture in developing its political and social theory — but this was not to argue that Marxism *rejected* all previous bourgeois thought, for while Marxism represented a sharp break with bourgeois ideology it was built upon the knowledge which the bourgeois class made possible: 'Proletarian culture must be the logical development of the store of knowledge mankind has accumulated under the yoke of capitalist, landowner and bureaucratic society.' At the 1920 Proletkult Congress Lenin was equally adamant. In his draft resolution he demanded that the Congress firmly reject 'as theoretically unsound and practically harmful, all attempts to invent one's own particular brand of culture, to remain isolated in self-contained organisations', and urged all Proletkult bodies to remain as auxiliary units within the Commissariat of Education. For Lenin, proletarian culture meant primarily the practical task of social and economic progress, of raising the appallingly low literacy and the standards of the broad masses, and the development of agriculture, industry and technique. Proletarian culture did not mean the invention of theories of culture, 'not a dilettante self-admiring, Proletkultish so-called science . . . but a serious education' lasting for years involving millions of workers and peasants.[23] It was precisely this aspect which was missing in Proletkult practice: there were few contacts with the working class and peasantry, only the elaboration of spurious theories concocted in studios, groups and the short-lived Proletkult University. The masses were merely the recipients of these ideas: reporting on the Proletkult University set up in Moscow in 1919, Bogdanov argued that its task was 'the elaboration and development of proletarian science'.[24] For Lenin, proletarian culture was possible only through the organised labour of the proletariat, by working *with* not *apart* from them. The theory was nonsense: Lenin was adamant that the value of creative writing did not hinge on the expressed ideology of the writer, whether he enjoyed an impeccable proletarian social background or a socialist vision. In a letter to Gorky, Lenin once remarked that 'an artist can glean much that is useful to him from philosophy of all kinds', arriving at conclusions valuable to the revolutionary party from an idealist philosophical position. Such a philosophy may well be in contradiction with the artistic truth embedded in his work, for the whole point is not what the writer thinks (his ideology) but what he creates.[25]

Trotsky shared Lenin's rejection of the Proletkult but linked his condemnation with the international fate of the Revolution. By 1924, when he published *Literature and Revolution*, a sharp conflict had broken out in the Communist Party over the question of socialism in one country: was it possible to build a socialist economy in economically backward Russia without help from a successful socialist revolution in Western Europe? By 1924 the latter seemed a distant hope, but Trotsky argued that the fate of the Russian Revolution nonetheless hinged on revolutionary possibilites in the economically advanced European countries: failure of revolution in the West, especially Germany, would mark the probable doom of a socialist Russia. In a series of articles collectively published as *The New Course* (1923) Trotsky pointed to the growing bureaucratisation of the party, its increasing divorce from the masses, and the threat which these tendencies posed to the Revolution. The theory of 'socialism in one country' Trotsky identified as the ideology of a bureaucratic caste whose interests ran counter to the internationalist revolutionary ideals of the 1917 Revolution: bureaucracy, for Trotsky, was the antithesis of proletarian democracy and the most serious obstacle for the creation of a genuinely socialist society. Lenin, too, had pointed to the dangers inherent in bureaucracy: in his *State and Revolution*, written on the eve of the 1917 Revolution, he had argued that proletarian revolution would smash the old state machine and instead of a privileged minority standing above the people — 'the essence of bureaucracy' — he envisaged an administration in which officials would be subject to recall, election and supervision by workers' deputies. The Revolution would immediately introduce 'control and supervision by *all*, so that *all* will become "bureaucrats" for a time in order that, *nobody* will be able to become a "bureaucrat".' And although Lenin continued to criticise and warn of the danger posed to the Revolution by bureaucratic tendencies in government and party (especially his identification of these tendencies with Stalin), it was Trotsky who analysed the bureaucratic phenomenon with the greatest prescience. In 1923 he wrote that bureaucratisation must separate the party from the masses, weaken revolutionary spirit, create a stratum of officials owing allegiance only to the administration and a career, and promote a profoundly conservative ideology. 'Bureaucratism', he argued, 'is not a fortuitous feature of certain provincial organisations, but a general phenomenon', rooted in the backward state of Russian culture, economy and technique, and the conflicting interests of peasants and urban workers.[26] Trotsky's theory of 'permanent revolution', in sharp contrast to Stalin's slogan of socialism in a single country, postulated a *transitional* proletarian regime in Russia as a prelude to world revolution, and his contribution to the debate on literature assumes major *political* as well as literary significance. His opposition to the Proletkult ideas flowed directly from a revolutionary, not bureaucratic, temper and his vision of a short-term, limited proletarian dictatorship. For a transitional period, he wrote, is one characterised by intense class struggle and civil war which, 'though preparing the way for the great culture of the future, is in itself extremely unfavourable in its effect on contemporary culture.' By its very nature a revolutionary epoch is inimical to artistic creation since it breaks all continuity of literary development. As for the 'formal analogy' drawn between bourgeois and proletarian culture, Trotsky dismissed it with contempt:

> The bourgeoisie took power and created its own culture; the proletariat, they think, having taken power, will create proletarian culture. But the bourgeoisie is a rich and therefore educated class. Bourgeois culture existed already before the bourgeoisie had formally taken power. The

bourgeoisie took power in order to perpetuate its rule. The proletariat in bourgeois society is a propertyless and deprived class, and so it cannot create a culture of its own.[27]

Proletarian art and culture were mere fictions, and could never exist precisely because of the temporary and transient nature of proletarian dictatorship. For Trotsky, the 'historic significance and the moral grandeur of the proletarian revolution consist in the fact that it is laying the foundations of a culture which is above classes and which will be the first culture that is truly human.'[28] Like Lenin, Trotsky saw 'proletarian culture' as the development of education, the growth of literacy and the general raising of cultural levels. But the conflict between Trotsky and the Proletkultist tendencies in VAPP went much deeper than mere political differences; it involved basic questions on literature and art.

In his polemics, Trotsky took up the important question of the literary 'fellow travellers', and he supported Voronsky's stand in *RVS*. Trotsky's intervention in the debate came at the moment when the *Octobrists* were vociferously attacking what they called 'bourgeois', anti-revolutionary writers such as Zamyatin and Pilnyak and their supporter, Voronsky. In particular, the *Octobrists* were hostile to one of the most important literary groups of the immediate post-revolutionary years, the Serapion Brothers, whose manifesto claimed the autonomy of art and its necessary freedom from the pressures of political ideologies and parties. Supported originally by Gorky, and containing both Zamyatin and Pilnyak, their credo was pure idealism: 'We believe that literary chimeras are a special reality, and we will have none of utilitarianism. We do not write for propaganda. Art is real, like life itself. And like life itself it has no good nor meaning; it exists because it cannot help existing.[29]

It was the Serapion Brothers whom Trotsky had in mind when he coined his term 'fellow-travellers', but for VAPP the group was alien and anti-proletarian. When they claimed that a literary work 'may reflect the epoch, but it need not do so and is none the worse for it', they struck at the very heart of Proletkult orthodoxy. But for Voronsky and Trotsky the value of literature did not hinge exclusively on the class and political ideology of individual writers. 'Of course', Trotsky argued, a class factor exists in literature, 'but this class criterion must be refracted artistically', it must conform with the dictates of creativity: 'Yes, art has to be approached as art, literature as literature, that is, as a quite specific field of human endeavour.' Politics and art, Trotsky went on, are qualitatively different human practices each with their own laws and structure, and in a passage of great significance he drew attention to the 'enormous role . . . played by sub-conscious processes' in artistic and literary activity. It followed that such processes by definition must fall outside the control of the Party and pose insuperable problems for those who saw the creative act strictly in terms of ideological cognition.[30]

It was in this situation of mounting opposition to the artistic 'fellow-travellers' that Voronsky, whom Trotsky described as 'our best literary critic', was forced to develop and clarify his own position on the fundamental question of the relationship between literature and society and in doing so he postulated arguments diametrically opposed to the crude pseudo-Marxist conceptions marshalled by his opponents. It has been said that in these debates of the 1920s the fundamental problems of Marxist literary criticism and aesthetics were raised for the first time[31] — the tragedy lies in their brutal resolution.

III

As we have seen, the fundamental argument of the *October* group was its concept of literature as a class weapon. In the struggle of bourgeoisie and proletariat no quarter could be given: literature formed an integral part of the class struggle and must be won by the proletariat; the 'fellow-travellers' should be replaced by genuine proletarian talent. And since 'writers are the conscious or unconscious warriors of various classes on the ideological front,' there was an obvious and essential need for organisation. Voronsky's magazine, *RVS*, was thus characterised in military terms as a 'fortress', a 'beachhead' of 'the class enemies of literature'.[32]

Voronsky agreed, of course, that the class factor was an important element in the genesis of literature. But whereas the *Octobrists* argued that literature must organise the reader's consciousness and orientate it towards class goals, Voronsky made a critical distinction between 'ideology' and the 'idea' underlying each literary creation. For Voronsky ideology was scientific, abstract and conceptual, the very opposite of art. 'Genuine art', he wrote, echoing Engels's analysis of Balzac and Lenin's comments on Tolstoy, 'always contradicts ideology'. It was clearly right to emphasise the influence of a class ideology on a literary work, but wholly wrong to argue that a bourgeois writer must necessarily serve an 'alien ideology' and that the task of the proletarian writer lay in consciously placing class values at the heart of his work. In doing this, Voronsky argued, the writer creates bad art for he portrays not the real world but his mind:

> The writer ought to know how to dissolve his ideological orientation artistically in the material. The class struggle in art is carried out not by the hatred or enmity of the artist toward man, not by praising his hero or cleansing him completely of sins, but by artistic sympathetic understanding of his living typical essence. The passion of the artist ought to be, in its own way restrained, objective and cold . . . the artist needs to worry about his results only in terms of the proper distribution of his material and the attempt to give it inner spirit.[33]

It was in this spirit that Voronsky defended the 'fellow-travellers', for not only were they the most gifted of all Soviet writers with a greater literary talent than so-called 'proletarian authors', but their art transcended their limited political understanding of the Revolution: they 'represent real life, they help make it known to us, and in this sense they are able to organise the mind of the readers along lines necessary to Communism'. The 'fellow-travellers', he argued, reflect through their literature the Revolution, sincerely attempting to describe the 'objective truth' of life in Soviet Russia.[34]

Na Postu would have none of this dallying with the class enemy: the basic criterion for the estimation of a literary tendency lay in its social significance; socially useful literature is that which 'organises the mind and consciousness of the . . . proletarian reader' towards the Communist goal. Voronsky also came under bitter attack from a new artistic organisation, *LEF*, an amalgam of Futurist and Proletkult ideas, grouped around Mayakovsky, a tendency which rejected literary tradition and called for a literature of fact. More sophisticated than the *Na Postu* group, *LEF* attempted to fashion a Marxist

aesthetic which defined reality dynamically so that art neither
'mirrored' nor 'represented' society since to do so implied stasis.
'Representational' art, the *LEF* theorists argued, characterised
societies which 'feared reality', recording the 'ossified or
decadent social forms' which obstruct the pulsating flux of
reality. This type of literature kills art, turning the reader into a
passive observer of a dead world; its social function is to
entertain and anaesthetise. In contrast genuine art is 'dialectical',
striving to transcend a simple recording of reality by organising
the emotions through artistically creating ('producing') an
object (novel, painting, poem,) serving a higher, future purpose.
In this way genuine art exerts an 'emotionally organising
influence on the psyche, in connection with the task of the class
struggle', and the true artist thus becomes a 'psycho-engineer',
'psycho-builder', actively aiding the one social class that can
serve reality — the progressive proletariat, a class which will
reject the surrogates provided by representative art.[35] For the
LEF, the 'fellow-travellers' were examples of decadent,
representational art; their baneful influence should be eliminated
from Soviet literature.

The key terms used by both *Na Postu* and *LEF* in their
polemic with Voronsky, 'infect' and 'organise', clearly point to
a dogmatic and profoundly non-dialectical understanding of art
and literature; to argue that genuine art is permeated by the
values of a specific class which then 'infects' the reader, is to
eliminate all contradictions and assume a simple, mechanical
and non-mediated relation between art and society. In contrast
Voronsky argued that art was fundamentally a mimesis of the
harmony which pervaded the world, enabling man to acquire
knowledge of that world through artistic devices, especially the
image. But although nature is patterned, ordered, harmonious,
the tedious and mundane experience of daily life prevents man
from grasping life's essential beauty, so that art's role lies in
reproducing 'the primitive and immediate sensations and
impressions' of a world man no longer knows:

Man preserves in his memory, sometimes perhaps only as a
distant and dim dream, unspoiled, genuine images of the
world. They break through into man despite all obstacles. He
knows about them because of childhood and youth; they
reveal themselves to him in special, exceptional moments, in

periods of social life. Man yearns after these virginally bright images, and he composes sagas, legends, sings songs, writes novels, tales and novellas about them.

Art, therefore, is not simply a 'reflection of class society and its social types', but a complex probing into the realms of man's unconscious: Voronsky daringly cited works by Dostoevsky, Tolstoy (*The Death of Ivan Ilych*) and Proust as artistic validations of his theory.[36] His defence of the 'fellow-travellers', therefore, rested ultimately on the view that genuine literature was not something to be ordered politically and that genuine art cannot conform to a single, utilitarian, propagandistic, agitational function. Literature was art, not ideology.

Voronsky's support for the 'fellow-travellers', however, was not sufficient. In May 1924, thirty-six prominent 'fellow travellers' protested to the Central Committee of the Communist Party against continuous harassment by 'leftist' critics. At the same time they affirmed their support for Soviet Russia, to Bolshevik ideals and their solidarity with proletarian and peasant writers.[37] But the increasing isolation of Trotsky and the left opponents of Stalin was mirrored by the isolation of their literary supporters, and while it was neither practical nor yet prudent politically for a complete bureaucratisation of writers to occur, the portents were clear. In 1925 the Bolshevik Party intervened; for the first time the Soviet state committed itself to a direct statement on literary questions. Superficially it brought to an end the bitter controversy prompted by the attacks of the VAPP leadership on the 'fellow-travellers'. But more significantly for the future, an earlier discussion at the 1924 Party Conference had disclosed a strong sense of sympathy with the VAPP organisation and its ideas, and while the 1925 Party resolution disclaimed any attack on Trotsky and Voronsky, arguing indeed for the freedom of artistic activity outside party control, it was clear that these ideas were in the minority.

Thus both Bukharin and Lunacharsky, now firmly on the right wing of the Party, attacked Trotsky's theories and, using carefully selected texts from Lenin's writings, argued that a proletarian literature was both possible and desirable; it should not, however, constitute the exclusive literary tendency, and

Lunacharsky stressed that while 'proletarian literature must be supported in every way as our chief hope . . . the fellow-travellers should by no means be alienated from us.'[38] Bukharin, political leader of the right wing and the main theorist of the N.E.P., accepted the broad arguments of the *Na Postu* group and quarrelled only with their tactics. He advocated free competition between all the literary groups; at the 1924 Party Conference he had argued for 'a general leadership and the maximum of competition'. Bukharin's standpoint was based on the belief that socialism in one country was possible and that the fate of the Revolution did not hinge on successful revolution in Western Europe. He was therefore implacably hostile to Trotsky's theory of permanent revolution arguing that the Soviet Union would develop proletarian and socialist institutions only slowly, and that a lengthy transitional period must ensue in which a proletarian culture would grow, mature and gradually conquer the residual remnants of bourgeois culture. On the question of culture, therefore, Bukharin was clearly retreating from the principles of revolutionary Marxism: without a revolution in the West, Trotsky had argued, a Communist Russia was impossible, and with it all ideas of 'proletarian culture'.

Thus, while Bukharin and Lunacharsky rejected the idea of the Party issuing directives to writers or giving exclusive support to any one group, it was clear that the ruling faction tacitly supported *Na Postu*. In June 1925 the central committee issued its document 'On the Policy of the Party in the Area of Belles Lettres', a compromise solution to the deep conflict between *Na Postu* and Voronsky. Supporting the idea of a lengthy transitional period during which time the Party must live with and utilise the non-proletarian intelligentsia, the statement admitted that a proletarian literature *already existed* and must be encouraged. Bukharin argued that proletarian literature 'should attempt to develop the fellow-travellers, to educate and attract them to our side, not beat them over the head with a club, nor hold them in a vice.'[39] But the *Na Postu* standpoint of the class war in literature had been tacitly accepted: the statement that a neutral literature was impossible coupled with the argument that a proletarian literature actually existed in embryo and should therefore be actively encouraged represented a rebuttal of Trotsky and Voronsky. One month after the resolution F. Raskonikov, a leading *Na Postu* theorist, was appointed to the editorial board of *RVS* and by 1926 Averbakh enjoyed wide support from the Party.[40] Voronsky's position at *RVS* and his influence on Soviet writing began to deteriorate: criticised aggressively by *Na Postu*, he was eventually sacked as editor in 1927 and control of the magazine passed to the *Na Postu* group.

Bureaucratic control of literature now became increasingly evident: in 1926 VAPP absorbed the independent writers organisations, the Union of Writers, the All-Union Society of Peasant Writers, LEF, Smithy, and in the new magazine of the *Na Postu* group, *On Literary Guard*, Voronsky was savagely attacked. The Trotskyist Left Opposition had been outlawed in 1927, their members arrested, their leader exiled. In 1928 (at the All-Union Congress of Proletarian Writers), VAPP became RAPP. In the deepening hostility towards Trotsky and Voronsky, Lunacharsky vigorously defended the claims and status of proletarian literature and with some reservations on RAPP's polemical approach to its critics, threw his weight behind the RAPP leadership. As the influence of Trotsky and Voronsky waned, the theoretical and bureaucratic basis for socialist realism was steadily augmented.

IV

It has been argued so far that the evolution to Soviet socialist realism cannot be treated apart from the broader socio-political development of Soviet Russia during the 1920s, as revolutionary Marxism was gradually supplanted by bureaucratism and nationalism. By the mid-twenties a conservative, bureaucratic stratum, dedicated to the slogan 'Socialism in One Country', had virtually routed the revolutionary left. In the literary field, dogmatic, utilitarian and non-dialectical theories surged to the fore. Indeed, two related tendencies dominated the cultural scene: the ideas of Proletkult stripped of their more extreme formulations, and those of the traditional fellow-travelling intelligentsia, the latter increasingly browbeaten by the former.

In 1928 the First Five Year Plan was suddenly announced. The N.E.P. policy, criticised by Trotsky and the Left Opposition for the dangers it posed to the Revolution but supported by Stalin and Bukharin, was now rejected. The rich

peasant (the kulak) was to be forcibly appropriated and
agriculture brought under complete state control. The aim was
the rapid industrialisation of Soviet society. Stalin's 'left turn'
in economics was reflected in a left turn in politics and literary
questions. From 1928 to 1933 an 'ultra-leftist' orientation
dominated the internationalist Communist movement: social
democratic parties were labelled 'social fascist' while in
literature the slogans were those of a refurbished Proletkult.
The rejection of Trotsky's fundamental theses on literature was
finally augmented by a 1928 Party decision which reversed the
1925 compromise. The Central Committee resolved that

> Literature, the theatre and the cinema should all be brought
> forward and into contact with the widest circles of the
> population, and should be utilized in the fight for a new
> cultural outlook, a new way of life against bourgeois and
> petty-bourgeois ideology, against vodka,
> philistinism . . . against the resurrection of bourgeois ideology
> under new labels, and against slavish imitation of bourgeois
> culture.

Literature must now serve the interests of the Party for only
through the Party were the interests of the masses adequately
represented. The reference to harmful bourgeois influences was
clearly aimed at what were now called the 'right' critics, whose
whole conception of literature was anti-utilitarian (Trotsky,
Voronsky). Literature was to be harnessed to the needs of the
Five Year Plan and RAPP was the organisation instructed to
wage war on all deviations from this historic socialist task. A
Pravda editorial in 1931 summed up the new approach:

> We must educate a type of literary man who can write for the
> newspapers, who can give a vital, gripping description of our
> socialist construction, of all its gigantic achievements, and of
> all its failings. We need a fighting literature on contemporary
> themes, one . . . which will daily mobilize the masses around
> the task of carrying out the general line of the Party.[41]

Averbakh was adamant that the advent of the first Five Year
Plan, with its basis in industry, the elimination of the kulak and
the collectivisation of agriculture must inspire new forms of
literature based on the Party's struggle against the class enemy
(kulaks and 'wreckers'), against nature and bad Russian

habits — laziness, drunkenness, and so on. The Fifteenth Party
Congress, held in December 1927, had urged the recognition of
'the necessity of the decisive raising of the cultural level of both
the city and the village population, the development of national
cultures among the peoples of the Union, and the inclusion of
the plan of cultural construction as an inseparable part of the
general plan for the socialist construction of the Soviet Union.'
Two years later Averbakh declared that the Five Year Plan in
industry necessitated a Five Year Plan in culture, a 'cult plan',
linked indissolubly with industrial reorganisation, for 'having
gained political power . . . we should "conquer" and "rule" in
the realm of culture.'[42]

The first Five Year Plan inaugurated in October 1928
concentrated on heavy industry: thus novelists turned away
from 'traditional' Russian themes to document the process of
socialist reconstruction. To comply with RAPP's ideology of
commitment, writers visited new construction sites and
participated in the literary and social life of the factories and
kolkhozes. The 'industrial novel' appeared, a new genre
glorifying machinery and industrial construction. The standard
plot had a sabotaging engineer or kulak disguised as a worker
whose reactionary, anti-Soviet plans are finally thwarted by
diligent Communists and the new industrial plant completed on
schedule. The literary emphasis was optimistic and progressive:
the author of one book described how 'shock-workers' at a
metalworks fought for the right industrial norms:

> Six o'clock sharp. The signal bell rings from the motor. The
> huge fly-wheel swayed, shaking the dust from its iron
> shoulders. The couplings moved with a chime, and the
> spindles began to sing their song. The sheet-rolling mill
> moved along, to fight FOR THE METAL, FOR THE FIVE-
> YEAR PLAN, FOR SOCIALISM.

The titles indicate their content and ideology: *Force of
Example, The Brigadier of the Hot Department, Meat
Factories* and *In the Fight for Metal.*[43]

By 1928 it was clear that Bukharin's idea of freedom for
all literary groups had become irrelevant: the 1925 Party
assertion that 'no literary current school or group must come
forward in the name of the Party',[44] was replaced by a

doctrinaire intolerance. By 1930 the multitude of independent literary groups which had characterised the early
1920s had been absorbed into RAPP: Pilnyak and Zamyatin,
respectively the Moscow and Leningrad leaders of the All
Russian Union of Writers, the main independent group
opposing RAPP, were accused of collaboration with émigré
Socialist Revolutionaries and publishing anti-Soviet novels
abroad (*We, Mahagony*). On the basis of these unwarranted
charges the Writers Union was wound up.

It would be inaccurate, however, to see RAPP as simply
the monolithic tool of the Stalin faction, for while literary
creativity was increasingly bent to the task of combatting
social and political 'evils' and describing the building of
industrial projects, criticism of the bureaucratic regime could
still be voiced. The magazine *October*, for example, published
the first part of Sholokhov's *The Quiet Don* and did not
concern itself exclusively with the literature of collectivisation. Averbakh himself resisted the idea that literature must
confine itself to one basic theme, while the novelist Fadeyev
(later to be a literary mouthpiece of Stalinism) opposed 'the
stupid and harmful identification of the tempos of reconstruction with the tempo and character of literary development.' For while RAPP's ideology was broadly nationalistic, its 'leftism', the emphasis on the class struggle in
literature, had the unintended consequence that many writers
criticised the growing bureaucracy and the loss of socialist
ideals. The contradictions in the situation were vividly
illustrated when the magazine *On Literary Guard* published
Yuri Libedinsky's novel, *Birth of a Hero* (1930). Libedinsky
was promptly attacked for a 'psychological realism' which
'falsely' depicted a Party official from the standpoint of his
personal, sexual relationships, for an excessive concentration
on the inner life. One of the first 'proletarian' writers
published by Voronsky in 1922, Libedinsky's fiction had
often described the conflict between revolutionary ideals and
bureaucratic sterility, but *Birth of a Hero* aroused the greater
hostility for its artistic portayal of a Party degenerating into
strict bureaucratic conformism, Party officials more concerned with material comforts than with revolutionary
socialism.[45]

As a leading member of RAPP, Libedinsky had clearly

voiced a left-wing criticism of bureaucracy that was not
congenial to the Stalinist apparatus, which saw in RAPP 'an
ideological-educational organisation' to lead and strengthen
proletarian writers and the working class in the battle with
class enemies.[46] Thus while Averbakh and the RAPP leaders
called for a committed literary realism embodying a
materialist philosophy and rejection of idealism, there
remained too many writers critical not merely of bureaucracy
but who in their work tended to the severe literary and
political crimes of 'pessimism and subjectivism'.

In 1930 the leaders of RAPP came under severe attack:
taking Libedinsky's novel as a typical result of RAPP literary
policies, critics argued that proletarian literature should not
concern itself with the 'inner life of heroes', or give
prominence to sex and the unconscious: its role must be bound
up with the immediate problems of socialist reconstruction.
Libedinsky's hero, one critic wrote, 'represents a revolt
against the epoch and like him those writers who go against
the epoch who . . . do not care to work on mass
journals . . . are contemptuous of present-day themes and
refuse to submit to discipline' must change.[47] The realism
propounded by RAPP was then depicted as passive and
criticised for its contemplative stance, for ignoring the basic
precepts of dialectical materialism that man himself is an
active agent not passive object in the processes of social
change. Realism should engage itself and aim at changing
reality. And to do this, realism must become 'romantic
realism', and produce a literature flowing with revolutionary
ardour and class consciousness. The first documented
involvement of Stalin in literary matters dates significantly
from this period. A leading *Na Postu* poet, Demyan Bedny,
had published a poem in September 1930 expressing criticism
of Soviet management and the labour force in the important
industrial area of the Don. The poem was greeted at once
with praise for its frank portrait of Soviet shortcomings.
Then Stalin intervened and the Central Committee banned
the poem as unpatriotic and slanderous. To Bedny, Stalin
wrote:

What have you done? Instead of understanding the meaning
of the greatest revolutionary process in history and rising to

the heights of a singer of the advanced proletariat, you've
gone off somewhere into the valleys . . . You announce to the
whole world that Russia in the past was a vessel of filth and
indifference, and that present day Russia is no better, that
laziness and desire to 'sit on the stove' are to all intents and
purposes national characteristics of the Russian people — and
that means, of Russian workers — who, after accomplishing
the October revolution did not cease to be Russians. And you
call that Bolshevik criticism! No, my honoured Comrade
Demyan, that is not Bolshevik criticism but a slander on our
people. It is the degradation of the USSR, the degradation of
the proletariat of the USSR, the degradation of the Russian
proletariat. And after that you expect the Central Committee
to be silent! Just who do you take us for?[48]

Such sentiments clearly presage the end of RAPP: for Stalin,
realism must become patriotic, nationalistic and agitational; a
literature was demanded which, by its very nature, had room
for willing 'fellow-travellers' but none for those who remained
critical of the bureaucracy and the Party.

The whole weight of the attack on RAPP, then, turned on its
concept of realism. Its errors were traced to Plekhanov whose
literary and sociological criticism, it was argued, represented a
form of 'passive determinism'. It was at this point that Lenin's
contribution to literature was introduced — the 1905
article — and transformed into a major source of Soviet
aesthetics: 'Leninism', distorted into dogma, now became the
touchstone of political, aesthetic and social 'correctness'.
Plekhanov's literary theories were roundly condemned and
'linked' with Menshevism and counter-revolution. A crude
concept of partisanship was soon invoked as the basic literary
norm for socialist art. RAPP was rendered obsolete and
politically dangerous. It had done its work: and like all other
organisations which facilitated Stalin's rise to supreme power,
its internal conflicts and contradictions had to be resolved by
disbanding it into a monolithic, bureaucratic structure. RAPP
was now dissolved and replaced by the Soviet Writers Union, an
organisation dedicated to Stalin and bureaucracy. It was a
self-conscious political act, for at the Seventeenth Congress of
the Communist Party in 1934 it was publicly admitted that the
decision had been Stalin's. Criticising the RAPP leaders for

impeding the development of creative writing, Kaganovich, one of Stalin's appointees, rejected the argument that RAPP could have changed its course, for 'this might have remained merely a good intention. Comrade Stalin posed the question differently: it is necessary, he said, to alter the situation in an organisational way.'[49] In April 1932 Pravda published the Central Committee's resolution disbanding RAPP:

> Now that the rank and file of proletarian literature has had time to grow and establish itself, and that new writers and artists have come forward from factories, mills, and collective farms, the framework of the existing proletarian literary-artistic organizations is becoming too confined and impedes the serious development of artistic creation. There is thus the danger that these organizations might be turned from a means of intensive mobilization of Soviet writers and artists around the problems of socialist construction into a means of cultivating hermetic groupings and of alienating considerable groups of writers and artists, sympathising with the aims of socialist construction, from contemporary political problems.[50]

A Pravda editorial was more specific: RAPP's basic error, apart from its 'clannishness and arrogance' lay in 'its insistence on individual psychology',[51] implying a subjective element dangerous to the Stalin regime. For RAPP was not a monolithic organisation, and while rejecting Voronsky and Trotsky its ideas still allowed some latitude in portraying both 'negative' and 'positive' features within Soviet life. With Stalin no such freedom was possible: literature must become an instrument of education and indoctrination. Literature, created by 'engineers of the soul', thus became a social control.

The fate of RAPP, however, was bound very closely to that of Bukharin. RAPP's programme, largely based on the 1925 compromise, had been inspired by Bukharin's theory that Soviet socialism would develop only slowly and therefore the task of the proletariat was one of 'peaceful organising work'. The sudden 'left' turn in 1928, the attack on the kulak and the collectivisation of agriculture, the Five Year Plan, put an end to tolerance, and literature was increasingly judged on its 'proletarian' virtues: the 'fellow-travellers', although not persecuted, were encouraged to write documentary novels and plays on the themes of industrialisation and socialist progress. Criticism of 'negative' elements in Soviet life continued to emerge in the great flood of bad literature devoted to reconstruction; the criticism of RAPP that it produced 'proletarian literature' as distinct from 'socialist literature', and therefore alienated 'progressive' fellow-travellers, is only half true. Stalin abolished RAPP because it represented a threat to his position and that section of the bureaucracy which supported him: for *all* proletarian organisations in the arts were simultaneously abolished (the proletarian musicians association, RAPM for example) and at one stroke a totalitarian control over literature established. But the attack on 'proletarian literature' also reflected the needs of the privileged layers within the Soviet bureaucracy whose secure social foundation had been laid in the Five Year Plan, bureaucrats with little interest in internationalism, socialism and democracy. This new, ideologically conservative social stratum constituted the source of Stalin's authority and helps to explain the nationalism, patriotism, and the socially inegalitarian policies pursued so zealously by the government during the 1930s: the introduction of fee-paying in grammar and higher education, a 'Victorian' stress on the virtues of family life, monogamy, sexual puritanism and the abolition of abortion. The rediscovery of Russia's 'great' past led to a vicious campaign against the 'heresies' of the Bolshevik historian Pokrovsky (1868–1932) for minimising the 'great' achievements of the Russian Tsars in territorial conquest and promoting Russian nationalism. Conservative historians (many of them ex-Mensheviks) were now charged with the task of rewriting the 'Marxist' history of Russia, glorifying the 'progressive' Tsars Peter the Great and Ivan the Terrible; in music the Composers Union demanded 'an implacable struggle against folk-negating modernistic directions . . . typical of the decay of contemporary bourgeois art', with the result that Shostakovich's opera, *Lady Macbeth of Mtsensk*, initially hailed as a Soviet masterpiece in 1932, was withdrawn from the opera repertoire after Stalin had objected to the 'tuneless', dissonant music and adulterous 'depravity' of its heroine. As with literature Soviet opera must now embrace a socialist topic treated in a realistic national musical language, and typify, through its heroes and heroines, the 'positive' achievements of Soviet society. The swing to the 'left' in 1928 was now followed by a swing to the 'right' which in Soviet foreign policy meant entering the League of Nations and concluding strictly pragmatic alliances with bourgeois political parties in Popular Fronts. The tactics Stalin had used so effectively to crush Trotsky (alliance with the 'right' led by Bukharin) and then eliminate the 'right opposition' by adopting the Left Opposition's programme for industrialisation were paralleled in the literary conflicts: RAPP crushes Trotsky and Voronsky, is then itself attacked and finally dissolved to prepare reconciliation with that section of the 'fellow-travellers' and intelligentsia prepared to compromise their principles.

A year before the dissolution of RAPP Stalin had announced a change in policy towards the non-proletarian intelligentsia. Justifying the previous policy of hostility on the grounds that some intellectuals had engaged in anti-Soviet 'wrecking' activities Stalin argued that as 'the intelligentsia are turning to the side of the Soviet power' they must be accorded 'greater attention and solicitude'.[52] For the new privileged classes in Soviet society 'proletarian' literature must be transformed into socialist realism, which meant simply an ultra-conservative emphasis on the models of a bygone age; the art of the first socialist state was to seek its inspiration from nineteenth-century bourgeois realism.

V

During the 1920s Soviet literature was largely free of any one single literary orthodoxy or political group. As late as 1929 the independent Russian Writers Association led by Pilnyak and Zamyatin still commanded an authority free of state interference. Within this 'liberated' era the novel developed in its own peculiar way. The twenties ended, in fact, with the novel as the major Soviet literary genre, but ten years previously it had been poetry and short stories which dominated the literary scene. Severe paper shortages and the hostility of prose writers to the Revolution were largely responsible for the early weakness of the Soviet novel, a situation which Marxist critics had found particularly worrying. It was hoped, indeed expected, that socialist society would revitalise the great nineteenth-century realist genre and critics were increasingly sceptical and hostile of the influence exerted by Symbolist writers such as Bely on potential Soviet novelists. Explicit in many of the sympathetic critiques of writers such as Pilnyak and Zamyatin, which appeared in the early twenties, was a yearning for the revival of traditional Russian realism, for a return to the 'monumental' forms of fiction associated with the great Russian masters which had seemingly run its course by the twentieth century. The predominance of fragmentary literary forms — short stories and the episodic plots of the first Soviet novels — was widely interpreted as a symptom of cultural stagnation, even decay, while the extensive, complex totality of the classical realist novel, as a reflection of cultural vitality. Bely's *Petersburg* was frequently cited as the antithesis of a good Soviet novel:

> The loss of plot, the loss of a basic organizing principle, the chaotic succession of impressions, isolated patches, reality bordering on the fantastic — these are the basic characteristics of the new 'realism'. It is based on a naturalistic way of creating things, which is incompetent to cope with details and blows them up entirely out of proportion to their meaning and value.[53]

But the influence of Bely and modernism was not so easily extirpated and it was only with the triumph of socialist realism that the Soviet novel finally freed itself of 'decadent' elements. But already in the middle twenties the novel had reasserted itself against the earlier fragmentary forms. With the end of War Communism, the New Economic Policy went some way towards healing the shattered Soviet economy; the novel reflected this transition, and in the work of Fedin, Leonov, Sholokhov and Fadeyev especially, it became once again the dominant literary genre. No longer an impressionistic and episodic rendering of the Revolution, the new novel seemed firmly grounded in the traditions of nineteenth-century Russian realism striving to depict the totality of a revolutionary epoch. Its realism, however, was highly problematical involving both a self-conscious organisation of plot and the sympathetic portrayal of what socialist realist critics later called 'negative' characters and social features. In particular there was an increasing emphasis on the overtly sexual, on morbid and eccentric characters, and a thinly disguised pessimism with the emerging society. Three novels especially exemplify this trend — Fedin's *Cities and Years* (1924), Leonov's *The Thief*

(1927), and Olesha's *Envy* (1927) all of them soon to be swept
into historical limbo by the optimistic and positive heroes
decreed by socialist realism.

A blending of modernist influences with realism, these three
works constitute the high point of the Soviet novel in the
twenties for, created at a time when the writer enjoyed a
relative freedom to choose his literary models, influences and
shape his style according to the inner dictates of art, they
reflect the deep tensions of a society ideologically committed to
socialism yet lacking the hegemony of a dominant class. Russia
was now a socialist society, but the heroes of its fiction were
not the proletariat, but rather rootless intellectuals,
twentieth-century versions of Turgenev's 'superfluous men'.
Many critics have observed the apparent irony of a socialist
society which fails to create a single distinguished work of
literature celebrating the proletariat as the new dominant class.
The October revolution had brought the working class to power
in an economy largely dominated by the peasant and by
agriculture. A severe distortion characterised the socialised
economy and, with the failure of revolution in the more
industrially advanced capitalist countries the bureaucracy
gradually substituted itself for the dominant class. It was not a
question, therefore, of literature arising organically from a
society saturated by proletarian hegemony, rather of imposing
from above, within the institutions of the state, the 'correct'
literary line. But the process was protracted: during the
twenties the Stalinist bureaucracy had yet to gain total control
and many of the novels written at this time reflect the absence
of any form of class hegemony; the pervasive theme is the
conflict between revolutionary ideals and the intellectual in
Soviet society. N.E.P. had spawned petty bourgeois speculators
and an atmosphere of disillusionment with the Revolution: the
typical hero is someone incapable of adjusting to the new
society, an outsider who lacks genuine, positive commitment. In
Cities and Years, Fedin's hero, Andrey Startsov, a rootless
intellectual interred in Germany during the war, returns to
revolutionary Russia only to find a conflict between the new
collectivism and his individualistic ideals, his sentimental and
vacillating character. Helping an avowed counter-revolutionary
escape, he is killed by his Communist friend, coldly and without
the slightest hesitation. In Leonov's *The Thief*, the hero,

Vekshin, a former Red commissar, becomes a highly successful
Moscow criminal, his courage and ingenuity placed at the
service of the underworld rather than the money-mad world he
associates with N.E.P. Portrayed as a rebel against the
bureaucratic deformations of revolutionary idealism, Vekshin
finally grows sick of crime, and turning to simple manual labour
is reformed. Leonov sugared the pill of this problematic hero.
Not so Olesha who portrays his hero Kavalerov in irreconcilable
conflict with the new society. Like Dostoevsky's 'Underground
Man', Kavalerov is thoroughly superfluous, his envy and hatred
of those he sees as successful (economically and sexually)
driving him into isolation and despair. Educated and sensitive,
Kavalerov craves success but rejects the 'sordid' means available.
He spurns his benefactor, the bureaucratic Andrey Babichev, a
successful, self-satisfied director of a Soviet food combine and
turns to Andrey's drunken, idealistic brother, Ivan, who has
invented a machine capable of destroying all machinery. Ivan
Babichev seeks 'revenge upon his age', and together with
Kavalerov hopes to organise a 'Conspiracy of Feelings' to
undermine the present order which he sees systematically
denying individual feelings such as jealousy, vanity and pride.
Arrested by the G.P.U. he defiantly asserts:

> I want to find the representatives of what you call the old
> world. I mean feelings like jealousy, love for a woman,
> vanity. I want to find a blockhead so that I can show you:
> here, Comrades, is an example of that human condition
> known as stupidity.
>
> Many characters played out the comedy of the old world.
> The curtain is coming down. The characters must gather on
> the proscenium and sing the final couplets. I want to be the
> intermediary between them and the audience. I will direct
> the chorus and the last exit from the stage.

He fails: the rebels Kavalerov and Ivan Babichev cannot reform
and the novel ends with them seeking refuge in a squalid
Moscow boarding-house.

It was not only the problematic hero which characterised the
new Soviet novel: in these three novels the author experiments
with character, time and point of view. *Cities and Years* plays
with traditional chronology beginning with the death of the
hero and then switching back to his arrival in Russia (1919) and

then later to his internment in Germany during the war. *The Thief* is more daring: like André Gide in *The Counterfeiters*, Leonov introduces a novel within the novel with one of the characters, Firsov, writing a novel about the characters in *The Thief* so that the reader is never quite sure if he is reading Leonov or 'Firsov'. *Envy* is in two parts: the first narrated by Kavalerov, the second, in third-person narrative, written from Ivan Babichev's point of view.[54]

These three novels represent a penetrating critique of a society on the way to bureaucratic collectivism. In contrast to the contemporary fiction of Western Europe — Joyce, Musil, Kafka, Gide — they assert the structural dominance of hero, of individual biography over community, and while experimenting with modernist trends remain essentially within the broadly humanist and liberal traditions of nineteenth-century realism. It is as if these early Soviet novels, bound to the ideals of individual freedom and liberal ideology, were forced to take issue with a collectivist society, which formally at least was aiming to put an end to injustice, unfreedom, illiberality. As will be argued later it is in this sense that these writers and novels are linked to Solzhenitsyn's realism and problematic heroes. But with the advent of the first Five Year Plan such problematic elements rapidly disappeared: traditional plot and character eliminated all modernist elements from the novels of the 1930s as Stalin's virtual monopoly of political control was paralleled by a totalitarian control of literature. In the place of a free choice of theme, treatment and style there was now ideological dictation by a bureaucratic caste whose usurpation of power demanded conformity in culture as well as politics. The transition from the relatively free literature of the 1920s to the dogmatic, one-dimension fiction of the 1930s and beyond is thus an outgrowth of the bureaucratisation of the October Revolution in which all the internationalist and democratic ideals were turned systematically into chauvinism, philistinism and political elitism. There was no room here for 'superfluous men' and problematic heroes: Soviet writers were urged to follow the inspiring ideals of Maxim Gorky who, returning from self-imposed exile in 1928, enthusiastically embraced the cult of optimism. Touring industrial centres and visiting factories Gorky saw progress everywhere. He now rejected his old friend Voronsky — then in disgrace — and co-operated with Averbakh

and the literary bureaucrats of RAPP. In 1917 Gorky had
fought for the rights of those intellectuals opposed to the
Revolution; now he remained silent as all vestiges of
independence within the intelligentsia were systematically
wiped out. Stalin had stirred Gorky's patriotism with the vision
of a truly great Socialist Russia: literature must now engage
itself as part of this historic transformation. For Gorky, critical
realism, a term introduced at this time to describe the
nineteenth-century bourgeois realist, was incapable of doing
justice to this gigantic task. The Soviet Union, Gorky argued,
must create a literature 'that can stir the proletariat of all
countries and stimulate its revolutionary awareness of its rights',
a task falling only to the revolutionary artist, 'the engineer of
the soul'. For Gorky, literature was defined in strictly utilitarian
terms, as helping the proletariat to develop class consciousness
and revolutionary ideals, a task made possible by the creation of
the 'positive hero', for only the positive man embodies the
historic truth of a revolutionary epoch: 'In our
country . . . there must not, and cannot be superfluous people',
Gorky demanded; literature must reflect this truth. The
weakness of critical realism, he argued, had been its emphasis on
the individual as a superfluous man, but socialist realism would
transcend these limitations by uniting criticism with practice.
Critical realism affirmed nothing: 'The contemporary world was
easy to criticise but there was nothing positive to assert except
the obvious absurdity of social life . . . ' In contrast socialist
realism 'proclaims that life is action, creativity, whose aim is the
unfettered development of man's most valuable individual
abilities for his victory over the forces of Nature.' By attacking
the corrupting influence of cultural survivals socialist realism
evokes 'a socialist, revolutionary understanding and
comprehension of the world'.[55]

The term 'socialist realism' was introduced for the first time
in 1932. During the fierce literary debates of the 1920s ideas
close to those embodied in the concept certainly existed, but as
we have seen they were at no point predominant. In sharp
contrast, the statute of the Union of Soviet Writers demanded
the allegiance of *every* writer to the methods of socialist realism
and 'the creation of works of high artistic significance, saturated
with the heroic struggle of the world proletariat and with the
grandeur of the victory of Socialism, and reflecting the great

wisdom and heroism of the Communist party . . . the creation
of artistic works worthy of the great age of Socialism.' With
Gorky as its first President, the Union of Soviet Writers met for
its first Congress in August 1934, addressed by leading Soviet
theoreticians and bureaucrats, prominent writers, critics and
various famous foreign guests. Later the records were
suppressed and the second Congress, due in 1938, was
postponed until after Stalin's death. By this time it was clear
what lay in store for socialist literature. In 1933 for example,
Lunacharsky had argued that socialist realism was an 'active'
force striving to change the world, purposeful, capable of
distinguishing good from evil and those forces which hamper
the forward movement towards the goals of socialism and
communism. 'It is realism plus enthusiasm, realism plus a
militant mood.'[56] And in a similar vein Bukharin argued that a
combination of the perceptive, educational and effectual
functions of poetry allowed it to be 'an extraordinary active
militant force'.[57]

The official government spokesman at the 1934 Congress
echoed these utilitarian sentiments, but Andrey Zhdanov added
the more insidious notion of 'partymindedness'.

> Our Soviet literature is not afraid of being accused of
> tendentiousness. Yes, Soviet literature *is* tendentious, for
> in the age of class struggle, a non-class, non-tendentious,
> would-be literature does not and cannot exist.
>
> And I think that every Soviet man of letters can say to any
> thick-headed bourgeois, to any philistine, to any bourgeois
> writer who will talk of the tendentiousness of our literature:
> 'Yes, Soviet literature is tendentious, and we are proud of its
> tendentiousness, because our tendency consists in liberating
> the toilers, the whole of mankind from the yoke of capitalist
> slavery.'

And it was here, too, that Karl Radek, old Bolshevik and
supporter of Proletkult, made his astonishing attack on James
Joyce and Marcel Proust. Echoing Gorky, he argued that
socialist realism went beyond mere criticism of decaying
capitalism, to portray the rise of the revolutionary
proletariat, its struggle and victory: for socialist realism 'means
not only knowing reality as it is, but knowing whither it is
moving.' Before 1934 Joyce had been admired by many Soviet

critics for presenting a realistic depiction of decaying capitalist culture — Radek corrected them. Joyce believed

> that there is *nothing great in life — no great events, no great people, no great ideas*, and that the writer can give a picture of life by just taking any hero any day and photographing him carefully. A heap of dung, teaming with worms and photographed by a motion-picture camera through a microscope — that is Joyce.

As the literary representative of the petty bourgeoisie, Joyce portrays not the Irish revolutionary movement but the brothel: 'Joyce stands on the other side of the barricades . . . I wish to say to Soviet and foreign writers: *'Our road lies not through Joyce but along the highway of Socialist Realism.'*[5][8]

At the heart of Radek's criticism lay the totalitarian precept, noted earlier in the Proletkult theory, that the writer must be *organised* if he is to make the right selection of material and weld it into a future-oriented art. In essence the Proletkult had believed that a proletarian culture must be handed down from above by administrative fiat. And it is in these ideas, not those of Lenin, that the origin of socialist realism lies: Lenin, Trotsky and Voronsky had firmly rejected the ideas of Proletkult as anti-Marxist, a position not shared by Bukharin and Lunacharsky who remained as opponents, both politically and culturally, of the Left Opposition and unhappy supporters of Stalin. Socialist realism, therefore, was not the result of 'Leninist *partiinost*', but one of the tragic consequences of the defeat of Marxism in Soviet Russia. Like Proletkult, socialist realism was not so much an artistic method bound up with socialist aesthetics, but an administrative means for the organisation and control of the literary imagination. In 1934 artistic freedom was over. Through the Union of Soviet Writers a tight government control over all forms of artistic creativity was established. Conformist writers could flourish: paid by bulk (as in the nineteenth-century), supported by massive government subsidies and published not because of popular demand but simply through a slavish following of the correct political 'line'. Soviet literature quickly degenerated into a stifling mediocrity in which the novel, far from celebrating man's struggle for freedom, became one of the means of chaining him to unfreedom. The great purges of the 1930s swept away what remained of the non-conformist writers, while former members and officials of RAPP were now accused of 'Trotskyism', of actively aiding counter-revolution. Many of Averbakh's former collaborators were classified as 'enemies' of the Soviet state. In 1937 an editorial in the *Literary Gazette* proclaimed that Averbakh and his 'paltry school' had operated as an agency for disseminating Trotskyist ideas in Soviet literature:

> RAPP, which in its time played a significant role in the consolidation of the forces of proletarian literature, had by the year 1932 been transformed into a brake on the development of Soviet literature, especially as a result of that heinous role played in it by the Averbakh school, which appeared to be in the leadership.

Thus the argument that RAPP had carried out good work for the Party against the Trotskyists before 1932 was completely reversed by the 1937 disclosure that the leadership had been Trotskyist all along.[59] Charged in April 1937 Averbakh disappeared from Soviet history. Other writers and critics were soon to perish, among them Babel, Pilnyak, the poet Mandelstam, Voronsky, Bukharin and Radek. Others remained silent, writing in the knowledge that they would never be published. The dark night of socialist literature had begun.

PART TWO

Introduction

In his study of European realism Lukács argues that the year
1848 demarcates progressive bourgeois 'critical realism'
from reactionary bourgeois 'naturalism' and modernism.
Without accepting Lukács's dogmatic and specious
historical-literary scheme it remains true that 1848 represents in
both a symbolic and sociological sense a turning point in the
evolution of European culture. The brutal suppression of the
proletariat by the victorious bourgeoisie powerfully affected the
leading European novelists. In his *Sentimental Education*
(1869) Flaubert portrayed with great fidelity to historical truth
the initial union of bourgeoisie and proletariat during the
February phase of the 1848 Paris Revolution and the sense of
equality which emerged briefly with it: 'The general casualness
of dress blurred the distinction between the various social classes,
hatred was concealed, high hopes were expressed, and the mob
was in a gentle mood.' But Flaubert's vision was not socialist:
the Paris workers are seen as a 'mob', a 'rabble', although
the novelist is scrupulous in describing the subsequent crushing
and slaughter of the bourgeoisie's erstwhile allies. Flaubert's
grasp of the complex mechanics of class struggle, as Edmund
Wilson has aptly remarked, is as prescient as Marx's analysis in
The Eighteenth Brumaire of Louis Bonaparte (1852) in spite of
his strong anti-socialist ideology. In *Sentimental Education*,
Flaubert pitilessly explored both the grasping, corrupt
bourgeoisie of the 1840s exemplified in the Dambreuse circle,
men who 'would have sold France or the whole human race to
safeguard their fortune, to spare themselves the slightest feeling
of discomfort or embarassment', and the equally mediocre and
dishonest socialists, who, proclaiming equality and justice, end
like Senecal in joining the victorious National Guard in their
bloody suppression of the working class.[1]
    In Russia both Turgenev and Dostoevsky hoped that
revolution would realise the ideals of 1789, but 1848 dashed
all such hopes. As a young writer Dostoevsky had joined the

Petrashevsky group of radicals and ardently championed the
socialist cause. 'Long before the Paris revolution of '48', he
wrote later, 'we were already consumed by the fascinating
influence of these ideas.' It seems that Dostoevsky went much
further than the gradualist radicalism of Petrashevsky and in
1848 became directly involved with a small band of
revolutionists whose expressed aim was the violent overthrow of
Tsarism. Secret cells, printing presses and vows to total
commitment anticipate Dostoevsky's harsh portrait of terrorism
in *The Devils* (1872). Indeed, Dostoevsky's involvement was so
deep he could write later that but for his arrest in 1849 he
might have become a Peter Verkhovensky.[2]

After 1848, with the class struggle between the rising proletariat
and dominant bourgeoisie forming a potential threat to
bourgeois society, the novel became the major literary form
through which this conflict finds expression. The post-1848
novelists, while rejecting the values of bourgeois society more
completely than any other generation, experienced the
profoundest difficulty in portraying the revolutionary
aspirations of the working-class movement: the realist novel, a
revolutionary genre, paradoxically foundered over this
intractable problem. As was argued in Chapter 3, while realism
presented character and ideas organically bound to
socio-historical change, as an art-form the realist novel
transcended this revolutionary content through its inherently
conservative form, the category of individual biography; the
antagonism between the individual and society which is
depicted against a background of social conflict and change
remains as the basic structural principle of the realist novel. It is
important to emphasise that those post-1848 novelists who
grapple with the question of revolution refuse *in general* to
dissolve the complex world of character and ideas into political
propaganda and ideology. The novel of potential revolution
invariably becomes either a novel of tragic conflict and
resolution or, as with those writers who fail to eliminate
satisfactorily from the fiction their own residual bourgeois
ideals, an entirely false, forced portrait of the
nineteenth-century socialist movement. It is in this sense that
the persistent weakness of proletarian hegemony exercises such
a decisive influence on the post-1848 realist novel.

Flaubert's *Sentimental Education* is a novel which relates

individual character to contemporary history, and although part of the novel is set during the 1848 Revoltion its problematic hero, Frederic Moreau, remains a largely passive and remote spectator. His ideals are not those either of the socialist left or bourgeois right: early in the novel, as a young gauche provincial in Paris, Frederic is reminded of Balzac's Rastignac and the need to conquer fashionable society. And while he succeeds in this ambition, Frederic's ideals remain as uncorrupted as the day he reached Paris. His one single passion, his dominant ideal — the romantic, unconsummated love for Madame Arnoux — prevents his complete assimilation into bourgeois society (i.e. his rejection of the widowed Madame Dambreuse). A romantic, absurd figure, Frederic's politics are those of strict pragmatism and his vision of the future is pessimistic: 'Perhaps progress can only be achieved through an aristocracy or a single man. The initiative always comes from above. The people are still immature, whatever you may say.'[3]

Turgenev's novels similarly depict an unheroic hero against a foreground dominated by political questions. But unlike Flaubert, Turgenev's heroes are driven into fundamental conflict with society precisely because of their values. 'Where ideas cannot be modulated through practice', writes Irving Howe, 'they keep their original purity; where intellectuals cannot test themselves in experience they must remain intransigent or surrender completely.'[4] Turgenev's Rudin and Bazarov retain their ideals only through isolation and ultimately death: Rudin's romantic gesture on the barricades of revolutionary Paris contrasts with Bazarov's hard-headed realism, but for both, the total absence of revolutionary possibilities in Tsarist Russia determines their superfluous and ultimately tragic character. Bazarov's materialist outlook, his utilitarian philosophy and nihilism which reduces love to physiology and raises natural science above poetry represent Turgenev's condemnation of Russia's impatient revolutionaries. 'We know approximately what our physical maladies are caused by', says Bazarov, 'but moral diseases are due to stupid upbringing, to all kinds of trash with which human heads are stuffed from childhood — to the monstrous state of society . . . Put society right, and there will not be any diseases.'[5] But as with Flaubert, Turgenev's own rejection of political radicalism remains hidden within the novel's structure:

character is not allowed to degenerate into simple extremes of good and bad; the subtle nature of men's relations with each other, the impact and influence of ideas, emerge and develop freely. Turgenev's sustaining vision is that of the genuine novelist for whom ideology is strictly subordinated to art.

No greater contrast of the ways whereby the novel form affirms man's freedom is provided than by comparing Turgenev's *Fathers and Sons* with a novel written by the radical, materialist philosopher, Chernyshevsky, *What is to be Done* (1863). Admired by Lenin and Plekhanov, *What is to be Done* portrays a 'positive hero', a professional revolutionary, Rakhemetov, whose qualities are strenuously ascetic: a raw beefsteak diet, a rigorous physical training programme and sexual abstinence combine with a penchant for the occasional bed of nails to produce a tough, impersonal and thoroughly unbelievable, wooden character.[6] There is no room in Chernyshevsky's novel for superfluous men or the tragic vision; a positive optimism superficially pervades the work and as with socialist realism later the tragic is identified quite simply with pessimism. Like Gorky's *Mother*, *What is to be Done* is more concerned with the future, with life as it should be not as it is: the novel form is thus transmuted into propaganda, its unfree structure, which eliminates all doubt and ambiguity, refracted through the prism of ideology. But the point is that Rudin and Bazarov are more realistic as examples of nineteenth-century Russian liberalism and radicalism than the absurd Rakhmetov; and more precisely, although tragic figures they are far from pessimistic, for although defeated by outside forces nonetheless they retain their ideals and refuse to compromise with 'reality as it is'. Turgenev's last novel, *Virgin Soil* (1877) is closer to Chernyshevsky and Gorky than his earlier work. Here Turgenev attempts to portray the revolutionary movement of the late 1860s when thousands of idealistic young Russians — socialists, anarchists, students — sought the regeneration of Russia by 'going to the people'. Historically inaccurate — the Populist movement had passed into political terrorism by 1869 — *Virgin Soil* represents an artistic failure for its too schematic delineation of character, motive and ideas: good and bad become the simple property of ideology and class position. To be sure, the typical Turgenev 'superfluous man' reappears, the anguished, melancholic and self-pitying student Populist,

Nezhdanov, who, having failed to communicate with the
'People' — 'It is difficult', he says, 'for an aesthetic creature like
me to come in contact with real life'[7] — gets drunk and,
concluding that he no longer believes in the cause itself,
commits suicide. But Nezhdanov is not the real hero of *Virgin
Soil*. For the first time in Turgenev's fiction a representative
from capitalist industry appears, Solomin, the socialist manager
of a local mill whose sympathy with the Populists is tempered
by his scepticism that revolution is neither imminent nor the
people revolutionary. Portrayed as a straightforward
non-problematic hero, Solomin defends the rights of workers
and criticises gentry and merchants: clearly he, not the
vacillating Nezhdanov, represents the future but it is a future
which Turgenev neither understood nor felt much sympathy
for. As a character, his 'positive hero' lacks depth and
complexity; representing the distant future of the
industrialisation of Russia there is no serious conflict between
the hero and society. His time is yet to come. This 'future
oriented' character thus remains apart from the abortive
Populist revolutionists who, directed by an anonymous political
centre, blunder into arrest and imprisonment.

As with other novels depicting revolutionary aspirations, the
exact source of political control remains ambiguous, the idealist
revolutionists mere pawns in a protracted struggle for power. It
is this aspect which links Turgenev's novel with *The Devils* and
The Princess Cassamassima (1886): Dostoevsky and James have
in common both the theme of anarchist terrorists subverting
bourgeois social order and a directing conspiratorial centre
foisting revolutionary ideology on a passive and indifferent
public. The nineteenth-century socialist movement is thus
largely absent from the mainstream of European fiction. In *The
Princess Cassamassima* the hero, Hyacinth Robinson, born in a
city slum — 'He sprang up at me out of the London pavement',
James wrote — emerges from the provinces to challenge society
and becomes involved with a strange Italian-American princess
and the unnamed leader of a terrorist revolutionary group
whose means to political power is assassination. Similarly in *The
Devils* the murder of Shatov is neither meant to raise mass
consciousness nor ignite any potential revolutionary movement,
but is rather an act of petty spite and revenge aiming to bind
the small group of revolutionists more tightly together.

Dostoevsky himself wrote that *The Devils* dealt with nihilism
not socialism, and the group of provincial revolutionists whose
fate becomes entwined with the fanatical Peter Verkhovensky
represent the network of secret cells which the revolutionary
groups founded during the 1860s by Sergey Nechaev and
supported by the anarchist leader, Bakunin, hoped would
foment the Russian revolution. Nechaev's theoretical work, *The
Catechism of a Revolutionary*, extolls the necessity for amoral
means to effect moral change — terror, arson, duplicity — and a
conspiratorial centre, a secret and hierarchical organisation
demanding total obedience. Unlike the socialist movement,
political terrorism is individualistic, rejecting the organised mass
movement and disciplined party as an agency for social change
in favour of secret societies; it has no coherent ideology, no
plans for a future society; its focus is on destruction not
construction. In *The Devils* Verkhovensky is quite explicit:

> Our party consists not only of those who kill and burn, or
> fire off pistols in the classical manner or bite their superiors.
> Such people are only in our way. Without discipline nothing
> has any meaning for me. You see, I'm a rogue, and not a
> Socialist. . . . The juries who acquit all criminals without
> distinction are ours.[8]

At one point in the novel Peter's father, the old liberal Stepan
Verkhovensky, is reading Chernyshevsky's novel, mistakenly
thinking it the 'catechism' of the nihilists: his son's
contemptuous dismissal indicates the great gulf which now
separated the new revolutionary terrorists from the earlier
impotent radicals. Neither Bazarov nor Rakhmetov would have
shared Peter Verkhovensky's authoritarianism: 'What we want is
one magnificent and despotic will, an idol of the people, resting
on something solid and standing outside everything.'[9] As with
Turgenev's fiction, the Russian working classes remain external
to the revolutionary movement while in *The Princess
Cassamassima* James's revolutionary workers, in the most highly
industrialised economy in the world, are not the factory
proletariat then (the 1880s) stirring into political activity but
skilled craftsmen, tailors, shoemakers, occupational groups from
which anarchist sympathies are more likely to spring, but
largely unrepresentative of the English working-class movement
as a whole. Of course, anarchism never actually penetrated

English socialism as it did in Spain, Italy and to a lesser extent, Russia. The point is rather the attribution to an indigenous political culture of a movement entirely foreign to that culture.[10] James's concern with the threat to bourgeois society was widely shared although largely misplaced: the English working-class movement was far too weak to impose its hegemony while in Russia the proletariat hardly existed.

Thus the novel of revolutionary *praxis* substitutes individualistic terror and nihilism for a non-existent threat from the nascent socialist movement. To portray revolution during a period when the only successful revolutions were those carried through by the despised bourgeoisie, when the proletariat constituted the only class capable of totally revolutionising society yet lacked the organisation, ideology and will to assert its hegemony, the novel form necessarily defined the socialist movement largely in bourgeois terms (individual terrorism). And bound to individualistic values and freedom, it portrayed the tragic clash of ideals and reality (*Fathers and Sons, The Devils*) or, abandoning its basic structural principle, the problematic character of the individual's relation with society, yielded a spurious, tendentious art (*Virgin Soil, What is to be Done*).

Part Two of this study will take up these themes in relation to those novels written against the background of genuine socialist revolution and the potential hegemony of the industrial working class. The twentieth century is the epoch of rapid industrialisation, imperialism, social democracy, fascism and Communism. For the nineteenth-century novelist there were only bourgeois revolutions: for the modern writer, there is October 1917.

5 The Novel and the Problem of Social Order: Gissing and Conrad

Towards the end of the nineteenth century the international working-class movement superficially seemed poised for a great victory: trade unionism had passed from its initial moderation into widespread strike action and a more positive commitment to socialism; working-class political parties were formed to contest elections and send representatives to parliament; and a more cohesive class-consciousness and sense of solidarity emerged. In England working-class agitation had revived during the 1880s, recalling the earlier class militancy of the 1840s and 1860s. An avowedly Marxist party, the Social Democratic Federation (S.D.F.) was formed in 1881; it was a time, too, of William Morris's Socialist League and the beginnings of the Fabian Society (founded in 1884 by Sidney Webb and George Bernard Shaw), an historical period characterised by immense contradictions — mass demonstrations, lockouts, strikes, violence — yet in 1884 the Reform Act extended the franchise to both the rural and urban working classes and set in motion the political assimilation of the masses into bourgeois culture. For industrial militancy provides only one side of working-class *praxis*: the founders of Marxism were quite clear that the nineteenth-century English proletariat were far from revolutionary. As early as 1858 Engels had written, '. . . the English proletariat is actually becoming more and more bourgeois, so that this most bourgeois of nations is apparently aiming ultimately at the possession of a bourgeois aristocracy and a bourgeois proletariat *as well as* a bourgeoisie'. And in 1894 he described the English proletariat as infected with bourgeois ideas and values and a jingoistic 'sense of imaginary national superiority'. The working classes, he concluded, have 'bourgeois "respectability" bred into [their] bones.' As for the trade unions, the skilled worders — 'the aristocracy of labour' — see in them not potential revolutionary organs but the means of improving their economic status within capitalism, and they quickly 'degenerate into mere sick funds and burial clubs', a conservative prop for the maintenance of bourgeois order.[1] Lacking a revolutionary political party with deep roots within the working class, strike action and militancy by themselves never posed a serious threat to bourgeois society; proletarian consciousness was *not* revolutionary but reformist. A proletarian challenge to capitalism was thus illusory, the labour movement too weak to generate its own revolutionary ideology and practice. Both Henry James and Conrad (in *The Secret Agent*) recognised the absence of an indigenous revolutionary movement in England by dramatising a breakdown of social consensus in terms of 'foreign', un-English anarchism and terrorism.

In general, the nineteenth-century English novel reflects a *fear of the masses*, of a potential, ever-present although remote threat to bourgeois order. In *Bleak House* Dickens had symbolised a deep crisis of bourgeois society through the vast, interlocking structure of Chancery (English society) which survives through political corruption and bribery, inequality and ignorance; there is neither justice nor the hope of attaining it; life has become alienated and devitalised. Dickens's contrived plot and happy ending should not disguise the profound pessimistic strain which dominates *Bleak House*: society is rotten, it must be torn down — yet society remains stable, seemingly impervious to the potentially explosive structures of social, economic and political inequality. By the 1880s, conservative writers, far more explicitly than Dickens, were dramatising a breakdown of social cohesion in terms of class inequality and conflict and the absence of a widely shared moral consensus. In this there is a parallel with sociology: the French positivist sociologist Emile Durkheim, writing in the 1890s, argued that a too rapid development of economic institutions (for example the growth of large-scale factories, extended division of labour) ran the risk of corrupting that consensus of moral values upon which a stable society depended. If economic institutions become 'unregulated' by shared moral beliefs, individual egoism and greed multiply and social order is threatened. For Durkheim the point of sociological inquiry was to discover the invariable laws of society so that man would submit willingly to their workings and thus limit any 'insatiable and morbid' demands.

These, then, are the themes of the present chapter. In the 1880s, George Gissing (1857–1903) portrayed the English working class with greater sociological detail than any previous English writer. His early novels, written from a profoundly conservative standpoint, confront the problem of social order with pessimism and resignation. Conrad's political novels bring us into the modern century and dramatise with greater artistic power than Gissing the conservative answer to the problem of bourgeois authority in the age of mass parties and mass democracy.

I

Gissing's novels of working-class life were all written in the 1880s; *Workers in the Dawn* (1880), *The Unclassed* (1884), *Demos* (1886), *Thyrza* (1887) and *The Nether World* (1889). The world they describe is uniformly depressing: the working-class characters lead lives of great physical squalour while Gissing's heroes are too readily defeated by the hostile forces ranged against them. The mood is a resigned pessimism — Orwell aptly called it 'a low spiritedness'[2] — a portrait of a social world dominated by the lack of money and incessant poverty. But the novels are more than reports on working-class life: Gissing worked firmly within the Victorian novel tradition with all its cumbersome paraphernalia of literary convention so that the dramatic structure of his novels revolves around legacies, murder and exaggerated coincidence. He departed from this tradition, however, in one important respect: his working-class characters and milieu lie at the heart of the novels; they are neither sentimentalised nor caricatured. The Goncourt's demand for a 'new novel' to resonate democratic, working-class aspirations is echoed strongly in *The Unclassed* when its novelist hero argues that the novel of ordinary experience is wearing out:

> We must dig deeper, get to untouched social strata. Dickens felt this, but he had not the courage to face his subjects; his monthly numbers had to lie on the family tea-table. Not *virginibus puerisque* will be my book, I assure you, but for

men and women who like to look beneath the surface, and who understand that only as artistic material has human life any significance.[3]

But Gissing's novels are not literary expressions of class conflict; they do not portray the struggle of the proletariat against the capitalist class. In Gissing's fiction the working class is not industrial but simply urban and at no point does he take the reader into a modern factory or trade-union meeting: the working class are the urban slum dwellers, existing in harsh poverty, described frequently as egoistic and dehumanised, exemplifying Hobbes's view of human life — 'solitary, poor, nasty, brutish, and short'. In *The Nether World*, Gissing describes a working-class street: 'On all the doorsteps sat little girls, themselves only just out of infancy, nursing or neglecting bald, red-eyed, doughy-limbed abortions in every stage of babyhood, hapless spawn of diseased humanity, born to embitter and brutalise yet further the lot of those who unwillingly gave them life.'

And elsewhere Gissing writes of 'the weltering mass of human weariness, of bestiality, of unmerited dolour, of hopeless hope, of crushed surrender', 'the intimacies of abomination', the 'filth, rottenness, evil odours' of slum life.[4] There is nothing in Gissing of a potentially revolutionary working class, only a brutalised and apathetic mass totally incapable of alleviating let alone changing their mode of existence.

It was argued earlier that one problem for the nineteenth-century realist was to describe artistically the emerging conflict between bourgeoisie and proletariat without betraying the art of the novel to political ideology or determinism. Gissing's mechanical conception of the urban working class is as much a betrayal of the novel form as is Gorky's more 'progressive' commitment. For it is not that Gissing's 'workers' lack *praxis* but that the social world within which class action takes place is rendered oppressive, alien, hostile and unyielding. It is not a world created by man's labour and thus recognisably human, but an external and dominating power; in Gissing's novels society becomes *natural* rather than social and historical, a reified structure which confronts the individual, demanding from him complete acquiescence. There is, here, an important difference between Gissing and realist

writers such as Mrs Gaskell, Dickens and George Eliot: for
them, man was capable of changing society and rising above the
arbitrary character of his environment, but with Gissing the
external environment, combining with heredity, propel the
individual irresistibly towards his fate. In *Workers in the Dawn*,
the radical Mr Tollady expresses Gissing's fatalism: 'History
pursues its path, using us as its agents for the working out of
prescribed ends. To think that we men can modify those ends is
the delusion of ignorance or madness.' Such sentiments have
little to do with socialism but are bound up with Comte and
positivism, as the ultimate fate of the novel's hero, Arthur
Golding, shows — the son of an alcoholic Oxford graduate
brought up in the London slums he passively endures everything
which prevents a happy marriage and an artistic vocation. Of his
non-problematic hero Gissing writes that the essence of
Golding's life 'lay in the fact that his was an ill-balanced nature,
lacking that element of a firm and independent will which
might at any moment exert its preponderance in situations of
doubt.' Against adverse social conditions his 'fragile talent'
disintegrates, the forces of heredity and environment proving
too powerful for the exercise of initiative and will.[5]

During the 1880s positivism, especially in sociology, had
become fashionable among certain sections of the English
'radical' intelligentsia. Gissing had read Comte's *Cours de
philosophie positive* in 1878, and he certainly knew of Taine's
theory of environmental determinism.* The idea of the social
world as a structure of fixed, immutable laws, able to be
'modified' but not changed (Comte), is central to Gissing's
fiction: in *Workers in the Dawn* the heroine, Helen, rejects
religion and metaphysics in favour of a positive *science*: 'There
is something entrancing . . . in these firmly fixed laws, these
positive investigations.'[6] And although Gissing became
disillusioned with positivism shortly after completing *Workers
in the Dawn* he remained firmly committed to a wholly
deterministic, fatalistic and thus pessimistic *ideology*. Like
Durkheim's sociology, Gissing's novels portray a world of
rampant egoism, unrestricted competition and moral anarchy,
but because they depict a reified world and an urban working

---

*In *The Unclassed* the hero paraphrases Taine's theory: 'Every strong individuality is
more or less the expression of its age. This direction may be imposed upon me; for all
that, I understand why I pursue it.'

class strongly regulated by environmental forces there is little real threat to social order. The picture which emerges from Gissing's novels is of a working class incapable of developing the organisation necessary to effect social and political change. Thus political agitation *and* education must ultimately fail as means for a better future. Working-class radicalism is presented as utopian and futile.

In *Workers in the Dawn*, for example, the revolutionary John Pether, who calls for violent insurrection and bloodshed and opposes all reform, dies in isolation raving like a madman. And in *The Nether World*, the revolutionary John Hewett is equally presented as an eccentric and reviled figure, belonging to no political party or trade union; his fellow workers reject his ideas with indifference. Sydney Kirkwood, the hero of this, Gissing's last and wholly working-class novel, is described as maturing out of radicalism and setting himself 'the task of becoming a practical man, of learning to make the best of life as he found it, of shunning as the fatal error that habit of mind which kept John Hewett on the rack', although the novel ends with his every ambition destroyed in a dutiful but loveless marriage. His early involvement with radicalism is described simply as immaturity: 'It had its turn, and passed'.[7] In *Demos*, the working-class revolutionary, Richard Mutimer, inherits a large rural estate which he transforms into an industrial town organised along socialist lines (the co-operative ideas of Robert Owen rather than those of Marx). As with other Gissing heroes Mutimer quickly falls victim to his environment and poor heredity. He aspires to become bourgeois, to marry into the local gentry and enter parliament as a radical not socialist candidate. He abandons many of his former working-class friends, jilts his proletarian fiancée in favour of a loveless but socially advantageous marriage and strives unsuccessfully to inculcate bourgeois, individualistic ideals into all members of his family. Gissing's working-class revolutionary quickly learns that 'to have a "lady" for his wife was now an essential in his plans for the future, and he knew that the desired possession was purchasable for coin of the realm. No way of retreat any longer; movement must be forward, at whatever cost.'

Equally significant is the role and effect of money on working-class character: Gissing's fictional world is totally reified with social and human relations mediated through money, but whereas the bourgeoisie are protected by their culture, the proletariat are completely corrupted: Mutimer's younger brother turns to drink and petty crime; his sister makes a disastrous marriage to a cynical adventurer while Mutimer himself, after losing his legacy, naively invests money from working-men's clubs in fraudulent stocks and shares. Mutimer's egoism, his desire for notoriety, are symbolic of Gissing's pessimistic view of working-class revolution: Mutimer organises workers' saving clubs as part of 'a plan for giving them [the workers] a personal interest, a money interest, in me and my ideas', and justifies investment in capitalist enterprise as a pragmatic means to socialist ends. Calling his movement 'Democratic Capitalism', he advocates authoritarian leadership but at the end, when the investments have failed and the savings are lost, the workers become a wild, bestial mob: 'Demos was roused, was tired of listening to mere articulate speech; it was time for a good wild-beast roar, for a taste of bloodshed.'[8] Mutimer's death, at the hands of his working-class followers, is clearly intended to be symptomatic of socialist aspirations and socialist movements: Mutimer dies not because he defends socialist principles but through his failure to rise above the dominating world of money:

> The character of this young man was that of a distinct class, comprising the sons of mechanics who are ruined morally by being taught to consider themselves above manual labour. Had he from the first been put to a craft, he would in all likelihood have been no worse than the ordinary English artisan — probably drinking too much and loafing on Mondays, but not sinking below the level of his fellows in the workshop. His positive fault was that shared by his brother and sister — personal vanity.[9]

The novel's 'message' is clear, expressed through Mutimer's mother who, rejecting her son's bourgeois aspirations, house and servants, accepts the inviolability of the class structure, enduring and 'making do' with privation and distress. As with Gissing's other novels of the 1880s, *Demos* is less to do with the emerging conflict between the industrial proletariat and capitalists than with a sheep-like, irrational mass of urban workers led in the main by opportunistic socialists. The conflict is between themselves within an impersonal, overwhelming world of dehumanised relations; it is not Marx's theory of class conflict but a Darwinian struggle for existence — usually hopeless — which informs Gissing's novels. This is the basic difference between Gissing and earlier realists: in Gissing's world human *praxis* has been eliminated and determinism rules his fictional universe. Thus the absence of problematic heroes or deep conflict between hero and society. More precisely, the excessive concern with factual, sociological detail leads to the loss of historical perspective. Gissing's characters are not organically bound to historical, political and economic change; the present is not history, but simply a factual representation of *what is,* an unchanging, hostile environment which reduces man to the status of object. There is, in Gissing's novels, no hint of the great events of the 1880s, the rapid development of militant trade unionism and escalation of industrial conflict, of those organisations through which the working class might control and shape its fate. What emerges so strongly from these novels is not the potential for transforming society through trade unions and political parties but the total subordination and conservatism of the English proletariat. Such fatalism is anathema to the novel form: Gissing's working-class fiction is pre-eminently an ideological resonating of the values of bourgeois society through its central precept of an external, hostile social and historical world largely impervious to human will and purpose — *praxis*. Thus to argue in defence of Gissing that 'given the historical context, only a "depressing" (if that means "hopeless") novel could possibly be an honest presentation of the themes it contains . . . a world . . . in which money is omnipotent and the individual has only the choice between worshipping it or being sacrificed to it',[10] is to accept uncritically the unhistorical abstraction of a purely passive, inert and animal-like proletariat and to undervalue the fact that working-class struggle and political organisation is coeval with capitalism. In *Captial* Marx had written that 'the advance of capitalist production develops a working class, which by education, tradition, habit, looks upon the conditions of that mode of production as self-evident laws of nature . . . the dull compulsion of the economic relations completes the subjection of the labourer to the capitalist', yet at the same time capitalist society sets in motion forces that promote working-class resistance. Thus the series of Factory Acts which limited

working hours flowed not from philanthropic intention but
directly from the class struggle:

> The creation of a normal working day is . . . the product of a
> protracted civil war, more or less dissembled, between the
> capitalist class and the working class. As the contest takes
> place in the arena of modern industry, it first breaks out in
> the home of . . . England. The English factory workers were
> the champions, not only of the English, but of the modern
> working class generally . . .[11]

Gissing's is a one-sided, mechanical and ultimately ideological
depiction of the English proletariat *as a whole*. Like the
Goncourts he strove to revitalise realism by turning to the
submerged masses, but like them he succeeded only in rendering
working-class life *externally*, within a narrow, deterministic and
static framework. Yet the fact that he chose to 'revitalise' the
realist novel by placing working-class life at the centre,
depicting it in sober and factual terms, cannot be interpreted as
an indication of the breakup of bourgeois hegemony. Certainly
the late-Victorian age was a troubled period but the rising
working-class movement and agitation did not develop into a
broad cultural challenge to bourgeois society. Thus Gissing's
approach to this 'new' material was wholly orthodox: the values
which underpin his grasp of working-class culture and history
remain resolutely bourgeois. The realists' conception of the
present as history and the organic relation of the individual to
an historically evolving society is eliminated. The tragic conflict
between the hero's ideals and the pragmatic values of capitalism
is transformed into pessimistic resignation and a deep sense of
alienation and isolation withing a fundamentally hostile
universe, a world in which freedom and autonomy have been
shackled by an overpowering external necessity. The problem of
social order is thus rendered non-problematical through
Gissing's *ideological* depiction of a totally reified world. Man no
longer makes his world, for with Gissing *praxis* is mere illusion.

II

Like Gissing, the Polish born Joseph Conrad was equally
concerned with social order but conceived the problem almost
exclusively in terms of anarchism and terrorism; and he made
no attempt to portray working-class life, characters, institutions

or movements. And whereas Gissing had worked with
nineteenth-century literary conventions Conrad broke decisively
from them. Unlike his English contemporaries — Wells, Bennett,
Galsworthy — Conrad's vision of man and society is bleak and
pessimistic. He portrays a troubled and tragic universe in the
manner of Bely employing all kinds of juggling with time and
frequent, complex shifts of narration. Conrad's 'modernism',
therefore, distinguishes him formally from Gissing and, as will
be argued, only a writer exiled from another culture, who
settled in England after many years at sea, could reinterpret
those bourgeois ideals which had early sustained the novel form,
and yet create a fictional universe critical of those values.

Conrad's early fiction is set either in isolation from society
(the sea stories) or within non-industrial, non-capitalist
societies. Between 1895, when he published his first novel,
Almayer's Folly, and 1904 Conrad's fiction is characterised by
strong, romantic, pre-capitalist ideals, the simple virtues of
honour, chivalry and courage and the ways in which man's
worldly experience inhibits his fulfilment. But beginning with
Nostromo (1904) and especially in the two novels of European
anarchism and socialism, *The Secret Agent* (1907) and *Under
Western Eyes* (1911), Conrad became obsessed with the themes
of revolution and social order. The reading public, however, was
less than enthusiastic: after 1911 Conrad returned to his earlier
themes (*Chance*, 1913, *Victory*, 1915), winning public
recognition and achieving economic security. Why, then, did
Conrad turn to a critique of socialism, anarchism and
revolution? Was it self-doubt about his own talent? His early
stories and novels had not been economically successful and
may also have exhausted Conrad's own experience, but neither
of these two suggestions satisfactorily explains the
choice of war and revolution, autocracy and imperialism as
the subject matter of his middle-period novels.

Conrad was a life-long Conservative: as early as 1885 he had
attacked the Socialist International for promoting 'despoilation
and disorder', and 'the ruin of all that is respectable, venerable,
and holy . . . " Socialism, he concluded, 'must inevitably end in
Caesarism.'[1][2] Socialist ideas he dismissed as 'infernal doctrines
born in continental back-slums', whose aim lay in the
destruction of everything which sustains social order.[1][3]
This anti-socialist animus, however, is bound up with a

thoroughgoing hostility to bourgeois society which Conrad
identified with spiritual and intellectual mediocrity; the
excessive concern with profit-making he saw as creating a dull,
unheroic, middle-class culture in which values become those of
the market place. More specifically, Conrad rejected
industrialisation, refusing to accept the comfortable, philistine
optimism of nineteenth-century philosophers and writers who
had identified progress completely with industry and science.
Industrialisation, Conrad's novels suggest, destroys man's sense
of community, breeding alienation and chaos, producing
societies lacking a deep-rooted moral and social consensus. In
The Secret Agent, for example, London is described as an
'enormity of cold, black, wet, muddy, inhospitable
accumulation of bricks, slates, and stones, things . . . unfriendly
to man', and when Mrs Verloc has murdered her husband she
experiences the city as 'a black abyss from which no unaided
woman could hope to scramble out.'[14] London is symbolic of
social fragmentation within the wider society, the loss of human
spontaneity and the growth of psychological disorders from
which spring the urge to destroy. In the language of Durkheim,
Conrad's industrial world is *anomic*, its social institutions no
longer capable of regulating man's actions: in a situation of
normlessness anarchy displaces order and an unbridled egoism
holds sway.

Conrad's complex relationship with the bourgeois society he
had adopted is particularly brought out in his most political
statement, the essay 'Autocracy and War', written shortly after
completing *Nostromo*. The essay's significance lies in its
uncompromising rejection of nineteenth-century optimism.
Beginning as an attack on Tsarist Russia and to warn the West
of her political ambitions (1905 was the year of the
Russo-Japanese war), Conrad developed a far broader critique
of the aggressive, warlike propensities of Western capitalism; at
times the essay reads like a crude Marxist analysis of
imperialism: 'The "noxious idle aristocracies" of yesterday
fought without malice for an occupation, for the honour, for
the fun of the thing. The virtuous, industrious democratic
States of tomorrow may yet be reduced to fighting for a crust
of dry bread, with all the hate, ferocity, and fury that must
attach to the vital importance of such an issue.' True world
peace, he concluded, 'will be built on less perishable foundations

than those of material interests.'[15] The corrupting power
exerted by 'material interests' forms the major theme of
Nostromo: the foreign dominated silver mines of the Latin
American Republic of Costaguana drive their English and
American owners to plan and finance a bourgeois revolutionary
coup and thus augment the civilising role of imperialism. The
idealist manager of the San Tome mines is quite explicit:

> What is wanted here is law, good faith, order, security.
> Anyone can declaim about these things, but I pin my faith to
> material interests. Only let the material interests once get a
> firm footing, and they are bound to impose the conditions on
> which alone they can continue to exist. That's how your
> money-making is justified here in the face of lawlessness and
> disorder. It is justified because the security which it demands
> must be shared with an oppressed people. A better justice
> will come afterwards.

The mine 'was to become an institution, a rallying-point for
everything in the province that needed order and stability to
live', and so a conservative national government 'took a
practical shape under the eye of the administrator of the San
Tome mine.'[16] But a national party financed by American
capital can neither command broad popular support nor satisfy
genuine national aspirations: in the face of the ultra-right
military this weak comprador government collapses. The price
of imperialism is the constant threat of civil war and military
dictatorship in societies where even bourgeois democracy seems
an impossible dream.[17]

In *Nostromo* (and the earlier short story, 'Heart of Darkness',
1899) Conrad shows the 'civilising' mission of the capitalist
West as nothing more than barbarism. Although the final verdict
on revolution in *Nostromo* is pessimistic, Conrad's attitude to
and portrayal of revolutionary movements in non-industrialised
society is far more open than in *The Secret Agent* and *Under
Western Eyes*. And, as the essay 'Autocracy and War' makes
clear, his attitude to the 1905 Russian Revolution was more
positive than his general conservative ideology might suggest: if
revolution is the expression of a broad social movement of all
social classes against tyranny then it is justified: 'A revolution is
a short cut in the national development of national needs . . . '
However, he remained implacably hostile to the socialist

international revolution; for him, nationalism acted to bind the different, conflictive segments of society together into a single organic unity, while socialism tore them apart.

Conrad, therefore, rejected both socialism and capitalism and while it has been argued that through his relation with intellectuals such as the novelist Ford Madox Ford and the radical liberal M.P. Cunninghame Graham he adopted a more 'democratic conservatism', he remained firmly wedded to conservative ideals. Of Cunninghame Graham Conrad wrote: 'I do not share his political convictions or even all his ideas of art, but we have enough ideas in common to base a strong friendship upon.'[18] The fact that both Graham and Ford Madox Ford knew the leading socialists of the day — Graham together with the trade-union leader, Ben Tillett, and the future leader of the Labour Party' George Lansbury, was involved in the agitation for the release of the anarchist Malatesta in 1912, while Ford knew and spoke generously of the exiled Russian anarchist Peter Kropotkin — probably helped to shape Conrad's view of left-wing politics, but not to redefine his extreme anti-socialist standpoint. In both *The Secret Agent* and *Under Western Eyes* Conrad's anti-revolutionary bias is clear. In *The Secret Agent*, for example, the anti-hero, Verloc, employed by the Russian Embassy as a spy and *agent provocateur* within the London anarchist community, agrees to dynamite Greenwich Observatory as a means of provoking the British government into repressive action against the many exiled Russian revolutionaries living in England. Vice-President of 'The Future of the Proletariat Society', Verloc exudes an 'air of moral nihilism common to keepers of gambling hells', an apt enough description for a man largely responsible for the accidental death of his wife's simple-minded brother. Helping Verloc with his explosives Stevie falls and is blown to pieces. Winnie Verloc, who had married Verloc solely to provide a home for her brother, responds to her husband's callous indifference — 'The boy is gone . . . as much an accident as if he had been run over by a bus while crossing the street . . . What's done can't be undone' — by murdering him. And then, abandoned by one of Verloc's anarchist acquaintances, Ossipon, she commits suicide.

On the threads of these dramatic events Conrad spins a series of complex relations between the police, the anarchists and Verloc. Detective Inspector Heat of 'The Special Crime

Department', who knows Verloc's true identity, hopes to incriminate a genuine, although innocent, anarchist, Michaelis, and thus preserve Verloc's value as a source of police information on the anarchist groups. Unfortunately Michaelis has been patronised by a friend of the Home Secretary's wife and Heat's stratagem is quickly dropped. The novel ends with Verloc's 'immoral' savings safely appropriated by Ossipon and further terrorism planned, although as the novel makes clear such activity is doomed to failure. For Conrad's hostility against anarchism leads him both to oversimplify the doctrine and present its adherents as atavistic savages of a peculiarly slothful and opportunistic disposition. Thus the old Karl Yundt's expression is of 'underhand malevolence' and his bearing suggestive 'of a moribund murderer summoning all his remaining strength for a last stab'. Ossipon has 'a flattened nose and prominent mouth cast in the rough mould of the Negro type', while the 'Professor' enjoys the 'stunted stature' of an inferior and 'ludicrous' physique, a 'physical wretchedness . . . so obviously not fit to live', an 'unsuspected and deadly . . . pest'.[19] Conrad's London anarchists are further depicted as indolent and as such pose no serious threat to bourgeois society. 'I don't think that I've been satirizing the revolutionary world', Conrad wrote to Cunninghame Grahame, 'All these people are not revolutionaries — they are shams.'[20] And these 'shams' are genuine individualists, isolated from any form of collective struggle, seemingly incapable of communicating even among themselves, divested of the most ordinary qualities of humanity. Who can possibly accept Conrad's ironical portrait of 'The Professor', a man whose right hand permanently encloses a rubber ball in his trouser pocket: 'The pressing of this ball actuates a detonator inside the flask I carry in my pocket.'[21] He is quite simply a madman whose commitment to social upheaval flows from vanity and not a genuine compassion for the exploited proletariat. By thus reducing the ideology of anarchism to idiosyncratic character, Conrad's anarchists remain not of flesh and blood but mere caricatures based more on the novelist's conservative ideology than a really serious historical *understanding*.

It is true, of course, that following the expulsion of the anarchists from the First International in 1872, and the first anarchist Congress in 1881, anarchist practice inclined towards

the tactics of 'propaganda by deed', so much so that terrorist
acts and explosions became increasingly frequent: between
1894 and 1912 for example, six heads of state were murdered
by terrorists. The point, however, is that the terrorist phase of
anarchism, with its emphasis on clandestine, para-military
societies, never constituted the dominant anarchist
tendency — naturally it received the greatest publicity and
helped to form the conventional stereotype of the anarchist as
criminal. But anarchism as a movement embraced assassins and
bandits as well as pacifist intellectuals such as Tolstoy; by 1900,
Kropotkin was advocating evolutionary not revolutionary
change and arguing that only in the most exceptional
circumstances was terrorism justified: and in sharp contrast,
Errico Malatesta's Communist anarchism preached class conflict
and the necessity for open political organisation and struggle.
Conrad's grasp of anarchism, therefore, is narrowly partisan
rather than objectively artistic. Moreover, his overriding concern
with social order leads him to portray a non-problematic social
world: Verloc's shadowy character, his moral mediocrity, are at
root the result of Conrad's *insincerity*, his refusal *as an artist* to
treat all characters as equal. Verloc cannot attain tragic stature
since his values (and those of his wife) do not place him in
conflict with society: in this novel, the anti-hero is not free to
choose this or that action, he possesses neither will nor purposes
beyond those demanded by his superiors. Thus rather like
Gissing, Conrad's concern with social cohesion and order within
industrial society leads ultimately to an unfree literary
structure.

   The Secret Agent and *Under Western Eyes* were both written
during a period of mounting industrial, social, and political
unrest, involving thousands of trade unionists, suffragettes and
Irish nationalists. To Conrad such conflict must have suggested
the existence of a profound malaise and breakdown of a stable
society. In his fiction these apparent threats to social consensus
are transmuted into the futile gestures of infantile terrorists and
revolutionary 'fakes': Conrad's Geneva revolutionists in *Under
Western Eyes* are as equally counterfeit as his London anarchists.

   Under Western Eyes is the story of a poor Russian student,
Razumov, the illegitimate son of a nobleman who becomes
involved, through no fault of his own, with political
assassination and the Tsarist secret police. Razumov is no

revolutionist, believing rather in an enlightened despotism as the answer to Russia's problems. Lonely and ambitious, aspiring to the higher ranks of the Civil Administration, Razumov's hopes of winning the University's major prize are shattered when a fellow student, Haldin — unlike Razumov, 'not one of the industrious set' — having murdered a Tsarist official, seeks refuge in his lodgings. Razumov's first thought, 'There goes my silver medal!' places him within the same moral universe as Verloc and as the novel unfolds a similar determinism and fatalism comes to dominate his existence. For with his future career apparently ruined Razumov betrays Haldin only to find himself accepted by the revolutionary students as Haldin's accomplice. The Tsarist Secret Police, the Third Division of the Imperial Chancery, have no difficulty in convincing Razumov of his value to them and he becomes their spy.

Sent to Geneva he meets the leading revolutionists and infiltrates their organisation. But unlike other spies Razumov is ill-equipped for his appointed task: already burdened by guilt over the betrayal of Haldin he falls in love with Haldin's idealistic sister, Natalia, who worships his 'revolutionary ardour'. The strain proves too much and Razumov confesses his true identity and role both to her and the revolutionaries. Retribution is swift: a terrorist and police agent, Nikita, breaks Razumov's eardrums, and he returns to Russian to die.

Like Verloc, Razumov is a non-problematic hero. In his 'Author's Note' Conrad described him as 'an ordinary young man, with a healthy capacity for work and sane ambitions. He has an average conscience.' A solitary individual 'as lonely in the world as a man swimming in the deep sea', Razumov seeks integration within the existing society; his ambitions are neither impelled by high ideals nor a sense of frustrated egoism. He has no will to assert and his ready acquiescence in a fate burdened by remorse makes him a pathetic rather than tragic figure. By choosing such a mediocre hero and treating him sympathetically, Conrad throws into sharper relief the utter banality of his Geneva revolutionaries — 'apes of a sinister jungle' as he called them in his 'Author's Note' — and the inhuman, autocratic power of the Russian government. The first part of the novel, set wholly in Russia, is magnificently done, its concentrated, tightly knit structure rendering an acute, pervasive sense of despair and isolation. But in the remaining three parts, Conrad fails to communicate a similar urgency or comparable atmosphere: the novel sinks into bathos.

Conrad's portrait of the revolutionaries is designed to show their political impotence, hypocrisy and venality. But more significantly, they emerge as barely credible figures; certainly they pale in comparison with the Tsarist bureaucrat, Councillor Mikulin. Conrad's revolutionaries are absurd because they belong not to the twentieth but to the nineteenth century. The lack of an historical dimension in the novel is decisive: Conrad had not grasped the significance of the 1905 Revolution, and the sharpening ideological conflicts within European Social Democracy, between the Bolsheviks and Mensheviks and the Malatesta and Kropotkin wings of the anarchist movement. Peter Ivanovitch's character and ideas, for example, are clearly modelled on Bakunin and Kropotkin, his ardent feminism contrasting with his evident sexual impotence (Bakunin), while his fatalistic philosophy has little in common with the ideas of class struggle advocated by Lenin and Malatesta. His companion, Madame de S —— , whom Conrad's narrator describes as 'more fit for the eighteenth century' with 'its atmosphere of scandal, occultism, and charlatanism' and whom Razumov sees as 'a galvanised corpse',[22] provides the necessary financial support for Peter Ivanovitch's futile and parasitic existence. In public the champion of women; in private a petty and spiteful man full of self-deception and vanity. As for the other revolutionaries — the odious police spy, Nikita, who acts as the group's assassin and executor, and the idealistic and naive Sophia Antonovna whose uncritical admiration for her leader ends the novel ('Peter Ivanovitch is an inspired man') — they are characters invested with the most superficial political depth. As in *The Secret Agent*, complex problems of political ideology are simplified by reducing them to a personal, idiosyncratic level; Conrad's absurdly sinister revolutionaries are anachronistic precisely because what ideology they profess is compounded not from twentieth-century thought but from a curious blend of Bakunin, Dostoevsky and Kropotkin. Conrad's 'shams' are political 'strawmen' and the novel cannot rise to anything other than a parody of those genuine and sincere revolutionary parties and movements which dominated the international socialist movement during the first decade of the twentieth century.

Conrad's sceptical attitude to socialist revolution is stated early in the novel through the language teacher—narrator:

> . . . in a real revolution — not a simple dynastic change or a
> mere reform of institutions — in a real revolution the best
> characters do not come to the front. A violent revolution
> falls into the hands of narrow-minded fanatics and of
> tyrannical hypocrites at first. . . . The scrupulous and the
> just, the noble, humane, and devoted natures; the unselfish
> and the intelligent may begin a movement — but it passes
> away from them. They are not the leaders of a revolution.
> They are its victims: the victims of disgust, of
> disenchantment — often of remorse. Hopes grotesquely
> betrayed, ideals caricatured — that is the definition of
> revolutionary success.[23]

It is the classic conservative concept of revolution — nothing
changes. History, however, is not a cycle of failed revolutions; to
judge revolution *only* by its most negative results is not merely
to distort the truth of historical change — the English
Revolution created the political culture necessary for capitalist
development while the 1789 French Revolution generated
democratic institutions and ideology as well as the Terror — but
to reject out of hand the possibility that socialist revolution
could be justified in certain circumstances. Thus in *The Secret
Agent* and *Under Western Eyes* revolutionary ideas and groups
are depicted as alien forces within Western European society:
the London anarchists have foreign names or none at all, while
the Geneva revolutionists define revolution strictly in
nationalist terms. *Under Western Eyes* describes revolutionary
ideas outside the broader, international socialist movement with
the result that private and personal issues dominate the novel's
foreground to the virtual exclusion of the ideological. Here lies
the fundamental weakness of Conrad's two novels: his
anarchists and revolutionists are insincere, ludicrous or
outrageously idealistic without any form of ideological conflict.
In the political novels of Serge, Koestler and Orwell the
individual exists as a political being only through dominant
ideological beliefs and conflict. But Conrad cannot accept
socialist ideology as a serious political force within modern
society because of his prior commitment to social order. The
ultimate failure of *The Secret Agent* and *Under Western Eyes*
lies here.

III

Verloc and Razumov are anti-heroes lacking in tragic stature, mediocrities whose values and social aspirations are entirely individual, wholly unconnected with a specific social group or class. The heroes and 'superfluous men' of Balzac, Stendhal, Turgenev, Flaubert were not individual in this sense, their ideas, ideals and fate bound up concretely with historical change and the social/political position of groups and classes. But in *The Secret Agent* and *Under Western Eyes* this organic link between hero/anti-hero and society has disappeared so their fate becomes entirely personal and not, as was the case with the nineteenth-century realists, emblematic of a generation, group or class. Only when his political fiction dwells on the underdeveloped non-capitalist world does Conrad come close to protraying a hero whose social and political existence, ambitions and ultimate fate are those of a specific social class — the working man, Nostromo, who, forced by circumstances to become leader of a popular movement, defender of the liberal Costaguan capitalists and finally guardian of the San Tome silver — Nostromo rebels against his imperialist bosses and hides the silver to use for himself. But Nostromo's ambition to 'grow rich very slowly', corrupts the incorruptible 'fellow in a thousand'. 'Nostromo had lost his peace; the genuineness of all his qualities was destroyed. He felt it himself, and often cursed the silver of San Tome. His courage, his magnificence, his leisure, his work, everything was as before, only everything was a sham.'[24] Nostromo's 'theft' is symbolic of a social class dominated by foreign capital and thus incapable of asserting any genuine independence from imperialism.

In *Nostromo*, therefore, Conrad succeeds in portraying the organic relation of individual to society, and history, delineating society as a complex totality of political groups, social classes and economic forces held together by 'material interest'. And he does so without betraying the individual to external, deterministic forces. The personal histories of Charles Gould and Nostromo while bound up with the Gould concession on the one hand and the nascent Costaguan proletariat on the other, are not the passive results of these forces. It is Conrad's achievement to have created the free literary structure in *Nostromo* which his ideological animus against revolutionary *praxis* within the industrialised West had denied in *The Secret*

Agent and *Under Western Eyes*. Revolution, imperialism and
nationalism have their human agents, but in *Nostromo* Conrad
does not reduce them merely to the properties of these
movements, neither revolutionaries nor the representatives of
imperialism are caricatured but depicted with *sincerity*. They
thus emerge as partially autonomous individuals who, through
illusion, ambition, vanity make their choices and pursue their
ends.

But in the industrialised, capitalist world neither Conrad nor
Gissing grasped the real historical significance of the socialist
movement. Their dominant concern with social order led
them to portray a reified world of social relations and
communities of egoistic, vain and weak revolutionaries. Their
choice of mediocre, non-problematic anti-heroes is one way of
resolving the problem of social conflict and class war; the other,
of course, was to treat the socialist movement *sincerely* in terms
of *praxis* and genuine political ideology.

6 Anti-Utopia and Revolution

In the fiction of the great masters of the nineteenth-century novel — Stendhal, Balzac, Flaubert, Turgenev, Dostoevsky — revolutionary ideas and experience are transmuted into the dominant structures of bourgeois realism. On the one hand the nineteenth-century novel reflected the prevalent concerns of bourgeois ideology buttressed by the firm belief in *progress* and the educative powers of reason; yet the novel was also criticism of the institutions and indeed the ideology of bourgeois society. Epistemologically the realist novel was securely anchored in an external, objective and knowable world; it thus developed a strong sense of *community* in which character was concretely related to such tangible things as class, social and political institutions, ideology, values. The conflict which emerges between the individual and society is structured within this totality of relations.

Not all nineteenth-century fiction, however, can be accommodated within this generalisation. The utopian novel, which emerged as a distinctive genre during the nineteenth century, clearly falls outside the prevailing concerns of realist fiction. Nineteenth-century realism was fundamentally critical of and hostile to bourgeois society: in contrast, utopian novels tended towards an uncritical portrayal of a world made perfect for man through science and education. As a secularised form of the City of God, utopian fiction substituted social order and a broad consensus on values and ends for the conflict and tension of the realist novel, eliminating the responsibility of the individual for his actions and ultimate fate. The concept of the individual undergoes significant changes in nineteenth-century utopian fiction; the emphasis falls on the collectivity and the wise leadership of society's 'guardians' and general overseers. To be sure, previous utopias had stressed the collective nature of the perfect society but for those utopias written after the 1789

Revolution, happiness is identified with collective, not individual, responsibility; equally important is the role of science and technology and the humanising effect of education. And because these utopias project much further into the future trends already existing they are more realistic, and informed by a greater sense of history than the pre-1789 utopias. But unlike the nineteenth-century realist novel, utopias have no problematic hero, their structures are not dominated by a deep sense of conflict between the individual and society. The 'hero' is usually a shipwrecked traveller falling upon a remote island or a visitor from another planet or century, objectively observing the progress in mankind's salvation. The question of how these societies evolved to such perfection is never raised: Samuel Butler's *Erewhon* (1872), Edward Bellamy's *Looking Backward* (1887), William Morris's *News from Nowhere* (1890) and certain of H. G. Wells's utopian romances ignore the problem of social change.

This lacuna, together with the other features of nineteenth-century utopias, is carried over into a new genre, the anti-utopia (or dystopia), a transformation which takes place at the close of the nineteenth century in some of H. G. Wells's writings and in E. M. Forster's satire on the optimistic Wells, 'The Machine Stops' (1907). In these early anti-utopias human beings survive in subterranean caverns, their lives wholly dependent on machines, or the vast mass of the population labour beneath the surface of the earth for a privileged ruling elite. But anti-utopia as a distinctive literary form only reaches maturity after the First World War and the Russian Revolution with Zamyatin's *We*, Capek's *R.U.R.*, and Huxley's *Brave New World*, all written during the 1920s. In these fictions the nineteenth-century belief that science, technology and education must eventuate in a boundless happiness is challenged. This chapter will explore the nature of this challenge and attempt to relate the literary structure of anti-utopia to the problems inherited from utopian fiction, especially the question of social change and revolution.

I

Unlike the classical utopia and nineteenth-century realist novel, the novel of anti-utopia is about power and authority, the political and social physiognomy of a ruling class. In his *A*

Modern Utopia (1905), H. G. Wells depicted a society rigidly bureaucratic and hierarchical, buttressed by a pervasive conformism in which class divisions have ceased to exist except in purely functional terms; a meritocracy of talent rules through reason and scientific humanism. Shorn of its scientific innovations, Wells portrayed a typically nineteenth-century utopia where the authority of reason had subverted the material interests of power and domination. Yet the same writer was capable of describing a more sombre future: in stories such as *The Time Machine, The Sleeper Awakes*, and 'A Story of the Days to Come', Wells clearly anticipated the modern anti-utopia. In *The Sleeper Awakes* (1898, revised 1910), there is little of the benevolent meritocracies descibed in his other fictions, but a world dominated by parasitical élites — capitalists, managers and bureaucrats — who live off the toiling masses enslaved in massive underground factories. It is a nightmare world where the proletariat have been rendered politically harmless through a pervasive propaganda broadcast by 'babble machines' and 'oval discs' (modern television) and where 'the ancient antithesis of luxury, waste and sensuality on the one hand and abject poverty on the other, still prevailed.' It is a world dominated by the struggle of capital and labour, a world characterised by economic exploitation, misery and oppression. In the vast, inhuman cities the individual enjoys no private life, the family has been eliminated and euthanasia is widely practised. Wells's vision here is anti-utopian and the novel anticipates many of the features of twentieth-century totalitarianism.[1]

Yet Wells's picture of the year 2100 is somehow false. As in his other science fiction fantasies, Wells's hero was not born either into the society or the century the novel describes. He is the classic traveller from another age, who thus resists the horrors that he sees around him to become the symbol of revolt against oppression. He is a man from our century, from the world of H. G. Wells and his readers, an advocate of Parliamentary Democracy, individual freedom, justice. Thus the novel is genuinely unreal; the result is a portrait of the future which remains mere fantasy. It is in this sense that Wells's anti-utopias remain firmly within the traditions of nineteenth-century utopias.

This assessment is especially borne out with regard to Wells's depiction of the dominant class. For the rulers seem to have little if any purpose to their lives, their domination over society apparently based on nothing more than sheer hedonism. Wells, like other utopian writers, never grasped that power is always related to purpose, that a ruling class must believe that it rules not merely to justify and legitimise its own interests but those of society as a whole. George Orwell observed that Wells was quite incapable of understanding that if a dominant class is to subjugate a subordinate class successfully then it must appeal to the sentiments associated with nationalism, patriotism and religion. Without such ideology a dominant class in a society rigidly stratified would soon collapse. Orwell went on to argue that irrespective of its scientific predictions, *The Sleeper Awakes* is far less prophetic and historically accurate in its depiction of future totalitarianism than Jack London's dystopic *The Iron Heel* (1907), a novel markedly weaker in both its literary qualities and grasp of science.[2] But it remains more realistic than Wells's *The Sleeper Awakes* precisely because London grasped that no society can function without ideological legitimation, that while the power of a ruling class must ultimately rest on force (army, police, and so on) its authority must flow from its own belief that it rules for humanity. *The Iron Heel* can thus be seen as forming an important link between the naive and anti-utopias of Wells and the genuinely totalitarian visions of Zamyatin and Orwell.

On one level *The Iron Heel* is a crudely written, badly constructed novel seriously lacking in genuine characters. Yet it remains the one single prophecy in fiction of the political, economic and social structure of Fascism years before the advent of Mussolini and Hitler. The novel sets out to describe the conflagration which results from a deepening crisis in American society, of the savage struggle between capital and labour which precipitates the ruling class of industrialists, bankers and ideologists into combining as an all-powerful Oligarchy. Using the weak and vacillating trades union and Labour leaders the Oligarchy crush the organised working class. The result is a fascist-style government ('The Iron Heel') which effectively eliminates all vestiges of democratic government and individual rights. An organised struggle now ensues led by the hero of the novel, Ernest Everhard, and other revolutionary socialists. Everhard, however, is caught and executed. The novel, which is in the form of a journal kept by Everhard's wife, ends suddenly with his death and the plans for another, apparently abortive revolution.[3]

Sociologically, the major interest in London's novel lies with his remarkably prophetic portrait of totalitarianism and the way in which his dictatorship of the Oligarchs arises organically from the class struggle. The novel rejects the mechanical Marxist view, held by many of the most eminent theoreticians and politicians of the Second International such as Eduard Bernstein and Karl Kautsky, that capitalist society would necessarily collapse under the strain of its own internal contradictions.[4] In contrast London adopts, at least superficially, a 'Leninist' position: the capitalist class, the novel suggests, would fight tooth and nail to maintain their privileges and it is only through a 'correct' leadership that the working class can hope to combat the military and economic strength of the bourgeois state. Unlike Wells, London understood that a capitalist class will seek not merely to protect its own interests but justify such action as the defence of civilisation:

> They, as a class believed that they alone maintained civilisation. It was their belief that if ever they weakened, the great beast would engulf them and everything of beauty and wonder and joy and good in its cavernous and slime-dripping maw. Without them, anarchy would reign and humanity would drop backward into the primitive night out of which it had so painfully emerged. . . . Many . . . have ascribed the strength of the Iron Heel to its system of reward and punishment. This is a mistake. Heaven and hell may be the prime factors of zeal in the religion of a fanatic; but for the great majority of the religious, heaven and hell are incidental to right and wrong. . . . Prisons, banishment and degradation, honours and palaces and wonder-cities, are all incidental. The great driving force of the oligarchs is the belief that they are doing right.[5]

Thus the emergence of American totalitarianism (the novel spans the years 1912–32) is not simply the result of capitalists crushing the workers through superior military strength. For certain sections of the labour force believe in the ideology of the capitalist class and accept its legitimacy. And while the trade union leaders cling to their belief in the peaceful road to socialism as a world-wide economic crisis creates increasing class conflict, the capitalists revert to simple repression — tightening of censorship, execution of labour leaders, breaking of strikes by armed bands. The trade union leadership holds fast to its 'democratic illusion' that salvation lies through the ballot box. In 1933 the leaders of the German labour movement met the challenge of Nazi government not through mobilising the entire working-class movement in a general strike but by asking the courts to rule on its 'legality'. Everhard's understanding of the pitiable weakness of Social Democracy in the face of totalitarianism is beyond the grasp of any fictional character from a nineteenth-century novel, utopian or otherwise: 'We are beaten. The Iron Heel is here. I had hoped for a peaceable victory at the ballot-box. I was wrong. . . . We shall be robbed of our few remaining liberties; the Iron Heel will walk upon our faces; nothing remains but a bloody revolution of the working class.'[6]

The revolution fails: the Oligarchy, supported by a privileged stratum of workers (the 'labour aristocracy') and its leaders defeat the revolutionary elements and gradually introduce a system of industrial slavery. A secret police force recruited from the old regular army — the Mercenaries — spring up to maintain a vast spy network devoted to tthe maintenance of social order. It was this aspect of London's novel which so impressed Trotsky:

> In this picture of the future [he wrote], there remains not a trace of democracy and peaceful progress. Over the mass of the deprived rise the castes of labour aristocracy, of praetorian army, of an all-penetrating police, with the financial oligarchy at the top. In reading it one does not believe his own eyes: it is precisely the picture of fascism, of its economy, of its governmental technique, its political psychology:

The Iron Heel had described the emergence of a fascist regime 'as the inevitable result of the defeat of the proletarian revolution.'[7]

Yet conflict is not eradicated, but develops both within the 'labour castes' who remain as exploited labour and among the great mass of labour slaves. Even when the 1918 uprising is brutally defeated the spirit of revolutionary *praxis* still remains.

'Tomorrow the Cause will rise again', says Everhard, 'strong with wisdom and discipline.' The eventual overthrow of capitalism, however, lies well in the future — three more centuries!

London's pessimism echoes George Orwell's picture of a wholly static society in *Nineteen Eighty-Four,* where all hopes of social change, revolutionary or otherwise, have been systematically eliminated by the diligence of the 'Thought Police'. Orwell was probably influenced by *The Iron Heel* but he undoubtedly rejected London's insistence that even under the most totalitarian regime the class struggle goes on, the capitalists must exploit labour and the workers will organise and struggle: revolution is always possible. It is characteristic of the modern anti-utopia that while it similarly portrays a totalitarian system it is one 'from which change is absent', in which the 'structurally generated conflict' of class societies has been replaced by a managed but universal consensus.[8] It is this concept of *praxis* and the related sociological understanding that a society based on privilege and inequality must of necessity generate conflict and thus a source of change, which distinguishes *The Iron Heel* from the anti-utopias of Wells. For Wells's vision, irrespective of its many contradictions, was typical of the late nineteenth-century middle-class reformer: a Fabian Socialist who held to the virtues of reform and the evils of revolution, Wells had no deep relationship with the organised Labour movement, and only a rudimentary understanding of its history. Reform from the top rather than revolution from below was his credo. London, in contrast, had lived his life up to becoming a writer as an ordinary worker; when he wrote *The Iron Heel* he was closely involved with the American socialist movement. He declared himself unequivocally a revolutionary: 'The Revolution is here now', he wrote, 'stop it who can'.[9] For 'ballot box socialism', for 'respectable' socialists who hated the word revolution, he had nothing but contempt, and like his revolutionary contemporaries Rosa Luxemburg, Lenin and Trotsky he firmly rejected the reformist theory that capitalism would pass peacefully into socialism: 'History shows that no master class is ever willing to let go without a quarrel. The capitalists own the governments, the army and the militia. Don't you think the capitalists will use these institutions to keep themselves in power? I do.'[10]

The Iron Heel reflects London's *praxis*, his understanding of Marxism and the character of revolution. In his essay on 'Revolution' written after the 1905 Russian Revolution he paints a picture of a worldwide proletarian movement against capitalism in which the intellectual plays a role only as part of the working-class movement. To be sure, London's hero, Everhard, is never portrayed as an active member of the socialist movement: we are told simply that he is and that he believes in proletarian revolution. Given the polemical intent of *The Iron Heel* it is not surprising that the hero is a 'kind of human gramophone' (Orwell), spouting set speeches on the conflict between capital and labour; and more seriously, London portrays him as a socialist 'superman', an ex-blacksmith with the physique of a 'prize-fighter', self-taught translator from German and French, prolific author and brilliant orator and debater. Thus although London's grasp of the structural basis of social conflict and change was sociologically superior to contemporary utopian and anti-utopian novelists, he was unable to create a genuine novel. *The Iron Heel* is of interest solely for its sociology, not for its characters or its insights into the human condition. It is a report on some possible events in the future: and for that reason it is more an example of *naturalism* than of realism. Its significance, however, lies in its influence on the development of the modern anti-utopia.

II

Zamyatin's *We* (*My*) has been described as the first major anti-utopia, 'the first novel of literary importance that presented a relatively complete vision of the negative results involved in the realisation of utopia.'[11] The relationship between Zamyatin's novel and *The Iron Heel* is not as remote as it might appear from the existing critical literature. Zamyatin edited the Soviet edition of London's novels in the early twenties; he knew of and may have been influenced by *The Iron Heel* in his portrait of the One State. But two other connections exist: both writers were strongly influenced by the 1905 Revolution. Zamyatin as an active Bolshevik revolutionary, London, at a distance, emotionally and theoretically. Zamyatin, as will be argued later, drew largely negative lessons from his experience, while for London 1905 showed the means whereby a few hundred socialists became an army of thousands after the first bloody skirmishes; and perhaps more significantly, that the transition to socialism would be bloody, violent and protracted. The rapid development of revolutionary consciousness and organisation fired his imagination and is largely responsible for the sustained belief in proletarian revolution in *The Iron Heel*. The second connection lies in their attitude to creative writing. London firmly believed in the social value of literature, seeing it as a part of man's *praxis* driving him into battle with the class enemy.[12] Discussing Gorky's early novel, *Foma Gordayev*, London argued that its realism was 'less tedious' than that of Tolstoy and Turgenev(!) for 'so fearful is its portrayal of social disease, so ruthless its stripping of the painted charms from vice, that its tendency cannot but be for the good. It is a goad, to prick sleeping human consciences awake and drive them into battle for humanity.'[13] London's activist conception of literature seems prophetic of Zhdanov and socialist realism, and *The Iron Heel* clearly reflects this crude utilitarianism. Yet the idea that literature must become revolutionary is echoed also in Zamyatin's writings, although the emphasis is different. Like London, he stressed the social function of literature and the artist's broad commitment to criticise the social and scientific forces that assail the integrity of the individual. *We*, he wrote in 1932, was written as 'a warning against the two fold danger which threatens humanity: the hypertrophic power of the machines and the hypertrophic power of the State'.[14] Literature must attack the forces of stagnation and philistinism *artistically*: Zamyatin's is not a call to action in the manner of Jack London, Gorky and socialist realism.

We is the culmination of Zamyatin's literary career and he wrote little of importance afterwards. This novel, which greatly influenced Orwell's *1984*, illustrates both Zamyatin's theory of revolutionary literature and his basic ambivalence towards revolutionary theory and practice. Like Jack London and Maxim Gorky he was attracted to the ideals of revolutionary socialism. He had joined the Bolshevik faction of the Russian Social Democratic Party as a student, playing an active role in 1905 as agitator in working-class areas and helping to foment the mutiny in the battleship *Potemkin*. Arrested in a police raid on Bolshevik headquarters, Zamyatin was beaten up and imprisoned in St Petersburg. The events of 1905 stirred his youthful imagination and, recollecting his experiences a year later, he wrote that 'the Revolution was not yet a lawful wife who jealously guarded her legal monopoly of love ... [but] a young, fiery-eyed mistress, and I was in love with the Revolution.'[15] His attachment to the Revolution was from the first romantic and idealistic. Released from prison in 1906, Zamyatin gradually moved away from his early support of Bolshevism and later came to reject it completely. In the years up to 1917 he lectured in marine architecture at the St Petersburg Polytechnic, wrote satirical tales on the torpid quality of Russian provincial life and in 1916 went to England to supervise the building of Russian ice-breakers in Newcastle. He returned to Russia after the February Revolution.

Unlike the great majority of Russian writers, Zamyatin gave critical support to the new regime although he disagreed with Bolshevik politics in favour of the peasant oriented Socialist Revolutionary Party (the S.R.s). At the same time he refused to endorse every aspect of the Bolshevik programme. In 1918 he criticised the use of terror, the widespread destruction of cultural monuments, and voiced his scepticism of Lenin's plans for electrification. Many of his criticisms echo those of Gorky, who, like Zamyatin, was bitterly critical of the Bolsheviks during the years 1917 and 1918. In his article, 'Tomorrow', Zamyatin graphically described his disillusionment with the new regime:

> Yesterday there were tsars and there were slaves; today there is no tsar but the slaves remain; tomorrow there will be only tsars. We march in the name of tomorrow's free men, the new tsar. We have lived through the age of the suppression of the masses; we are living in an epoch of suppression of the individual in the name of the masses ... The proud *homo erectus* is getting down on all fours, is sprouting tusks and fur; the beast in man is triumphant. The Brutal Middle Ages are returning; the value of human life is falling steeply; a new wave of European pogroms is rolling on.[16]

In the same year as this article was written, the S.R. leaders were arrested and their newspapers closed down. Zamyatin was among those questioned by the Cheka but asserting his beliefs in Communism and pointing to his Marxist past he was quickly freed. Like Gorky, he now ceased to write political articles and concentrated all his energy on literature, editing an ambitious series of translations and lecturing at the Petrograd 'House of the Arts'. He was largely responsible, too, for forming the All Russian Writers Union in 1920 which throughout the next ten years remained as the leading writers' association. *We* was written in 1920 and revised the following year but never published in the Soviet Union. It was published, however, in English (1924), Czech (1927) and French (1928), although none of these translations were authorised by Zamyatin himself.

Throughout the twenties he remained critical of Bolshevism and later of Stalinism. A leading fellow-traveller whom Trotsky rather unkindly called an 'internal émigré', Zamyatin was frequently attacked by the Proletkultists and by RAPP. In 1922, together with 160 other intellectuals the Soviet government considered undesirable, he was re-arrested; but unlike the others who were given their passports and sent abroad Zamyatin's friends interceded and the charges against him were dropped. His subsequent request to be deported was refused.[17] But by the end of the twenties Zamyatin's Soviet career was virtually over: his work was little published, his name maligned by the newly appointed guardians of Soviet culture. Incapable of orienting himself to the literary demands of the bureaucracy he was finally removed from the leadership of the Writers Union in 1929. Zamyatin was charged with publishing abroad a 'vicious slander' against the Soviet Union (*We*) in Russian, and having White émigré connections. He had neither émigré connections nor had he sanctioned the Russian edition of *We*. But although cleared of these two charges he resigned from the Writers Union he had helped form and lead, arguing that he could no longer belong to an organisation which even indirectly persecuted the members it was supposed to defend. In 1931 he wrote his famous letter to Stalin requesting permission to leave Russia:

> My name is probably known to you. To me as a writer being deprived of the opportunity to write is nothing less than a death sentence. Yet the situation that has come about is such that I cannot continue my work, because no creative activity is possible in an atmosphere of systematic persecution that increases in intensity from year to year. . . . I know that life abroad will be extremely difficult for me, as I cannot become

a part of the reactionary camp there . . . I know that while I have been proclaimed a Right Winger here because of my habit of writing according to my conscience rather than according to command, I shall sooner or later probably be declared a Bolshevik for the same reason abroad. But even under the most difficult conditions there, I shall not be condemned to silence. . . .[18]

With Gorky's help the request was granted and in 1931 Zamyatin left Russia for the last time. His name and his works were soon erased from Soviety history and even during the 'thaws' of the 1950s and 1960s Zamyatin remained a non-person vilified as anti-Soviet, his ideas declared hostile to every principle of socialist literature.

In the 1920s Zamyatin had defended the freedom of artistic creation against the crude theories of the Proletkult and RAPP which saw art largely in terms of ideology and agitational propaganda. Superficially at least, he shared Trotsky's defence of literature as literature, the right of the artist to create outside the narrow confines of political pressure and conformism. Indeed he argued for the continual revolutionary renewal of literature forged from the creative and anarchical spirit of 'heretics' and dreamers. In 1919 he wrote that

Every today is at the same time both a cradle and a shroud; a shroud of yesterday, a cradle for tomorrow . . . Today is doomed to die — because yesterday died and because tomorrow will be born. Such is the wise and cruel law. . . . Cruel, because it condemns to eternal dissatisfaction those who already see the distant peaks of tomorrow; wise, because eternal dissatisfaction is the only pledge of eternal movement forward, eternal creation. He who has found his ideal today is, like Lot's wife already turned into a pillar of salt, has already sunk into the earth and does not move ahead. The world is kept alive only by heretics: the heretic Christ, the heretic Copernicus, the heretic Tolstoy. Our symbol of faith is heresy . . . Today denies yesterday, but is a denial of tomorrow. This is the constant dialectic path which in a grandiose parabola sweeps the world into infinity. Yesterday, the thesis; today, the anti-thesis; and tomorrow, the synthesis.

The same themes inform his essay 'On Literature, Revolution and Entropy' (1924): without the heretic, society would ossify and culture degenerate into stagnation and decline. Heretical literature, he wrote, is too often judged socially harmful because it damages dogma yet such literature is far more useful than 'useful' literature because it 'is anti-entropic, it militates against calcification, sclerosis, encrustedness, moss, peace.' Utopian and absurd, it challenges the habitual and the banal, restlessly searching and questioning, never at peace: literature that is truly alive, he wrote, is a 'leap', a 'wound', a 'pain'.[19] Literature, then, forms part of a never-ending pattern of cosmic revolution in which the triumph of heresy will be followed by ossification and entropy unless new heretics arise and challenge the inevitable tendencies towards social, political, scientific, and religious dogma. In 1921 he wrote that 'as long as human thought lives, there will never be ideological entropy and there will be revolution, storms, rebellions, explosions, whirlwinds, no matter how many others may desire constant zephyrs'.[20]

Zamyatin's formulations would seem both a criticism of Bolshevism and the trend towards the bureaucratisation of literature, stagnation and the reliance on traditional literary forms explicit in socialist realism. His emphasis on the dialectical pattern of literary development is superficially close to some of the themes in Trotsky's *Literature and Revolution*. In his essay 'On Synthetism' Zamyatin applied these ideas to the question of modernism which, as was seen in Chapter 4, presented a major problem for Soviet Marxists in the 1920s. Like Trotsky he saw the complex relation of form and content, arguing that revolutionary literature must go beyond the 'primitive realism' of the nineteenth century: to express revolutionary content the writer must assimilate artistically the highly complex character of modern life, especially its scientific discoveries which create new conceptions of what is 'fantastic' and what is 'ordinary'. The 'ordinary' would no longer suffice as it had for the older realism; neo-realism, as Zamyatin called his approach, served as a synthesis of nineteenth-century Realism (the thesis) and twentieth-century Symbolism (the anti-thesis) in which the realists' straightforward depiction of surface reality and the Symbolists' portrayal of a higher reality is fused dialectically in a qualitatively higher literary practice:

Realism saw the world with the naked eye. Symbolism glimpsed the skeleton through the surface of the world — and Symbolism turned away from the world . . . Synthetism approaches the world with a complex assortment of lenses, and grotesque, strange multitudes of worlds are being revealed to it. Tomorrow we shall calmly buy a ticket for a journey by sleeper to Mars. Einstein broke space and time themselves from their anchors. And the art which grows out of this present-day reality — can it be anything but fantastic, dreamlike?

Neo-realism, Zamyatin wrote, is the depiction of 'the other, true reality that is concealed under the surface of life', a constant juxtaposing of the *everyday* with the *fantastic* in a way which alerts the reader to a consciousness of the world.[21] In 1920 he concluded that the Revolution had become 'philistine' and might lead to an epoch of entropic literature. His opposition to Bolshevism was total and he clearly blamed Lenin for 'betraying' the Revolution, for instituting a 'new Catholicism', a 'disease' which, should it prove incurable, meant simply 'that Russian literature has only one future — its past.'

All Zamyatin's preoccupations, his hostility to Bolshevism, his experiences in the early years of the Soviet state and his doctrine of neo-realism find their ultimate literary expression in *We*. In this novel Zamyatin satirises the emerging Communist state with literary concepts antagonistic both to bourgeois and socialist realism: Zamyatin's dystopia is thus an expression of that modernist movement distrusted by both Marxist and Stalinist critics.

Although never published in the Soviet Union, *We* was widely circulated and read by many prominent writers and critics. Its reception reflected the political and literary climate of the twenties. Gorky declared it 'hopelessly bad' and 'sterile', its anger 'cold and dry; it is the anger of an old maid.' Marxist critics were divided: for some Zamyatin had portrayed the Revolution 'through the eyes of a malevolent intellectual whose finer feelings had been insulted', while sympathetic 'leftist' critics such as Voronsky defended the novel, arguing that from an artistic point of view it was excellent. However, Voronsky had reservations: Zamyatin's attitude to the 1917 Revolution

was hostile — 'the Revolution was alien to him not in its details
... but in its essence' and this severely detracted from the
novel's undeniable merits.[22] In contrast, Western critics have
usually admired the novel as a prophetic indictment of Stalinist
totalitarianism which they see implicit in the works and ideas of
Marx and Lenin; for others, *We* represents a more general
criticism of the modern technological age, 'the implied aims of
industrial civilisation', a study 'of the machine, the genie that
man has thoughtlessly let out of its bottle and cannot put back
again.'[23] *We*, indeed, involves both as interrelated structures:
for Zamyatin's opposition to Bolshevism was partly due to his
belief that its programme must lead to the development of an
alien, Western-type mechanised industrial society in which the
virtues of Old Russia would be irrevocably doomed. But
Zamyatin, like Jack London, saw himself as a revolutionary, in
deed as well as in the word. He was one of his 'heretics', a
'rebel' and 'dreamer' from whose visions great literature springs:
as a revolutionary writer he therefore challenged every
orthodoxy, suggesting new and striking ways of looking at and
understanding the world.

Before discussing *We* in more detail it is clearly important to
establish the way in which Zamyatin's specific orientation to
the 1917 Revolution is translated into literary and artistic
terms. Two stories in particular provide important insights into
Zamyatin's artistic conception of the October Revolution. *The
Cave* (1920) is a surrealist portrait of a starving and beleaguered
St. Petersburg, the landscape likened to an ice-age wasteland of
roaming mammoths and ragged cavemen, 'a confusion of beasts,
clean and unclean, thrown together by the flood' in which a
bourgeois steals logs to warm his dying wife, the 'cave man's'
values triumphing over those of civilisation. In *A Story About
the Most Important Thing* (1923) Zamyatin depicts a bloody
episode from the civil war as part of a broader cosmic
movement involving a dying star on which four people are
themselves dying.[24] Here, and elsewhere, Zamyatin's
understanding of the revolutionary epoch through which he was
living is episodic and fragmented. Symbolically the stories
suggest the utter futility of revolution — men senselessly killing
one another, mass starvation and deprivation. And they do so
because Zamyatin has isolated mere episodes and left them
unrelated to the broader social movement which alone can

invest them with meaning and significance. Without this the episodes suggest only chaos and futility; but every great epoch has to be grasped not in bits and pieces but as a whole, as a totality.

It is in this important sense that Zamyatin's literary theory fuses with his partial grasp of the Revolution, the one related organically to the other. The fact that he understood October 1917 in this way, however, is clearly the result of his separation from the revolutionary movement and his close support of literary, intellectual groups such as the Serapion Brothers. All these different elements find their expression in *We*.

III

We is set in the twenty-sixth century in a society known as the Single State ruled by a dictator called the Benefactor and his secret police (The Guardians) who maintain strict social order. A totalitarian state located within a vast, domed glass city, it houses the survivors of a two-hundred year global war which has effectively reduced the world's population to one-tenth of one per cent. Artificially walled from nature by a Green Wall which separates the city from the world outside, the inhabitants of the Single State live in glass houses, have no names but numbers, wear identical uniforms and survive entirely on synthetic food. It is a society built around the ideal of conformity and strict regimentation; the piped anthem music of the One State, the daily routine of marching in fours and the scientifically assessed sexual needs of each number attest to the One State's thoroughness. All emotion is suspect: love has been defined as irrational and the rational beings of the One State satisfy what remains of their emotional life through the 'Right of Blinds', following precise diagnosis by the scientists of the Sexual Bureau where 'the content of sexual hormones is determined with the utmost exactitude, and a corresponding table of Sexual Days is worked out.'[25] Science, and especially mathematics, constitute the basis of social action and morality with the One State's 'system of ethics founded on subtraction, addition, division, multiplication.' In this mathematically perfect society the Tables of Hourly Commandments strictly regulate mealtimes and the number of chewing motions necessary to digest the regulation food, the hours of sleep, physical exercise and the sexual ('personal') hour — for

everyone. With all individual decisions eliminated and the word
'liberty' defined as 'crime' the One State claims for its numbers
the mathematically logical utopia of happiness without
freedom. There is no choice between 'Happiness without
freedom or freedom without happiness'.

Zamyatin's One State is a totally dehumanised society: love,
sex, art, individual relations have become mere objects, things.
Initiative has virtually vanished in a society where social change
has ceased. Yet this is not strictly true: for the novel attempts
to portray the conflict generated between its hero and a society
which is dedicated to the suppression of every vestige of
criticism. The focus of the novel is thus on the problematic hero
and the contradictions and tensions he discovers between
human values and the social world of the One State. It is this
aspect which distinguishes Zamyatin's anti-utopia from the
utopias and anti-utopias of Bellamy, Morris, Wells and Huxley.

The novel is written in the form of a diary kept by D—503,
the builder of the space-ship Integral through which the
Benefactor hopes to subjugate other planets and civilisations to
his benign and enlightened rule. Members of the One State have
been urged to compose poetry to be carried by the Integral, and
D—503's diary is his substitute for a poetic paean of praise for
the 'mathematically infallible happiness' of life in the One
State. At first the diary catalogues D—503's day-to-day
impressions, but it quickly becomes a record of his rebellion
against the Benefactor. He meets a strange and fascinating
woman, 1—330, who introduces him to members of what the
State newspaper calls an 'elusive organisation' whose aim is the
overthrow of the Benefactor. Under 1—330's influence D—503
becomes more and more individualised; he experiences the
'irrational' emotions of jealousy and hatred and begins to
dream. He has developed a 'soul'. A doctor diagnoses his
problem and recommends 'fantasiectomy', the surgical
elimination of fantasy, but he refuses: 'I don't want to be cured
of this ailment', he asserts. The transformation of 'We' to 'I'
continues with a journey outside the Green Wall where he meets
the primitive, healthy creatures, untouched by technology,
science and mathematics whom the rebels — they call
themselves the Mephi, presumably after Mephistopheles — see
as the sole revolutionary force: 'All this was extraordinarily
strange, inebriating; I felt myself superior to all, I was I, a world
by itself, I had ceased to be an item, as I had always been, and

had become an integer.' (p. 155) The rebellion ultimately fails: the State Gazette announces the discovery of a cure for 'fantasy' (now widespread) and demands that everyone submit to the Grand Operation. Many reject the order: D—503's diary is found and he thus betrays the revolutionaries. After undergoing the operation he cheerfully watches 1—330's execution under the Gas Bell Glass:

> Her face became very white and, since her eyes were dark and large, this created an extremely beautiful effect. When they started pumping the air out of the Gas Bell Glass she threw her head back, half closing her eyes and compressing her lips: this reminded me of something. She kept looking at me as she gripped the arms of her seat — kept looking until her eyes closed altogether. (p. 221)

The particular details of Zamyatin's totalitarian society clearly distinguish it from other utopian satires. It is often pointed out that Zamyatin, like Wells, predicted the development of certain scientific innovations which then existed only in embryonic form (brain surgery, electronic music, spaceships, etc.) as well as many of the basic features of twentieth-century totalitarian societies (the secret police, the Iron Curtain of the Green Wall, the unanimous re-election of the great leader in periodic elections). There is, however, another prediction related to the structure of the novel form itself which is even more significant. In the majority of utopias social change has been eliminated and society conceived in largely static terms. Morris's *News From Nowhere*, for example, begins with the class war between capital and labour, a conflict which eventuates in revolution and the emergence of a socialist utopia from which every problematic element has been removed. In *We*, however, the conflict between the individual and society functions as a major organising principle: D—503, like Winston Smith in *Nineteen Eighty-Four*, is the problematic hero whose rebellion against the overpowering and crushing weight of the One State is in the name of genuine human values and freedom.

The essence of totalitarian societies lies in their systematic attempts to annihilate all form of individuality and impose a uniform collective identity. But no society can effectively stamp out individuality and opposition, and the evidence from

the Soviet and the Communist states of Eastern Europe clearly
suggests that intellectual and political dissidence constitute the
unintended effects of modernisation, that societies which
depend so much on science and technology will necessarily
produce individuals critical of those societies (although the
strenuous efforts to restrict the scope of dissidence in these
societies, such as the use of psychiatry to define the
oppositionists as insane, is reminiscent of Zamyatin's One
State). Zamyatin's *We* is important in this sense: that the One
State has not succeeded in reducing society to a pliant, uniform
mass but rather that its own overwhelming repressive norms
acting as a focus for dissent generate opposition and rebellion.
This is especially true of two particularly sensitive areas which
all totalitarian states have striven to eliminate — eroticism and
the unconscious.

The One State has brought scientific sexuality to a fine pitch:
pink coupons allocate the biologically right partners to one
another with bureaucratic efficiency, a fact which militates
against widespread promiscuity. Sexuality is thus highly
controlled and human relations no longer subject to the
irrational passions aroused by eroticism. Sex is dehumanised,
mere technique, based on the principle that 'every number has
the right of availability, as a sexual product, to any other
number.' All sexual taboos have gone; pleasure and thus
happiness is equated with 'having' a particular individual. This
institutionalisation of sex is similar to that portrayed in *Brave
New World* where human and social relations are mediated
through a pervasive hedonistic promiscuity and while the *free*
choice of partners characterises Huxley's dystopia sexuality has
become a commodity, one fetishised to the exclusion of
virtually all other activity. In both dystopias sexual relationships
have become objectified, thinglike, mechanical and devoid of
human passion. The erotic has been reduced to the single
dimension of sexual experience, to mere physical satisfaction,
to pleasure. The individual is thus no more than an object for
others, part of the collective mass, incapable of differentiating
himself as an identifiable person through his own individual
passions. In this sense the apparent freedom of sexuality
depicted by Zamyatin and Huxley is repressive, since it
demarcates and distorts the range of the erotic. Thus in the One
State repressive sexuality has the effect of making the erotic a

potentially liberative force. It is certainly true that authoritarian societies strive to regiment sexuality, to promulgate rigid sexual norms and thus impose a deadening conformity. But it is precisely the irrational element of eroticism which escapes such control. It is this aspect which Zamyatin brings out quite sharply in his novel, and when D—503 meets 1—330 it is the erotic attraction of her *individual* attire which disturbs him:

> She was clad in a fantastic costume of some epoch of antiquity: a black, clingingly enveloping garment that strikingly emphasized the white of her bared shoulders and bosom and that warm, shadowy valley, wavering with her breath, between her — And her teeth, too — dazzling, almost wicked . . . (p. 34)

Like many contemporary totalitarian societies the One State has standardised every aspect of social life, its numbers wear identical light-blue 'unifs'. The liberative erotic power of individualised clothing is thus obvious: 'She was in a saffron-yellow dress of an ancient cut. This was a thousandfold more wicked than if she had had absolutely nothing on. Two sharp points, glowing roseately through the thin tissue: two embers smouldering among ashes. Two tenderly rounded knees.' (p. 65)

Linked to the suppression of the erotic is the attack on fantasy, imagination and the unconscious. D—503 rediscovers the submerged human feelings of passion, jealousy, envy, and when fully aware of his 'illness' makes the 'irrational' decision to remain a 'deviant'. Indeed, he discovers that many other numbers are suffering from the same malaise, and that the basis of the Benefactor's rule is profoundly unstable. The role of unreason in the novel is of great significance, for some critics have drawn a parallel between Dostoevsky's 'Underground Man' and the revolt of D—503, arguing that both Dostoevsky and Zamyatin are satirising rationalist and utopian socialist ideas and ideals and defending the concept of man as essentially an irrational being.[26] Yet there seems nothing irrational in the normal human feelings associated with love or the desire for individuality, to be a *person*. Rather, the whole structure of the One State, far from embodying rational norms, has institutionalised unreason. The Benefactor, for example, is shown to be invested with almost divine attributes. Society is held together through fear of the Machine as by conformist obedience to the science of mathematics; for human sacrifice, the public executions of deviants, has become almost an end in itself, cruelty which in the scene describing it 'is given deliberately the colour of the sinister slave civilisations of the ancient world' (Orwell). Zamyatin's problematic hero, far from accepting the irrational side of totalitarianism, rebels against it and in this sense *We* is not a paean of praise for irrationality.

It is these feelings against the Benefactor's domination which link the diarist with the revolutionary movement. But it is here also that the fundamental weakness of *We* lies. D—503 rediscovers his human essence through his liason with 1—330 and the heretical rebels; thus the novel implies that social change is still possible. Yet what is this revolution which threatens the basis of the One State? In his literary theory Zamyatin had asserted that only through madmen and heretics was truth and great literature possible. 1—330 is the spokesman for this doctrine: when D—503 argues that opposition to the One State is mere madness she assents, 'We must all go mad', as quickly as possible. And later she tells him of 'the two forces in this world — entropy and energy. The first leads to beatific quietism, to a happy equilibrium; the other, to the destruction of equilibrium, to excruciatingly perpetual motion.' (p. 161) *We* is the literary expression of Zamyatin's theory of cosmic revolution which, embodied in the flesh and blood figure of 1—330, appals the conformist D—503: 'It's preposterous because there can't be any other revolutions. Everybody knows that — '. (p. 169) The ultimate revolution, mocks 1—330, what nonsense. 'You're a mathematician', she tells D—503, 'Well, then: name the ultimate number for me.' What ultimate number, he replies bewildered, and she tells him, the greatest number of all. That is absurd, D—503 replies: 'Since the number of numbers is infinite, what number would you want to be the ultimate one?' 'Well, and what revolution would you want to be the ultimate one? There is no ultimate revolution — revolutions are infinite in number.' (p. 169)

The result is that the revolutionary Mephis have no programme, no ideology to sustain their opposition; it is merely an instinctual revolt against total repression, an assertion of individual human values over the machine, a spontaneous illustration of perpetual renewal through heresy and rebellion.

Rebellion is a thing in itself; the Mephi's revolution springs not from structurally generated conflict (the economic expoitation of one class over another) but has its source in the intellect and the heart. Zamyatin's theory of endless revolution is thus wholly different from Trotsky's theory of permanent revolution with which it has sometimes been mistakenly compared: Trotsky envisaged a succession of international revolutions generated by one in backward Russia spreading to the more advanced industrial capitalisms and eventuating in a socialist Europe.[27] Rather, Zamyatin's concept of revolution is more the emanation of his philosophical and literary ideas and as such contrasts quite sharply with Jack London's more sociological approach. For the principle which underlies the Mephi's revolution is fear of dehumanisation, a disgust with the scientific barbarities of the One State. Yet because the sustaining vision behind *We* is Zamyatin's notion of cosmic not social revolution, the novel is far more optimistic than either *Nineteen Eighty-Four* or *Brave New World* for it suggests that some form of opposition must always emerge to 'negate' the repressive state. The members of Zamyatin's One State have not been totally subjugated: Mephi sympathisers and agents are shown almost everywhere, they have even infiltrated the Guardians. The state poet, R−13, whose real feelings are carefully concealed but whose admiration for Dostoevsky clearly hints at rebellion (p. 56),[28] and D−503's biologically matched female partner who suddenly rediscovers atavistic maternal feelings, indicate the weakness of the One State's domination. Total control of the population has not been achieved and although the novel ends with D−503 submissive after the Grand Operation to eliminate the 'soul', revolt and revolution rend the One State, 'everything was perishing, the greatest and most rational civilisation in all history was crashing', the city full of chaos, 'roaring corpses', of numbers 'who have betrayed rationality'.

   Nineteen Eighty-Four and *Brave New World* portray societies in which all possibility of *praxis* has been systematically destroyed, in which total domination renders every faint flicker of rebellion futile. In *Brave New World* a utilitarian mass culture combined with the pleasure-drug soma have made both the working masses (Gammas, Deltas, and Epsilons) and the technicians and administrators (Alphas and

Betas) politically docile and content; consciousness has become totally anaesthetised, one-dimensional. And in *Nineteen Eighty-Four* the 'proles' are a passive, degraded mass kept in check by the 'Thought Police', incapable of even the futile rebellious gestures of Winston Smith. But in the One State *praxis* remains possible in spite of the secret police, conformist norms and institutionalised cruelty; the Mephi's proclamation of revolt is answered at once by a purely spontaneous uprising against the One State and its inhuman values. The 'Great Operation' is ordered as a last desperate measure, and the awful spectacle of the patients as they emerge from surgery on wheels, attests to the fundamental weakness of the Benefactor's rule. Pure coercion and fear hold the One State together and they do so imperfectly, thus providing the source of rebellion and revolt.

Zamyatin's conception of power is at once the strength and the weakness of *We*. Sociologically the novel is superior to all previous utopias and anti-utopias in its understanding that social relations in any society must be regulated by social institutions. *News from Nowhere*, for example, describes a future society largely based on craft industry yet characterised by an anarchic system of social regulation and a total lack of planning. In contrast, Huxley's *Brave New World* retains the profit motive and remains a highly rationalised, global capitalist system with a strictly functional class structure, a civilisation dedicated to the norm of planning, social efficiency, scientific management, yet a society where each individual exists independently of the regulative authority of the family, work, religion, politics; the norms which govern each person's conduct are merely the function of his biologically determined social status and no longer flow from political, familial or religious authority. The individual has become regulated and social stability functions through rigorous conditioning. In contrast, the citizens of the One State are urged to devote themselves to the Benefactor, to vote for his rule, and thus invest his authority with legitimacy. The secret police — the Guardians — further maintain the power of such social regulation. The numbers of the One State are thus regulated *socially* by repressive political institutions, an insight which distinguishes Zamyatin from Huxley. But what Orwell praised in Zamyatin, his grasp of the irrational elements of totalitarianism and the glorification of cruelty as an end in itself, is precisely his weakness. No state can exist *solely* on pure force, on the terror and fear of the population, especially if its credo is universal happiness. For the very existence of such a society demands an ideology to sustain the beliefs of its slaves. It is in this important sense that *We, Brave New World* and *Nineteen Eighty-Four* fail as convincing sociological portraits of future societies. Every dominant class believes in the rightness of its rule, that its actions are committed in the interests of the whole population, that its values are those of the future. Unless such beliefs are welded into a cohesive ideology no ruling class can hope to survive as a political force, for cynicism and contempt for the human race are not the stuff of political stability and strength but rather of corruption and weakness.

If Zamyatin's *We* was intended as a satire on the Bolsheviks or the ideals of revolutionary socialism, as some critics maintain, then it must fail, for not merely were the Bolsheviks supported by broad sections of the urban proletariat and peasantry in the actual act of revolution but their rule was legitimised by the authority of an ideology which Stalinist totalitarianism might distort but has never been able to eliminate. But Zamyatin never intended that *We* should bear such a narrow interpretation. It was far more a satire on mechanisation, on the social power of machines, on the dehumanising society built around the alienation and reification of human labour in which man is reduced to pure servitude, to exist as an instrument, as a thing.

IV

In his appreciative essay on H. G. Wells written in the early 1920s, Zamyatin described him as an example of the modern revolutionary artist, a 'heretic' without whom all art and culture would be impossible. Wells, Zamyatin wrote, was both prophet and artist of the modern city, its asphalt his literary 'territory'. In particular Zamyatin admired Wells's ability to portray the future 'through the opaque curtain of the present', to describe civilisations dominated by machines, technology — aeroplanes, loud-speakers, television — and atomic energy; yet these utopias were stratified into rich and poor, rulers and ruled.[29] Zamyatin was clearly influenced by Wells, but the important point is the way in which he departed from him on the portrayal of the social significance of the machine. In Wells's utopias social evolution is both social and technological, a standpoint shared by many of the pre-1914 utopian writers such as Bellamy and Morris. *We*, however, clearly suggests that technology rather than liberating man from a lifetime of degradation and toil will only enslave him further so that he ceases even to be a human being. Both Zamyatin and Huxley see the roots of a greater subservience not in political or economic organisation but in the overpowering authority of technology and science.

At first sight this seems to contradict the Marxist theory which identifies the realm of genuine freedom with the advances made by science and technology, the whole linked to a socialist economy in which man's 'free time' expands at the expense of 'labour time'. Marx's concept of the 'abolition of labour' implied a social organisation that allowed man to develop all his faculties and abilities free from the debilitating effects of capitalist exploitation. Work would become an expression of man's humanity involving all his latent creative talents and not the means solely of earning money. The worker is free only outside work, Marx argued, in his leisure time, and that too can exist both as degradation (drink) and alienation (organised leisure). But Marx's analysis of capitalism emphasised not only the alienation which necessarily flowed from the worker's exploited status, but also suggested that technology itself can form an important link in the worker's alienation. For technology and science become part of the system of exploitation; and in the same way as the alienated worker comes to see capitalist social relations as natural rather than social, so too does he perceive technology. The essence of alienation lies precisely in this vision of the *social* world as natural and thus external and ineluctable. Science, Marx wrote, 'thus appears, in the machine, as something alien and exterior to the worker'; and the world of machinery and technology take on the appearance of independence, external to man, beyond his control. In such circumstances *praxis* is almost impossible. But 'Nature does not construct machines, locomotives, railways, electric telegraphs, self-acting mules, etc. These are products of human industry; natural material transformed into organs of the human will to dominate nature . . . organs of the human brain, created by human hands, the power of knowledge made into an object.[30]

This is a truth beyond the alienated numbers of the One State and the conditioned Alphas, Betas of *Brave New World*, all of whom exist within societies dominated by an overpowering reification. The human world, human action, *praxis*, has been transformed completely into the social world of commodities; man is an object to be manipulated at will. Consciousness is thus uncritical, one-dimensional. In *Brave New World* leisure time is fully organised; there is no free time, only servitude to a mindless hedonism.

In *Brave New World*, *Nineteen-Eighty-Four*, and *We* technological reification is overpowering: all human resistance against it is futile. Yet Zamyatin contradicts his fictionalised reified world by depicting rebellion and revolt against the One State. The rational, objective narrator of *We* writes a diary which becomes not merely a record of his rebellion but his struggle against reification, towards consciousness, freedom and some form of *praxis*. Yet given that in the One State there is no structurally generated conflict and the absence of both political programme and ideology from the Mephi's revolution how can such a struggle take place. In the One State — as in *Brave New World* — there is total administration and reification; the social sources of conflict are either controlled or have been eliminated. In such a society the problematic hero is incapable of sustaining his rebellion; he becomes non-problematical. The ultimate failure of Zamyatin's novel lies here: that while he created the first anti-utopia in which the hero is himself part of the society described (and not a traveller or awakened sleeper) his rebellion which thus gives him his problematical status is the result not of social change (there is none) but rather of Zamyatin's idealist philosophy of history.

As a genre anti-utopia is conservative, extrapolating real historical trends deterministically into the future and thus removing the human element in social development, technology, science and political organisation. The genre of anti-utopia does not build on the strengths but on the degeneration of nineteenth-century realism (for example Wells), separating man from history and *praxis*, transforming him into mere object. Thus the problematic hero in a society from which all structurally generated change has disappeared, where reification penetrates every sphere of human and social activity, leads ultimately to a literary structure which is fragmented, episodic and incapable of grasping revolutionary ideas and practice as organically bound up with man as both a social and historical agent.

7 The Revolution Betrayed: Koestler and Serge

In Chapter 4 it was argued that the literary debates between the Proletkult faction and those grouped around Trotsky in Soviet Russia during the 1920s reflected a much deeper political division within the ruling Communist Party. Ultimately the question of whether 'proletarian literature and culture' was possible for a society in which the proletariat formed a minority of the working masses was resolved bureaucratically. Proletkult theory was transcended by the more completely totalitarian precept of socialist realism and literature firmly welded to the state. By 1929 the internationalist wing of the Bolshevik party had been defeated by the nationalist Stalin group and henceforth the slogan 'Socialism in One Country' became the guiding principle of Soviet domestic and foreign policy. The consequences on other Communist parties were disastrous, and by 1938 the exiled Trotsky concluded that the Third International, founded by Lenin in 1919, no longer represented the interests of the international working class: Russian Communism, having subordinated all other Communist movements to its interests, was now effectively a counter-revolutionary force. A Fourth International was duly formed; its task to maintain the revolutionary Marxist tradition of Marx, Engels and Lenin.

It is, perhaps, something of a paradox, that the greatest influx of writers to the Communist cause came during the 1930s when the Party no longer embodied revolutionary ideology and practice; the philistine Stalin and the totalitarian creed of socialist realism drew fulsome praise from sympathetic Western writers while the brilliant and cosmopolitan Trotsky attracted few creative writers to the cause of his new International. In the Soviet Union the writer was simply an ideologist; artistic criticism of the regime had ceased and Babel discovered the new genre of silence. But for many Western

writers totalitarianism wore a progressive face: at the First
Writers Congress Malraux had praised the White Sea canal
project (built on slave labour) and a few years later declared
that 'Stalin has lent dignity to mankind; and just as the
Inquisition does not detract from the fundamental dignity of
Christianity so the Moscow trials do not detract from the
fundamental dignity of communism.' In France, Louis Aragon
celebrated GPU terrorism in verse, while in England Auden
wrote of the 'conscious acceptance of guilt in the necessary
murder.' Upton Sinclair was grateful that Stalin had abandoned
world revolution for 'a wiser and saner point of view', while
Heinrich Mann, Lion Feuchtwanger, Theodore Dreiser and
Dashiell Hammett accepted the 'necessary judicial murders' of
the old Bolsheviks and vigorously defended Stalin's rigged
Moscow trials; Gorky, Sholokhov and Ehrenburg echoed the
gutter sentiments of Stalin's Attorney-General Vyshinsky (a
former Menshevik and opponent of Bolshevism), who declared
Old Bolsheviks the offspring of 'bulls and pigs', to be shot 'like
mad dogs'. During the 1930s George Bernard Shaw,
Hemingway, Dos Passos, Sherwood Anderson, André Gide,
Stephen Spender, Sartre, Camus and other eminent novelists,
poets and critics expressed their sympathies with, and in some
cases found their way into the Communist movement.[1] But for
many of these 'literary fellow-travellers' allegiance to Stalinism
proved short-lived: disillusioned with the failure of the Spanish
Revolution and the Nazi-Soviet pact their faith in proletarian
revolution turned into pessimism, quietism and in many cases a
virulent anti-Communism.

The effect on literature, and particularly the novel, of 'fellow-
travelling' political commitment, however, was largely negative,
and Koestler's *Darkness at Noon* (1940) is one of the few
significant fictions written out of this experience. Unlike
Heinrich Mann who saw in the Moscow Trials 'a psychological
battle for the possession of buried truth',[2] Koestler portrays the
ebb-tide of revolutionary ideals and revolutionary theory,
disillusionment with Marxism and a lack of faith in a socialist
future. Victor Serge's *The Case of Comrade Tulayev* (1945) is
equally concerned with Stalin's assumption to power, but
unlike Koestler, Serge had lived through the tragic events of the
1920s and, joining the Left Opposition, remained to the end of
his life hostile both to Stalinism and capitalism. Both novels

attempt to portray an epoch of revolution at the moment of
defeat, to salvage something from apparent barbarism and
chaos. This chapter will explore the ways in which the greatest
revolutionary epoch of modern times finds expression in these
novels; for Koestler and Serge are portraying the present as
history, man as an agent of social change transforming his
society and himself through *praxis*. And because these novels
are pre-eminently based on specific historical events and
persons, non-fiction fiction which strives to generalise about
political ideology and revolutionary *praxis*, they must be judged
against the particular political background they describe.

I

The October 1917 Revolution was the culmination of a broad,
popular movement embracing the urban proletariat and the
great mass of peasantry. By the summer of 1917 Russian
society had broken down and traditional social institutions were
increasingly replaced by local Soviets, workers' committees and
rank-and-file army committees. The Bolshevik Party came to
power not conspiratorially but openly as the one political force
capable of providing coherent expression to mass discontent;
the seizure of power was not the work of a small group of
professional revolutionaries but the combined efforts of the
broad mass of the urban working class. Yet the practice seemed
to confound Marxist theory, in which socialist revolution was
invariably linked to the highly industrialised capitalist world
and not with an economy, eighty per cent dominated by
peasants. But neither Lenin nor other leading Bolsheviks
expected the Russian Revolution to remain isolated: a
revolution in Germany was confidently anticipated. 'Without a
world revolution we will not pull through', wrote Bukharin in
1918,[3] a sentiment echoed four years later by the ailing Lenin:
'We have always proclaimed and repeated this elementary truth
of Marxism, that the victory of socialism requires the joint
efforts of workers in a number of advanced coutries.'[4] But by
1922, revolutionary movements in Germany, Hungary, Bulgaria
and Estonia had suffered defeat while the economies of the
advanced European capitalist countries had stabilised. The tide
of world revolution was clearly ebbing, at least for the time
being. And in a Soviet Russia surrounded by hostile capitalist
states, the social and economic structure lay in ruins. Between

1917 and 1921 the country had endured a savage civil war, war with Poland, peasant uprisings, mass starvation and a staggering fall in industrial production. These were the years of War Communism, when a highly centralised state regulated virtually every sphere of political, economic and social existence, years which drained away much of the initial enthusiasm for Bolshevism. By 1921 the Party was decimated, many of its leading cadres dead, the proletariat exhausted and ready for peace. The Russian working class no longer represented a revolutionary force; and increasingly the Soviets and workers committees were absorbed into the burgeoning bureaucratic state. Massive nationalisation of private property combined with the need to fight internal and external enemies created the foundations of bureaucracy: bourgeois specialists were recruited as managers of industry replacing collective, working-class control; former Tsarist officers became military advisers to the systematically organised and centralised Red Army; and trade unions became administrative organs of the state.

Impatient for pure socialism and deeply disturbed by the apparent 'right wing' policy of the Bolsheviks, Leftist Opposition groups emerged demanding a return to workers control of industry and an end to one-man factory management, work discipline and the efficiency methods copied from American industry (Taylorism): 'These are the elements that bring decay into our soviet institutions, breeding there an atmosphere altogether repugnant to the working class.'[5] The dangers posed to the Revolution by an omnipotent state dominating a weak civil society is a theme common both to the 'ultra lefts' (anarchists, syndicalists) and certain of the Bolshevik leaders. Groups such as the Workers Opposition and Workers Truth based their critique of bureaucracy largely on the increasingly non-proletarian content of the Soviet regime; bourgeois specialists must be purged from the administration and an immediate return made to direct democracy. The revolt of sailors at the Kronstadt naval depot in March 1921 had as its slogan 'All power to the local soviets', and called for an end to excessive centralisation. At the Tenth Party Congress in 1921 Lenin admitted the truth of these criticisms by declaring the Soviet state as one 'with a bureaucratic perversion'. Four years earlier, in *The State and Revolution*, Lenin had described future socialist society as a state 'without police, without a standing army, without an officialdom', a frankly utopian vision of a 'commune state' in which *all* will become "bureaucrats" for a time in order that *nobody* will be able to become a "bureaucrat" . . .' But in practice, through the rigours of War Communism, local and central administration had been swollen by former Tsarist functionaries working sometimes for, sometimes against the regime. In this critical situation the dictatorship of the proletariat was quite simply becoming a dictatorship *over* the proletariat.

Lenin's writings from 1919 to his death five years later are dominated by this problem: the lack of working-class hegemony in a society ruled by the dictatorship of the proletariat. Why is it, he asked, that Communists are swamped by red-tape and bureaucratic inefficiency? Because they lack *culture*, while Soviet society itself lacks the necessary 'civilisation' for an immediate transition to socialism. The Russian masses, he argued, exist in a state of 'semi-Asiatic ignorance', illiterate and ignorant, and 'without an entire cultural revolution' a genuinely co-operative organisation is impossible.[6] Thus although Lenin accepted many of the criticisms levelled at the Soviet state by the Workers Opposition he rejected their idealist assumption that the transfer of political power to the party of the proletariat automatically conferred on the proletariat the attributes of a dominant class. By the 1920s the bureaucratic domination of state-appointed functionaries over a decimated and politically weakened working class had taken firm foot. Lenin might criticise these developments but in a socialist Russia desperately short of the raw materials, machinery, technique and expertise essential for an industrial infrastructure there was little room for manoeuvre.

In 1921 severe food and fuel shortages and widespread resentment against the 'militarisation of labour' among the working masses produced a wave of strikes paralysing Moscow and Petrograd, while on the island fortress of Kronstadt the sailors mutinied. In the midst of this crisis Lenin sanctioned a ban on factions within the Bolshevik party, 'the rapid dispersal of all groups without exception which have formed themselves on one platform or another', for while the 'best Central Committee may make a mistake . . . this is less dangerous than the wavering which we see now.'[7] In the desperate situation of 1921 the prohibition of factions *within* the Party was probably

justified. With hindsight it is now obvious that this temporary
measure — during the similarly desperate Civil War and War
Communism phases freedom of discussion within the Party
remained — stifled criticism and strengthened the power of the
Party bureaucrats. Writing in 1939 Trotsky went further:
'Whoever prohibits factions thereby liquidates party democracy
and takes the first step toward a totalitarian regime.'[8] For as
the single ruling party, the Bolsheviks had created a state
proletarian only in name; instead of 'withering away' it was
growing to gigantic proportions.

Effectively the ban on factions weakened the power of the
Party Central Committee in favour of the Politburo and its
Secretariat. It was the Politburo which increasingly became the
major forum of decision making. Appointed General Secretary
in 1922, Stalin made good use of his extraordinary bureaucratic
authority, gathering around him loyal, pragmatic, down-to-earth
Party executives, owing their privileges and career to him and
the apparatus. As for Lenin, while criticising bureaucracy he
failed to grasp its great significance for the future course of the
Revolution. Sometimes he described it as a residual element
from the Tsarist regime, and at other times he agreed with
Trotsky's analysis, arguing that bureaucracy was the logical
outcome of the lack of proletarian hegemony. He could not see
that by the 1920s power was no longer invested in the
revolutionary working class and its party, but increasingly
within a bureaucratic apparatus. In 1924 Lenin's death allowed
Stalin to flood the Party with political followers (the 'Lenin
Levy'), bureaucratic careerists firmly controlled by his
Secretariat; now less than one per cent had belonged to the
Party in 1917, and by 1926 the Central Committee was
dominated by Stalin's appointees. Thus although Lenin in his
'Testament' (1924) urged the Party to replace the 'rude' and
intolerant Stalin, the document was suppressed in the interests
of 'unity'. But by 1924 the battle between the Left Opposition
(which included the Workers Opposition as well as those who
followed Trotsky) and the right wing of the Party was already
well developed; while Trotsky demanded rapid industrialisation
Bukharin and Stalin urged a more moderate compromise course,
a policy of 'growing into socialism' through a flourishing
agricultural capitalism and weakened industry. At issue was
Trotsky's belief that socialism in Russia was impossible without

a European revolution; Bukharin and the right wing, however, claimed that 'we *can* build socialism even on this wretched technical base . . . we shall creep at a snail's pace, but . . . all the same we are building socialism . . .'[9] Permanent revolution came under attack as 'a variety of Menshevism', although in practice Trotsky's theory had formed the basis of the October Revolution. The theory of 'Socialism in One Country' had the support of a majority within the Central Committee and Politburo, in the State Commissariats of Agriculture, Finance and Trade, the State Bank and Gosplan, the latter staffed largely by former Mensheviks with little enthusiasm for permanent revolution. Defeat of the Left was inevitable. Even the alliance of Trotsky with Zinoviev and Kamenev (former supporters of Stalin against Trotsky) proved abortive; Trotsky was expelled from the Party and the Left Opposition banned.

It was now that Stalin's policy moved to the left by a brutal policy of forced collectivisation. The right wing led by Bukharin was flung into a state of bewilderment. Too late Bukharin discovered the true face of Stalin: 'He is an unprincipled intriguer who subordinates everything to the preservation of his power. He changes theories depending on whom he wants to get rid of at the moment.'[10] In his battle with the Left, Stalin had relied on Bukharin's arguments to answer Trotsky's criticisms and lend intellectual credence to his bureaucratic intriguing and nationalist policies. Now the editor of Pravda, Lenin's and the Party's 'favourite', was curtly dismissed as 'a half-educated theoretician' and leader of 'the most repulsive and pettiest of all the factional groups that have ever existed in our Party.'[11] Bukharin, however, was neither expelled from the Party nor arrested. Like other Old Bolsheviks (for example Zinoviev, Kamenev, and those members of the Left Opposition who, believing that the new policy marked a decisive shift to the left made their peace with Stalin — Smirnov, Rakovsky, Radek), he remained within the Party hoping to effect changes from within, certain that Stalin's policies must end in disaster. Judging Stalin's military solution to the agricultural crisis as 'idiotic illiteracy', Bukharin concluded, prophetically, that they must result in 'a police state'. Yet as late as 1936 he could write that if the Stalinists 'are acting badly now, it is not because they are bad, but because the situation is bad.'[12]

Bukharin's optimism clashed ominously with the facts. By

the late twenties the secret police were busily arresting
'saboteurs' and 'wreckers', discovering 'imperialist plots'
among mining engineers, former Mensheviks and industrial and
scientific specialists: there is no doubt that the Shakhty trial
(1928) and 'Industrial Party' trial (1930) were deliberately
planned both to deflect responsibility for severe food and fuel
shortages from the Party bureaucracy and to implicate
suspected Trotsky sympathisers (for instance David Riazanov).
Repression was gradually escalating: in 1932 Stalin
reintroduced the Tsarist Internal passport system and the death
penalty for violations of state property, and three years later he
extended the death penalty to twelve-year-old children. These
totalitarian, police-state trends finally culminated in the mass
arrests, torture, and deaths of Old Bolsheviks, innocent
Communists and Stalinist bureaucrats who knew too much.
Between 1936 and 1938 Zinoviev, Kamenev, Radek, Bukharin,
Rykov and Rakovsky were accused and found guilty of the
most ludicrous criminal acts, from attempting to spread pig
plague to throwing glass into Soviet butter supplies (in 1932 the
entire meteorological office staff were accused of distorting
weather forecasts and so damaging Soviet agriculture).[13] Old
Bolsheviks confessed in court to their links with the Gestapo,
Trotsky and international capitalism: previously dedicated to
the overthrow of capitalism they now sought its restoration in
Soviet Russia. But of those brought to public trial none were active
Trotskyists; the majority of defendants had long capitulated to
Stalinism, and in the case of Radek actually defended Stalin's
purges to the extent of demanding the death penalty for those
in the Kamenev-Zinoviev trial. Defeated and demoralised,
lacking a coherent Marxist perspective, the Old Bolsheviks were
ripe for Stalin's Inquisition. In every trial Trotsky and
Trotskyism was defined as the chief enemy: from exile, Trotsky,
acting in concert with Hitler, the Emperor of Japan and British
military intelligence, seemingly controlled the leaders of Soviet
industry, transport and agriculture. Trotsky's ironic comment
that 'if all the key positions were occupied by Trotskyists who
submitted to me, why, in that case, is Stalin in the Kremlin and
I am in exile?'[14] sums up the absurd, yet terrifying, public face
of Stalin's show trials. But far away from public scrutiny in the
labour camps and cellars of the GPU a mass slaughter of
Trotskyists and other oppositionists was ruthlessly carried out.

After 1938 there was no political group left to challenge Stalin. 'No centre of independent political thinking had been allowed to survive', writes Isaac Deutscher, 'a tremendous gap had been torn in the nation's consciousness; its collective memory was shattered; the continuity of its revolutionary traditions was broken; and its capacity to form and crystallize any non-conformist notions was destroyed.'[15]

The brutal suppression of every single socialist opposition to Stalin, the use of military force to impose policies on minority groups, the nationalist domestic and foreign policies, and reliance on bureaucracy for rule indicate clearly enough the gulf between Leninism and Stalinism. Victor Serge wrote:

> It is often said that 'the germ of all Stalinism was in Bolshevism at its beginning'. Well I have no objection. Only, Bolshevism also contained many other germs — a mass of other germs — and those who lived through the enthusiasm of the first years of the first victorious revolution ought not to forget it. To judge the living man by the death germs which the autopsy reveals in a corpse — and which he may have carried in him since his birth — is this very sensible?[16]

Trotsky sought a different explanation: Stalinism triumphed because of Russian 'backwardness', isolation and the progressive weakening of revolutionary will: 'The tired and disappointed masses were indifferent to what was happening on the summits'; the October Revolution had 'devoured' individual and collective energies, the leading revolutionary party cadres were decimated by war and famine and 'the ebb of the "plebeian pride" made room for a flood of pusillanimity and careerism.'[17] But the history of opposition to Stalin suggests another significant factor: in 1924 at the height of the battle between the left and right factions Trotsky, submitting to the will of the Party, arguing that 'in the last instance the party is always right, because it is *the only historic instrument which the working class possesses for the solution of its fundamental tasks.*[18] Eight years later, however, at the time of the capitulation of Zinoviev and Kamenev, he concluded that 'the party can be served only by serving its ideas, not its degenerated apparatus.'[19] It was loyalty to the Party, however, which proved far stronger than Trotsky's Marxist understanding and with it the fate of the Revolution.

II

During the 1930s a current saying among the GPU was 'Give us a man, and we'll make a case'. *The Case of Comrade Tulayev* and *Darkness at Noon* have as their theme the collapse of revolutionary idealism and submission to the Stalinist bureaucracy of former revolutionaries and Old Bolsheviks. Why did these men, whose lives had been given selflessly to the cause of international socialism, now degrade their past as counter-revolutionary and fascist? Koestler's answer provides the single, all-embracing structure of *Darkness at Noon*. The old revolutionaries, having identified the Party with man's future, lacked the inner strength to question its claim to historical omniscience. As with Conrad, Koestler rejects revolutionary action as a means for social progress, arguing quite simply that revolutionary power ultimately corrupts every ideal through the revolutionist's belief of the end justifying any means. Thus trapped by their own 'revolutionary logic' the Old Bolsheviks submitted to Stalin as a final service to *their* Party. Serge, too, depicts the seeds of totalitarianism in the failure of the old revolutionaries to distinguish between the apparatus and the Party; instead of fighting Stalin they succumbed to Party loyalty.

Darkness at Noon and *The Case of Comrade Tulayev* have thus a significance quite apart from their literary value, for these are novels of political terrorism and ideology written by two men who, unlike the literary fellow-travellers, knew totalitarianism *from within.* During the late 1920s Serge suffered the fate of other unrepentant Oppositionists, arrest, exile, prison. Having gone to Russia in 1919 to work firstly as a political journalist (with pro-Bolshevik — anarchist sympathies) and later for the Comintern in Germany, Serge never wavered in his opposition to Stalinism and bureaucracy. As other Left Oppositionists made peace with Stalin, Serge resisted, refusing to implicate others in 'terrorist' plots and sign his 'confession'. He survived largely through pressure from abroad and the fact that the real terror had yet to start. Koestler, too, worked as a journalist, but not for the socialist press. The Russian Revolution seems to have had no impact on his ideas until 1931 when fascism threatened bourgeois society. Knowing nothing of Russian politics or of Marxism, he joined the Communist movement as it entered its most sterile and bureaucratic phase. Until his

break with the Party in 1938 Koestler in effect became a
Stalinist agent, his membership kept secret, his 'revolutionary'
activity largely confined to the journalistic fringe of the
Communist movement. He repressed all doubts — such as the
Party's 'social fascist' policy — faithfully carrying out his orders
even to the extent of deliberately distorting the truth. In his
autobiography Koestler wrote of his 'fanatical allegiance' to the
Party and admiration for Communist organisation and power.
Visiting Russia in 1932 he betrayed and denounced to the GPU,
as Rubashov does in *Darkness at Noon*, a girl he had fallen in
love with, and although disturbed by this first taste of
totalitarianism, remained within the largely clandestine and
conspiratoral organisation which was now the exiled German
Communist Party. Thus although describing himself later as 'a
born Trotskyist', he clearly rejected Trotskyism; and equally
important he had no real contact with the working-class
movement, his political practice confined exclusively to the
intellectual (journalistic) wing of Stalinism. His report on the
Spanish Civil War (*Spanish Testament*) contained deliberate
distortions. Visiting Spain again in 1936, ostensibly as
correspondent for English and Hungarian newspapers, he was
arrested by the fascists and imprisoned in Seville. In Russia the
purges had started and this, together with his knowledge of
Stalinist mendacity in Spain and elsewhere, provoked his final
break with the Party — in 1938![20]

For both Koestler and Serge, then, totalitarianism was a lived
experience, a horrific reality engulfing hundreds of their
comrades in secret trials and mass executions. For them,
totalitarianism meant the destruction of the individual and the
complete rewriting of history. At such a time, wrote Serge, the
writer has a duty to speak up and not seek refuge in a
'principled but impotent silence', for while 'the witness passes'
his testimony survives: 'He who speaks, he who writes is above
all one who speaks on behalf of those who have no voice.'[21]
For without sincerity and a respect for the individual, literature
must lose all critical functions and, accommodating itself to the
dominant interest, become mere ideology. Thus Serge and
Koestler's choice of the novel form as the genre through which
the fate and meaning of October 1917 is rendered is
indissolubly linked with the necessity to affirm individual
freedom against totalitarian ideology and state. Like Orwell,

both Serge and Koestler worked within a variety of genres, from political pamphlets and journalism to memoirs and the novel. Both turned to the novel form only when their practical involvement in politics began to wane: Serge's first novels, *Men in Prison* (1930), *Birth of Our Power* (1931), *Conquered City* (1932), composed in exile are rambling, impressionistic fiction which relates revolutionary movements to society through an episodic narrative structure: 'I knew that I would never have time to polish my works properly', Serge wrote, and because they would never be published in Russia only abroad, 'I had to construct them in detached fragments' so they might reach Europe. Koestler's first published novels, *The Gladiators* (1939), *Darkness at Noon* (1940), reflect his political break with Stalinism, the abrupt transition finding its expression in his one major significant fiction. Serge's development was more gradual. Exiled to France he returned to political activity and journalism (mainly exposing the Stalinist Show Trials) and it was only when the Nazis forced him to his final exile in Mexico that he wrote his single significant novel. No longer the reluctant defender of Bolshevism and Trotsky, belonging to no identifiable political tendency nor professing a coherent ideology, Serge gradually came to reject Russia as a socialist society although remaining committed to revolutionary politics. While Koestler abandoned every vestige of revolutionary thought to embrace a virulent anti-Communism, Serge, for all his pessimism, retained hope for a socialist future; his belief in October 1917 remained unshakeable, its 'enormous moral capital', and 'the storehouse of intelligent resolute energy which it had built up'.[22]

Comrade Tulayev, like *Darkness at Noon*, is an exploration of totalitarian power, the means whereby the decisions of a few bureaucrats decisively affect the lives of millions: killed on impulse by a petty clerk, Tulayev's death provides 'The Chief' with the opportunity for removing the few remaining political opponents to his rule as well as those who, serving his cause, know too much; within a few weeks loyal Stalinists, former Oppositionists and security chiefs are drawn into the net until the whole country reverberates with the Tulayev case. There is, of course, no wide-scale plot but no one is safe from a bureaucratic, centralised authority which seems to have an existence and a logic of its own. *Comrade Tulayev* is

pre-eminently a novel which expresses the futility and
hopelessness of a genuine political *praxis* in the face of
totalitarian power. It is a pessimistic not tragic view of the
world, for Serge portrays not men holding firmly to their values
and refusing compromise but men broken in spirit, unable to
articulate any consistent moral or political resistance to
Stalinism. There is Rublev, former member of the Party's
Central Committee, academic historian, ex-Bukharinist who in
the late twenties defended Stalin against Trotsky arguing that
the Party of the proletariat cannot degenerate; but now he
argues for the 'cultivation of consciousness' among the masses,
refusing to accept that the Revolution has been betrayed. For
him the Party may commit 'mistakes' but ultimately history
will vindicate it: 'Nothing remains for us, then, but to go on
serving nevertheless, and, if we are murdered, to submit.'[23]
Imprisoned, knowing he will die, Rublev composes a history of
the inner conflicts within the Party, hopefully for future
generations, a futile gesture from a man who does not
understand his own predicament. Thus arguing that 'it is
better to be murdered by the Chief, than to denounce him to
the international *bourgeoisie*', Rublev's final message to the
Party affirms his fetishised and degenerate concept of the Party:

> That I have lived my whole life only for the Party. Sick and
> degraded though it may be, our Party. That I have neither
> thought nor conscience outside of the Party. That I am loyal
> to the Party, whatever it may be, whatever it may do. That if
> I must perish, crushed by my Party, I consent . . . But that I
> warn the villains who are killing us that they are killing the
> Party . . .'[24]

Rublev's insane logic is echoed in the 'confessions' of the two
Stalinists, security chief Erchov, and provincial bureaucrat
Makayev, both loyal administrators owing their careers entirely
to an unswerving support for the Chief. Men of the apparatus,
enjoying no power outside it, their past stained with purges and
trials, they quickly capitulate, agreeing that resistance to Party
can aid only the enemy. 'We build on corpses, but we build',
Makayev had argued, justifying forced collectivism in an
economically backward country. Similarly, the Old Bolshevik
Kondratiev, returning from Spain and critical of the Stalinist
policy, decides to fight his impending 'frame-up' but ends by

justifying 'crimes and errors' through the 'feeble' political
consciousness of a backward country. Having told the Chief,
'You are the Party', Kondratiev seeks refuge in fatalism and
determinism: there are no great Bolsheviks left, for 'History
takes millenniums to produce men so great! Incorruptible,
intelligent, formed by thirty or forty decisive years, and pure,
pure!'[25] All Kondratiev can do is accept an administrative post
in Siberia.

In Spain, fighting with the Republicans, Kondratiev was
called, ironically, General Rudin, a 'superfluous man' who
compromises and yet survives. There is, however, one figure in
the novel who rejects all compromise, Ryzhik, an old Left
Oppositionist for whom revolution has degenerated into
bureaucratic counter-revolution. Brought from exile to
complete the 'scenario' in the Tulayev trial, he cleverly starves
himself to death and thus cheats the Chief. But Ryzhik, too, is a
fatalist: this sixty-year-old veteran, while vigorously defending
the October Revolution, seeks an historical justification for
Stalinism: 'The old revolutionary proletariat ends with us. A
new proletariat, of peasant origin, is developing in new
factories. It needs time to reach a certain degree of
consciousness and, by its own experience, to overcome the
totalitarian education it received.'[26] Serge's pessimism is total:
in the face of totalitarianism men must capitulate or die in
silence; there is hope neither for political nor inner resistance;
crushed in spirit, Serge's characters seek solace in historical
determinism. It is a vision almost identical to Orwell's in
Nineteen Eighty-Four, a world in which a future made by men
is no longer possible. *Comrade Tulayev*, then, expresses on an
artistic level Serge's final political condemnation of Bolshevism
as 'authoritarian through and through' and the Russian
Revolution as 'the continuation of certain ancient traditions
stemming from the despotism it had just overthrown.'[27] His
own resilient political faith that the Russian people must
eventually discard Stalinist totalitarianism, finds its expression
in the novel's 'optimistic ending' as Kostia, the murderer of
Tulayev, finds happiness and possible fulfilment working for a
collective farm. Feeling guilty for the actions which have sent
innocent men to death, he is comforted by his girl-friend: 'Just
the same, we are going forward, aren't we? There is a great and
pure force in you. Don't worry.' This aspect of *Comrade*

Tulayev contradicts Serge's political ideology of the absolute power of totalitarianism and the hopelessness of any form of struggle against it. His carefully selected gallery of representative figures, each reflecting a clear ideological standpoint, supposedly embody the tragic destiny of a revolutionary epoch. But they do so mechanically, refuting Serge's own argument that 'if the novelist's characters are truly alive, they function by themselves, to a point at which they eventually take their author by surprise'.[28] Serge's naive, anarchical view of the Revolution, his assertion of a vague populism and his failure to grasp the complex historical nature of Stalinism leads him to depict typical characters whose fates are determined absolutely by his pessimistic ideology.

III

In his memoirs Serge describes his 'strong conviction of charting a new road for the novel'; the classical bourgeois novel was now an outmoded and impoverished genre. Serge's ambition, to create revolutionary literature capable of expressing his socialist belief in the revolutionary *praxis* of the working class, remained unfulfilled: *Comrade Tulayev* is a traditional, realist novel, its typical figures and sequence of parallel events evoke an objective, documentary and static vision of totalitarianism. In portraying a defeated revolution in terms of 'the inevitable triumph of Stalinism' and the absence of any viable political alternative, Serge's novel approaches the political conclusions of *Darkness at Noon.* Koestler's novel, however, is a more concentrated and dense structure, focusing not on 'typical figures' but on the one character of Rubashov; and whereas the concentrated horror and nightmare world of totalitarianism eludes Serge's diffuse literary form, Koestler's more subjective approach through Rubashov's inner and outer life grasps its essence economically and dynamically.

Koestler began writing the novel at the time of the Third Moscow Trial. He was not yet an anti-Communist and the Soviet Union still remained a socialist state. In a later postscript to the novel Koestler argues that while the action virtually wrote itself, 'I had only a vague and general notion of the reasons which would induce [Rubashov to confess]', and it was only through Rubashov's interrogation by Ivanov and Gletkin that these emerged. Undoubtedly it is this aspect which gives the novel its compelling power and immediacy, its supple qualities contrasting sharply with Serge's schematic structures. Whereas Serge depicts standard types and clear political positions, Koestler makes no attempt to delineate the differences between Stalin and the left and right oppositions. For Koestler is concerned with the nature of revolution *in general* rather than the particular dynamics of the Russian Revolution. His political intentions are clear from the beginning: Rubashov, he says, represents a synthesis of *all* Bolshevik trends, combining the intellectual qualities of Bukharin with the personality of Radek and physical appearance of Trotsky. A more absurd conflation is difficult to imagine — Radek, ex-collaborator of Trotsky who in 1929 capitulated to Stalin, betrayed Trotsky's secretary Blumkin, and became servile ideologist for Stalin; Bukharin, whose right-wing policies opposed him to Trotsky from the early twenties; and Trotsky, who held firmly to his Marxist beliefs, never capitulated nor betrayed anyone. Koestler emphasises that his account of Rubashov's final confession was not intended to exhaust all other reasons for capitulation — some hoped they or their families might be saved, while others were already worn out, broken and disillusioned. However, it is obvious that Koestler intended his analysis of Rubashov's motives as a general explanation for those Old Bolsheviks who agreed to a public trial and a 'voluntary confession' which they would not recant. Koestler's thesis is that the Old Bolsheviks confessed because they recognised the 'Marxist' logic in their captors' supremacy.

Who, then, is Rubashov? A right-wing Bolshevik who never joined the Opposition, Koestler depicts his past as that of a loyal Party bureaucrat who follows Party orders even though he knows their disastrous consequences. In 1933, for example, supporting the Party's 'social fascist' policy even after the Nazi conquest, Rubashov betrays a German comrade to the Gestapo for daring to question its validity. Others are equally sacrificed to the Party's shifting policies — Little Loewy and the girl, Arlova. It is important to note that Rubashov's political activity is conspiratorial and secretive and he has no contact with the masses. This Stalinist concept of *praxis* is clearly Koestler's own bureaucratic experience as is Rubashov's bureaucratic definition of the Party:

The Party can never be mistaken . . . You and I can make a
mistake. Not the Party. The Party, comrade, is more than
you and I and a thousand others like you and I. The Party is
the embodiment of the revolutionary idea in history. . . .
History knows her way. She makes no mistakes. He who has
not absolute faith in History does not belong in the Party's
ranks.[29]

For Rubashov the Party was necessarily monolithic and thus
totalitarian. The individual counted for nothing in the face of
definite, inexorable historical laws; history sides with the Party.
There is thus no need for *praxis* and Rubashov's Marxism is
quite simply historical determinism and fatalism. For Rubashov
the principles were always right, and if things have gone wrong
then 'history itself was defective'.[30] Koestler's grasp of the
Stalinist mind is here acute and exemplary, as he delineates
Rubashov's incredibly simplistic yet totalitarian equation of
ends justifying means: 'History has taught us that often lies
serve her better than the truth; for man is sluggish and has to be
led through the desert for forty years before each step in his
development.' Those 'in the wrong must pay', while those 'in
the right will be absolved'.[31]

   Thus faced with the similar logic of Ivanov and Gletkin,
Rubashov is trapped. When Gletkin tells him that Truth is the
Party he must acquiesce, for he shares Gletkin's identification
of the bureaucratic apparatus with Marxist ideas and practice,
and Rubashov confesses — voluntarily — as his final service to
the Party. For in the end Rubashov exonerates the Party and
places blame on the working class. The masses were not ready
for revolution: 'The mistake in socialist theory was to believe
that the level of mass-consciousness rose constantly and
steadily . . . The peoples of Europe are still far from having
mentally digested the consequences of the steam engine. The
capitalist system will collapse before the masses have
understood it.'[32] Having rejected permanent revolution and
accepted the possibility of socialism in a single country,
Rubashov (and Rublev in *Comrade Tulayev*) has no other
choice but capitulation. There are no alternatives. But is
Koestler's explanation adequate? Writing in the 1940s he
suggests support for his theory in the confessions of the Old
Bolshevik Mrachkovsky who, resisting physical torture, finally

capitulated to the more subtle logic of a Gletkin/Ivanov type interrogation. But Koestler is wrong: the ex-Oppositionist Mrachkovsky had long capitulated to Stalin and the bureaucratic apparatus. 'We need men like you', Stalin told him, and seduced by Stalin's 'forgiveness' Mrachkovsky bent his energies to railway construction. When Rubashov tells Gletkin, 'I will do everything which may serve the Party', he speaks as a member of that small group of Bolsheviks who, rejecting permanent revolution for socialism in one country, defended the bureaucratic apparatus against revolutionary Marxism and the totalitarian politics of a monolithic party against socialist democracy. Koestler's is not an explanation for those thousands of Old Bolsheviks, Trotskyists and other Oppositionists whose stand against Stalinism never wavered and who died anonymously at the hands of Stalin's secret police.

Koestler argues that Rubashov's final speech is a paraphrase of Bukharin's testimony at the Third Moscow Trial. The historical record, however, hardly supports Koestler's extravagant thesis. The transcript of the trial (which Koestler obviously read), far from showing Bukharin's sympathy for his accusers' philosophy, demonstrates his resolute opposition to it. Of course, there exist superficial similarities between Rubashov and Bukharin — Bukharin had capitulated to Stalin, reviled his own policies and admitted 'his guilt before the Party . . . the Central Committee . . . the working class and the country.' On the Shakhty trial he remained silent and later justified the early Stalinist trials. Equally he shares Rubashov's fatalism and blind faith in inevitable progress: 'It is difficult for us to live . . . But one is saved by a faith that development is always going forward. It is like a stream that is running to the shore. If one leaps out . . . one is ejected completely.' With Radek he wrote the Soviet Constitution and believed that 'the people will have more room . . . can no longer be pushed aside.'[33] Unlike Trotsky, Bukharin held, to the very end, his belief in the Party, the necessity to stay within it and fight (or hope) for reforms. He was, after all, the architect of socialism in one country and however brutal, Stalin's policy was one of industrialisation and technological development:

For three months I refused to say anything. Then I began to testify. Why? Because while in prison I made a revaluation of my entire past. For when you ask yourself: 'If you must die, what are you dying for?' — an absolutely black vacuity suddenly rises before you with startling vividness. There was nothing to die for, if one wanted to die unrepented ... And when you ask yourself, 'Very well, suppose you do not die; suppose by some miracle you remain alive, again what for?' Isolated from everybody, an enemy of the people, an inhuman position, completely isolated from everything that constitutes the essence of life.[34]

Equally significant is Rubashov's (and Bukharin's) rejection of specific crimes and acceptance of a broad *general* responsibility:

Rubashov — 'On a demand for a liberal reform of the dictatorship; for a broader democracy, for the abolition of the Terror, and a loosening of the rigid organization of the Party. I admit that these demands, in the present situation, are objectively harmful and therefore counter-revolutionary in character.'[35]
Bukharin — 'I plead guilty to being one of the outstanding leaders of this "bloc of Rights and Trotskyites".
Consequently, I plead guilty to what directly follows from this, the sum total of crimes committed by this counter-revolutionary organization, irrespective of whether or not I knew of, whether or not I took a direct part in, any particular act.'[36]

Unlike the fictional Rubashov, however, Bukharin systematically destroyed the prosecution case against him in *open court* and ended his final speech by pointing out that 'the confession of the accused is a medieval principle of jurisprudence'. It is here that the crucial differences between Rubashov and Bukharin emerge. Bukharin hated Stalin, 'a devil', he told André Malraux in 1936, who 'is going to kill me.' He feared for his young wife and newly born son, yet he resisted right to the end. At a Central Committee meeting he openly accused Stalin of deliberately fomenting political terrorism and torture, and urged that the Party 'return to the traditions of Lenin and to call to order the police plotters who conceal themselves behind the authority of the Party. It is the NKVD, and not the Party, which today governs the country.' Shortly before his arrest he wrote his letter, 'To a Future

Generation of Party leaders', and here there is no trace of the
helpless and defeated Rubashov.

> I feel my helplessness before a hellish machine, which,
> probably by the use of medieval methods, has acquired
> gigantic power, fabricates organized slander, acts boldly and
> confidently. . . . . At present, most of the so-called organs of
> the NKVD are a degenerate organization of bureaucrats,
> without ideas, rotten, well-paid, who use the Cheka's bygone
> authority to cater to Stalin's morbid suspiciousness . . .
>   Any member of the Central Committee, any member of
> the Party can be rubbed out, turned into a traitor, terrorist,
> diversionist, spy, by these 'wonder-working organs".[37]

Arrested, the defiant Bukharin refused to confess, and only
threats to kill his wife and child induced his participation in
Stalin's scenario. And knowing he must die, Bukharin, like
other revolutionaries before him, used the one available means
left, his open trial, to condemn his accusers before world
opinion and history. The 'Aesopian' language employed, his
utter contempt for Vyshinsky, the ex-Menshevik Public
Prosecutor, together with his last writings suggest that Bukharin
for all his opposition to the Left rejected Stalinism and held
firmly to the democratic principles of Bolshevism and Marxism.
  There is thus a hollowness, a deep falseness to Koestler's (and
Rubashov's) reflections on the means—ends 'dilemma'.
Rubashov's assertion that 'we are sailing without ethical ballast'
is an indictment of Stalinism not Bolshevism. Stalin's
'revolution from above', his policies of rapid industrialisation
and elimination of socialist democracy were not simply the
application of 'bad' means to the 'good' goal of a future
Communist society, but rather the result of his faction's need to
augment *its* power within the social framework erected by the
1917 Revolution. A workers' democracy is incompatible with
bureaucracy and nationalism. The right-wing Bukharin knew
that Stalinism was in no sense the heir to Bolshevism, and in his
last days affirmed his beliefs in Lenin, the Revolution and the
Bolshevik party. No greater contrast is possible than between
the broken, defeated and unfree Rubashov, the prisoner of his
Stalinist past, and Bukharin, who, in his last days, and with
great courage, affirmed *his* freedom, to stand by those values
which had first drawn him to Lenin and Bolshevism. Rubashov

speaks Bukharin's forced confession abjectly but *sincerely*.

Darkness at Noon, with its graphic and historically accurate descriptions of GPU interrogation techniques, embodies a pessimistic not tragic view of revolutionary ideas and action. It bears repeating that Koestler did not suggest one single explanation for the confessions, which 'only appear mysterious to those who look for one uniform explanation of the behaviour of men prompted by heterogeneous reasons.' There was, for example, brutal physical torture, widely used after 1937, but Koestler clearly believed (and the novel makes this explicit) that a Rubashov-type confession, voluntarily extracted in the end, was typical of a particular type of Bolshevik, a member whose whole life had been formed, moulded and determined by the Party. In truth, the strength of *Darkness at Noon* lies in Koestler's meticulous understanding of the bureaucratic *Stalinist* mind; its great weakness must ultimately rest with its selective and distorted historical grasp of Bolshevism and Stalinism.

IV

Comrade Tulayev and *Darkness at Noon* are novels of defeat and disillusion which fail to attain a genuine tragic stature. The choice of realism to render a conservative affirmation of individual freedom — Rubashov's belated discovery of his conscience, the 'I' — from within a pessimistic ideological standpoint is clearly linked with the relations of writer to socialism. For both Serge and Koestler the absence of proletarian hegemony within Soviet society is decisive; neither belonged to social groups able to generate genuine working-class, socialist values and through them affirm the historical meaning of the October Revolution. Serge lived his last years on the fringes of the socialist movement, while Koestler as he wrote *Darkness at Noon* was retreating to a firm bourgeois standpoint. Years later a genuine tragic vision would emerge from within bureaucratised socialist society, a vision which both affirms man's freedom and his irreducible autonomy as an active and moral agent. It will be the argument of the subsequent chapters that this tragic vision finds expression through the novel form, linking man organically with society as history. The rich historical dimension of this tragic view is precisely what is missing from Koestler and Serge.

8 Solzhenitsyn: The Tragic Vision

In 1953 Joseph Stalin died. During the 1930s he had
successfully eliminated all effective opposition to his rule by the
use of show trials, tortures, judicial murder, imprisonment, exile
and assassination. Shortly after his death the spectre of more
needless bloodshed and terror presented itself to the Soviet
people: in 1949 the Yugoslav Communist leader, Tito,
pursuing the right of socialist nations to political independence,
was declared an active agent of Western Imperialism, a fascist
for all his life-time service to Communism. The Communist
parties of the Soviet bloc were ruthlessly purged of Tito
sympathisers and 'lackeys of capitalism'. Many sincere
Communists were arrested and executed. And in the Soviet
Union a vicious campaign against 'rootless cosmopolitans',
'formalists' in art and literature (Pasternak, Shostakovich,
Prokofiev) culminated in the discovery of a 'doctors' plot', a
'Jewish conspiracy' to poison the venerable Stalin. In 1956, at
the Twentieth Congress of the Communist Party, Nikita
Khrushchev revealed for the first time the appalling magnitude
of Stalin's crimes: in his 'secret speech' Khrushchev spoke of the
extreme 'violations of socialist legality' perpetrated by Stalin, of
the imprisonment and execution of innocent victims of the 'cult
of personality'. He went further, arguing that in the Stalinist
atmosphere of terror and repression, Soviet science, industry and
culture had failed to develop its potential: Khrushchev's policy
of de-Stalinisation was clearly aimed at modernising a largely
inefficient industrial society. It seemed to many that the era of
Stalinism was at an end and the spirit of free inquiry and
creative imagination in science and art would now reassert itself.
But de-Stalinisation carried with it a problem posed by the
process itself but left unanswered by its proponents: was
Stalin's arbitrary rule the result of one man's paranoia, as
Khrushchev seemed to suggest, or was Stalin himself merely the

reflection of deep-rooted tendencies in Soviet society, made possible in the first place by the Bolshevik assumption of power? After all, a basic tenet of Marxism holds that the historic individual represents not merely himself but specific social and economic forces. Khrushchev had merely blamed the individual for thirty years of mismanagement, terror and stagnation. It was a question others could not ignore so lightly.

I

The immediate impact of Khrushchev's revelations was a relaxation in the rigid system of censorship established in the early thirties, and for the first time since 1934 writers openly questioned the basis of socialist realism. In his memoirs Ilya Ehrenburg remarks that among the liberal intelligentsia a feeling grew that Soviet letters would never again degenerate to the state when Zhdanov could publicly describe the great Soviet poet Anna Akhmatova as 'not exactly a harlot, but rather a nun, with whom harlotry is mixed with prayer.'[1] Ehrenburg's optimism was seemingly confirmed with the publication of his critical novel, *The Thaw* (1954), and Vladimir Dudintsev's *Not by Bread Alone* (1956); and also by the 'rediscovery' and re-publication of writers and artists whom the Stalin regime had classified as 'non-persons' (Babel, Olesha, Meyerhold, Pilnyak, Bulgakov) or as hopelessly 'reactionary' (Sologub, Bely, Bunin). In Stalin's time a full history of Soviet literature was never written, nor even attempted, and it was not until 1958 that the first tentative steps were taken and the rehabilitation of Soviet writers begun.[2] In the liberal magazine *Novy Mir* (New World) the genuine voice of criticism, howevever faint, was heard for the first time since the 1920s. Many of the younger generation of Soviet writers clearly associated de-Stalinisation with a renewal of the cultural vigour unleashed by the October Revolution, a return to the idealism of the early years of the Revolution which Stalinism had systematically distorted. And for the first time since those years an authentic opposition gradually emerged, at first hesitant and grateful for the new liberties, but increasingly critical of the rigid bureaucratically undemocratic structure of Soviet society.

During the 1960s Soviet writers, scientists and scholars formed themselves into groups and associations openly hostile to the totalitarian politics still practised by Stalin's successors. Unlike other opposition groups which from time to time had emerged in the 1940s and 1950s (for example 'Lenin's True Work' group and 'The Democratic Movement of the North of Russia'), largely composed of students and young workers, the opposition of the 1960s not merely *survived* physically but maintained and developed a critique of Soviet society. Denied free access to the organs of communication the opposition began to 'self-publish' (*samizdat*) and inform the growing community of dissident intellectuals of the many malpractices of the governing bureaucracy through extensive clandestine circulation of typescripts and mimeographed copies of books, articles and speeches. Underground journals had started appearing in the late 1950s but they reached a high point with the important *Chronicle Of Current Events* in 1968. Published bimonthly, until forced to cease publication in 1972 by the police, the *Chronicle* became the main forum for a wide spectrum of dissident opinion, providing a reliable and informative survey of recent arrests, activities of the K.G.B. (Secret Police), and critical commentary on current affairs.[3]

Unlike the explicitly political opposition of the 1920s and 1930s (the Left and Right Oppositions) the modern opposition is not unified by a common ideology and political standpoint but characterised by diversity in social, economic, and religious questions. The dissident historian, Andrey Amalrik, for example, describes the opposition as the 'Democratic Movement' and divides it into three distinct groups: Marxists who aim to restore genuine Leninist norms to society (Major General Pyotr Grigorenko who, among other things, has defended the right of workers to strike in a socialist society, Pyotr Yakir whose father, a Red Army general, was purged by Stalin, and the historian Roy Medvedev are the best known representatives of this group); Christians hoping to restore genuine religious values to society (including Solzhenitsyn and his fellow dissident novelist Vladimir Maximov); and finally, liberals who dream of transforming the Soviet Union into a market-type economy and Western-style parliamentary democracy (the leading exponent of this tendency is one of Russia's leading nuclear physicists, Andrey Sakharov, co-founder in 1970 of the Human Rights Committee).[4] Obviously there is some overlapping in interests and emphases: all three groups

while divided on their analysis of and solution for Stalinism —
Roy Medvedev calls for democratic change through a reformed
Communist Party, while Sakharov looks to the capitalist West
and a policy of detente as the only hope — are united in their
opposition to censorship and the obstacles to free expression.
The Marxists explicitly criticise the Soviet bureaucracy for a
betrayal of Marxism and Leninism and consciously raise the
questions which Khrushchev's secret speech had ignored; others
seek their inspiration in the socially committed traditions of
the pre-revolutionary Russian intelligentsia, and, in their search
for understanding, frequently invoke the nineteenth-century
Populist principle of 'going to the people', of self-sacrifice. It is
a measure of the great uncertainty and the internecine conflicts
which characterised the post-Stalin ruling élite that this
situation was tolerated for so long. It represents an ambiguity
partly the result of the heritage of Stalin's rule, but equally
flowing from the fact that a modern industrial society in
competition with the more advanced Western capitalisms,
especially the United States, has to permit some degree of
intellectual freedom and social consensus in order to harness the
energies and creative spirit so necessary for social development.
The Soviet bureaucracy clearly cannot afford a return to the
Stalin era when the leading Russian physicist, Pyotr Kapitsa,
lived under house arrest for seven years for refusing to work on
military oriented research, when the charlatan geneticist T. D.
Lysenko could dominate Russian science and condemn
scientists who disagreed with his ideas to prison and death, and
where Lev Landau, one of Russia's most brilliant theoretical
physicists, could be charged as a Nazi spy and imprisoned for a
year. The Soviet leadership thus fluctuates between granting
intellectual freedom and the right of cultural exchange to some
groups (notably scientists) while denying it to others. To allow
free expression to historians, political scientists and writers, must
inevitably lead to the kind of critical analysis of the rise of
Stalinism and the role played by the bureaucracy in the
elimination of all opposition and the augmenting of totalitarian
domination. Any critical assessment of the period of Stalin's
ascendency would manifestly challenge the legitimacy of the
present incumbents to power. And, of course, this is what
actually happened. Thus Roy Medvedev's massive study of
Stalinism, *Let History Judge* (1962—8), and his theoretical

work, *On Socialist Democracy* (1972), together with his
brother's detailed analysis of Soviet genetics under Stalin and
Khrushchev, *The Rise and Fall of T. D. Lysenko* (all published
in *samizdat*)[5] argue that 'violations of socialist legality' were not
the result of the 'cult of personality' but constituted an organic
part of bureaucratic domination:

> A bureaucrat is not simply a government functionary who
> sits in his office and directs certain affairs. A bureaucrat is a
> privileged functionary, cut off from real life, from the
> people, from the needs and interests of common folk. He is
> interested in his job as a position to be preserved and
> improved, not as a task to be done. He will knowingly do
> something unnecessary or even harmful for the people if it
> will preserve his position. Careerism and subservience, red
> tape and protocol, are his constant companions. Basic
> ignorance, especially of cultural achievements, emotional
> dullness, and a limited intellect are . . . typical characteristics
> of the bureaucrat.[6]

It is clearly this aspect of the Opposition's analysis which
terrifies the bureaucracy, that Stalinism represented a
degeneration of the proletarian state brought about, quite
consciously, by a powerful, anti-democratic and fundamentally
non-Leninist bureaucratic caste. Many of the imaginative writers
whose work is banned in the Soviet Union come close to this
theme, and through the power of art itself raise disturbing
questions not susceptible to the simplistic answers provided by
Khrushchev and other Party leaders. They are not satisfied, also,
by the kind of evasions practised by life-long liberals and
apologists of the Stalin regime: Ehrenburg, for example,
admitted unease with the Stalin cult as it developed in the
thirties, but, as a 'mere intellectual' out of touch with 'the
needs of the age' and 'the psychology of the masses', he
gradually accepted what he knew to be phony trials and
confessions ascribing them conveniently 'to the moral climate
of our time'. Silence was thus a 'curse', a necessary evil for evil
times.[7] The result of such pragmatism avoids precisely the kind
of question which must lie at the heart of any contemporary
Soviet novel: how was Stalinism possible? Who are the guilty
men? The tragic vision emerges precisely in the work of those
novelists who, seeking to understand the years of terrorism and

dictatorship, reflect the fragmentation and political weakness of the contemporary opposition. The positive hero of socialist realism becomes the problematic hero of tragedy in the novels of Andrey Sinyavsky, Lydia Chukovskaya (*The Deserted House*, 1940, *Going Under*, 1957) and Solzhenitsyn. It is Solzhenitsyn's achievement to have gone beyond the 'critical' but 'safe' novels (Ehrenburg, Dudintsev) of the immediate post-Stalin years to pose the fundamental questions of past and present Stalinism within a profoundly tragic artistic structure. It will be the argument of this and the following chapter that Solzhenitsyn's two major novels, *The First Circle* and *Cancer Ward*, cannot be understood adequately unless firmly grounded in the history of the post-Stalin opposition.

II

Alexander Solzhenitsyn was born in 1918. His father died six months before he was born, and during the 1920s his mother found great difficulty in earning a regular income. Mother and son survived through her work as a typist in Rostov. During the 1930s, at a time when the Old Bolsheviks were being systematically purged by the Stalinist bureaucracy, Solzhenitsyn studied mathematics and physics at the local university, going on to win one of the first post-graduate Stalin scholarships. Although this fact suggests that the local Party trusted him, there seems no doubt that Solzhenitsyn was deeply disturbed by the events of the late 1930s and particularly by the insane glorification of Stalin as the great leader and brilliant theoretician. It was during this period that Solzhenitsyn conceived what he now calls 'the principle project of my life', a massive survey of the social forces that precipitated the collapse of the old Russia in 1917 and the rise of the Soviet state. But then his deep interest in literature and philosophy was subordinated to the more practical requirements of mathematics and science. In 1941 he graduated in mathematics and was married. A year later he joined the army, rising to the rank of Captain by 1945. From 1942 to the end of the war Solzhenitsyn fought permanently at the front, and, for his personal bravery, was awarded the Order of the Patriotic War as well as the Order of the Red Star. Ironically, it was now that serious doubts entered his mind on Stalin's tactics during the early stages of the war, when the Soviet Union had been brought to the brink of defeat. 'I thought he had betrayed Leninism', Solzhenitsyn later recalled. The letters he wrote at this time were full of poorly disguised criticism, for although the 'great leader' appeared as 'the whiskered one' or 'boss' Soviet censorship quickly grasped their real meaning. Solzhenitsyn was arrested, and following a summary and illegal trial, sentenced to eight years hard labour and perpetual exile.

He should then have spent his years in one of Stalin's labour camps. But having written on his prison registration card the occupation of nuclear physicist ('I had never been a nuclear physicist in my life, and what I knew of the field I had heard in the university before the war — just a little bit, the names of the atomic particles and their parameters'), Solzhenitsyn was transferred in 1946 on the orders of the Minister of Internal Affairs, to the special Moscow prison, Marfino, to join a number of eminent Soviet scientists who, for various reasons, had fallen foul of Stalin, brought together and used for scientific research and experiment. This is the setting for *The First Circle*, a prison research institute 'where the standard was so high that any scientist would have been proud to work there'. Solzhenitsyn spent four years at Marfino enjoying the kind of free intellectual discussion that would have been impossible on the outside. One result seems to have been the collapse of Solzhenitsyn's belief in Marxism. In 1949 he refused to help in the development of a secret telephone coding device on the grounds that to acquiesce was to augment Stalin's repressive rule. He wrote later that he 'could not make moral compromises', a decision punished by four years in the Karlag labour camp in Karaganda. Released in 1953 he began his perpetual exile in Kazakhstan, far from European and Central Russia, becoming a teacher in a local school. Remarkably he had survived the onset of a cancerous tumour in the labour camp but now it flared up again. In 1954 Solzhenitsyn, a dying man, travelled to Tashkent to undergo a successful course of treatment (the setting for *Cancer Ward*). Finally in 1956 he was freed from exile and the following year, together with thousands of other victims of Stalin's purges, 'rehabilitated', acknowledged as the tragic victims of 'violations of socialist legality'. During the court proceedings which rehabilitated him Solzhenitsyn took the unusual step of answering questions by reading from the manuscript of *One Day in the Life of Ivan Denisovich* on which he was then working:

it is ironic to read, in view of subsequent events, the court's statement that 'when Solzhenitsyn in his diary and the letters to his friend discussed the problem of the correct interpretation of Marxism—Leninism . . . he was opposing the cult of the personality of Stalin and was referring to the artistic and ideological inadequacy of many works by Soviet authors and their sense of unreality.'

In the same year Solzhenitsyn joined the Ryazan branch of the Writers Union and, teaching physics in a local school, completed the manuscript of *One Day*. But it was not until 1961 that this remarkable first novel was submitted to the liberal magazine *Novy Mir* at a time when the Soviet Union was passing through its most liberal stage since the death of Stalin. At the Twenty-Second Congress of the Communist Party in 1961 Khrushchev had decided to speed up the process of de-Stalinisation, to promote economic efficiency by a shake-up of the ossified Party bureaucracy. Never one to shirk melodrama, Khrushchev announced the removal of Stalin's body from the Mausoleum on Red Square. Such actions clearly worried the die-hard Stalinists who still remained firmly entrenched within the inner circles of the Party. As support for his policies Khrushchev sought allies within the progressive sections of the intelligentsia and it was at this crucial point that Alexander Tvardovsky, the editor of *Novy Mir*, brought Solzhenitsyn's novel to him. For the only way that *Novy Mir* could publish the story was by a direct appeal to Khrushchev, thus circumventing the Soviet secret censorship system (Glavlit). When he had read it, as well as Yevtushenko's poem 'The Heirs of Stalin', Khrushchev saw it as ammunition against the dogmatic Stalinists. The novel was actually authorised for publication by the Presidium of the Central Committee, although not without a struggle. To those who opposed publication — and these included the man who, some twelve years later, would finally order the exile of Solzhenitsyn from the Soviet Union, Leonid Brezhnev — Khrushchev shouted, 'There's a Stalinist in each of you, there's even some Stalinism in me. We must root out this evil.'[8] Thus in November 1962 *Novy Mir* published Solzhenitsyn's story: within one day all ninety-five thousand copies of the magazine had sold out and Solzhenitsyn, the unknown school teacher, had become both a national and world figure.

The critical reception of *One Day* was startling. Liberals, of course, were delighted, greeting it as a masterpiece, but even the most reactionary Stalinist critics, aware of Khrushchev's support, gave enthusiastic notices. To many it seemed that the Zhdanov period was really ended.[9] Such optimism was quickly stifled. In 1962 Khrushchev had sent nuclear missile heads to Cuba; the Americans threatened war and Khrushchev backed down. In December 1962, a depressed Khrushchev visited the Manezh exhibition of modern art. The exhibition itself was hardly modern by Western standards but it was sufficiently *avant-garde* to distress Khrushchev's simple aesthetics. Of the painter Zheltovsky he asked, 'Are you a paederast or a normal man?' while his general comment on abstract art was quite simply, 'I am entitled to think you are all paederasts and for that you can get ten years . . . We aren't going to spend a kopek on this dog shit.'[10] In a 20,000 word speech in March 1963 to the Central Committee Khrushchev particularly defended Stalin ('those were bright and happy years') and attacked Ilya Ehrenburg, the poet Voznesensky and many other liberal writers for what he called 'formalism' and 'ideological co-existence'. This attack had the effect of bringing certain artists into line: the sculptor Ernest Neizvestny, the composer Shostakovich and the poets Robert Rozhdestvensky, Yevtushenko and Voznesensky, published statements accepting the guiding role of the Communist Party in all matters of education and culture.

This pragmatic policy of 'freeze' following 'thaw' had characterised Soviet culture since 1953. Each successive thaw had given writers and artists greater confidence in attacking the basic tenets of Soviet art. In October 1953 Ehrenburg, for example, felt free enough to declare that 'the author is not a piece of machinery' and that novels cannot be ordered or planned like new factories but only created, for 'can anyone imagine ordering Tolstoy to write Anna Karenina?' A year later Ehrenburg published his aptly named novel, *The Thaw*, which quickly became the symbol of the changes which seemed inevitable in Soviet society. But perhaps the most significant event of the immediate post-Stalin years was the publication in *Novy Mir* of the article 'On Sincerity in Literature' by the young critic Vladimir Pomerantsev, which attacked in forthright terms many of the prevailing shibboleths of socialist realism. In *Cancer Ward* this article plays an important role in emphasising the choice between the pragmatic and compromised values of Stalinism and those of a genuine moral awareness. Pomerantsev wrote that the:

> primary task of criticism today is that of leading writers toward a broadening of themes and a change in the treatment of problems. This is the chief thing, because the reader must be able to get something from literature that he can't get elsewhere.[11]

These criticisms met an immediate response from the die-hard Stalinists. Tvardovsky was sacked as editor of *Novy Mir* and at the Second Congress of Soviet Writers in December 1954 (the first since 1934) the chief spokesman for the Party, Alexey Surkov, reasserted the Zhdanov line, insisting that literature was part of the class struggle and its function pre-eminently educational and ideological. But criticisms of socialist realism and its purely utilitarian approach to literature continued to be heard. In 1956 *Novy Mir* published Vladimir Dudintsev's *Not By Bread Alone*, a novel which dramatised the conflict between the innovatory ideas of a dedicated Communist scientist and the stifling of these ideas by the bureaucratic structure and organisation of Soviet science. To the inventor Lopatkin, the narrow-minded, dogmatic bureaucrat Drozdov says:

> You are a truly tragic figure. You personify an age which has vanished never to return . . . We can do without your invention, even if it is an important one. And we shall lose nothing because strict planning and calculation ensure steady progress . . . If your invention is one of genius our collective will none the less solve the same problem when it becomes necessary. We are builder ants and necessary. You are a solitary genius, and not needed . . .[12]

Dudintsev's novel was a powerful attack on privilege and careerism, on the snobbery, servility to authority and arbitrary use of power induced by bureaucracy. Other writers began to pillory bureaucracy, but already a new freeze was coming: Khrushchev's secret speech had never been published in the Soviet Union but the 'leaks' widely publicised in the West were enough to help promote widespread unrest in Eastern Europe. In Poland and Hungary opposition to the Stalinist bureaucracy culminated in the emergence of Gomulka in Poland and Soviet military intervention in Hungary. Late in 1956 Khrushchev's de-Stalinisation was temporarily halted and a dogmatic line on literature reasserted. Dudintsev was upbraided for his 'slanderous book' and socialist realism defended as a whole for providing 'unlimited possibilities', for communicating the 'pathos of labour' to the people and 'for waging a relentless struggle against the penetration of alien ideologies into our art and literature'.[13] Pasternak's *Doctor Zhivago* was refused publication in *Novy Mir* and the author accused of 'bourgeois ideology', while other writers were more simply criticised for playing directly into the hands of the 'counter-revolutionaries'.

That the situation was not simply a return to the worst excesses of Stalinism was made clear in 1959, when Khrushchev now praised Dudintsev, arguing that the battle against the 'revisionists' in 1956 was over and won. The Third Writers Congress held that year again illustrates the wild oscillations which characterised the Soviet bureaucracy's ambivalent attitude towards cultural matters. Khrushchev rehabilitated a number of 'forgotten' writers (purged for 'anti-socialist' activities in the 1930s) and announced that 'angels of reconciliation' were at hand and a new liberal policy in the offing. But once again certain inviolable rules must be respected:

> Soviet writers must inspire the people in their struggle for Communism, must educate them according to Communist principles, must develop in them high moral virtues . . . writers must become passionate propagandists of the seven year plan and bring cheerfulness and vigour into the hearts of man . . . We need art capable of inspiring millions and millions of builders of Communism . . . Life showed the fruitfulness and stability of creative principles of socialist realism.[14]

The result was a compromise: the liberal writer Konstantin Fedin replaced Surkov as Secretary General of the Writers Union; Tvardovsky once again assumed editorial responsibility for *Novy Mir*. Solzhenitsyn's novel and Ehrenburg's *Memoirs* (which discusses modernist and purged Russian writers) were now published, both indeed sanctioned by Khrushchev himself.[15] Other novels and stories published at this time hinted at the nature and extent of the Stalinist concentration camps and practices, the system of police frame-ups which had sent thousands of innocent Communists to prison and death.[16] But following Khrushchev's disastrous decision to send nuclear missiles to Cuba combined with the failure of his agricultural policies — price rises had triggered off widespread industrial unrest in 1962 — the pro-Stalinist elements again asserted themselves. No more prison camp stories were to be published and many other critical novels and memoirs dealing with the 1930s and the period following the death of Stalin were suppressed.

In 1963 Solzhenitsyn's 'Matryona's House' and 'For the Good of the Cause' (both stories dealing·with contemporary Russia) were published in *Novy Mir*. The picture the latter gave of present-day Stalinists and Stalinist practices immediately drew savage criticism from the dogmatists — *One Day* had been set firmly in the Stalin era. The fact that Solzhenitsyn's critical story had been published at all seemed to justify Tvardovsky's optimism, even though the novelist was increasingly attacked in the Soviet press. Recommended by Tvardovsky for a Lenin Prize, *One Day* was rejected on the testimony of one S. P. Pavlov, First Secretary of the Young Communist League and friend of the K.G.B. chief, who announced that Solzhenitsyn had surrendered to the Germans during the war (i.e. was a traitor) and sentenced to prison had never been fully rehabilitated. When Tvardovsky gathered the evidence disproving these slanders it was too late. Yet even Tvardovsky, the champion of many of the more critical Soviet writers, still believed that the liberal tendencies which had manifested themselves so uncertainly since 1953 could not be denied. When Khrushchev was replaced by Kosygin and Brezhnev in 1964, he hoped for an improvement in artistic freedom and in the pages of *Novy Mir* published a history of the magazine in which a sharp contrast was drawn between the period 1934—53 and the 1920s, when writers such as Pilnyak, Pasternak, Babel, Leonov and others were regular contributors, a brilliant and seemingly free decade so swiftly succeeded by the epoch of socialist realism and Stalinist dogma:

By 1936, every issue opened with a portrait of Stalin, a *skaz* [folklore, epic] on Stalin, 'folk songs' about Stalin. Nothing

is more depressing than to read today . . . of a meeting held
in the editorial office, at which members of staff made
confessions and admitted not having been vigilant enough to
notice the 'enemy activities' of [certain] contributors . . .
The December 1936 issue did not have the usual annual
index — too many of the contributors had become
unmentionable.[17]

But the fall of Khrushchev was not followed by a new 'thaw'.
On the contrary, the oppositional intelligentsia were now
attacked and persecuted by the bureaucracy and increasingly
forced to publish their work in *samizdat*, underground journals
or send it abroad. Solzhenitsyn was one writer who refused any
form of compromise with the regime. His work has thus
disappeared from the Soviet scene, even though he remained
protected and defended by Tvardovsky (who died in 1971),
who believed that *Cancer Ward* would be published and actually
set up the type for its inclusion in *Novy Mir*. But the Khrushchev
era was over: a new repression was under way, engineered by a
regime wholly hostile to the liberal tendencies which Khrushchev
had patronised.
    Under Khrushchev the social role of literature had been
defined in similar terms to those of the RAPP period
(1928—33) — 'social command' — useful for criticising
bureaucratic mismanagement and 'errors'. (In 1963 Khrushchev
had even agreed with Tvardovsky on the need to abolish Glavlit
but nothing came of it.) The point here is that a relaxing of the
Party's dogmatic attitude to writers did not entail any
abandonment of the fundamental bases of socialist realism. But
under the new regime de-Stalinisation was halted: it was clearly
impossible to allow intellectuals the freedom to pose those
questions which threatened the basis of bureaucratic authority.
In the late 1960s a partial rehabilitation of Stalin thus occurred:
his military strategy during the Second World War was
reappraised and books which had documented his mistakes and
general incompetence were now withdrawn from circulation.
Novels extolling the 'heroism' of the Stalin era were published
in large printings; the twentieth anniversary of Stalin's death in
1973 was celebrated by the publication of Alexander
Chakovsky's novel, *Blockade*, which portrays Stalin as a wise,
modest leader caught off guard by the Nazi invasion; and

ironically, Sholokhov's new novel *They Fought for the Motherland*, in which one of the characters describes Stalin's illegal purges, has been cut by the censor and the location changed to the fishing industry. In 1970 a life-size bust was unveiled over Stalin's previously unadorned grave.[18]

In 1964 the trial of the Leningrad poet Josef Brodsky heralded the new repression. Described as 'an idler and a parasite' engaged in no 'socially useful work' other than the writing of 'anti-Soviet' verse and translating foreign literature, he was sentenced to five years forced labour. In fact, a year later, after world-wide protests, he was freed. More significant, however, was the trial in 1966 of the two writers Sinyavsky and Daniel for the 'crime' of publishing abroad works 'hostile' to the Soviet Union. Not even under Stalin had writers been tried for something which the Soviet constitution does not define as illegal. Pilnyak and Zamyatin in the twenties, Pasternak in the 1950s, had published outside Russia work which could not be published inside. But this was the first time that a writer's actual work — fiction — was brought against him in legal proceedings. Under Stalin writers were 'administratively silenced'; under the new regime at least they could plead, defiantly, 'not guilty'.

Sinyavsky's two novels, *The Trial Begins* and *The Makepeace Experiment*, together with his essay on socialist realism and Yuli Daniel's short stories were held to constitute 'vicious slanders' on both Marxism and Communism. During the trial proceedings both writers vigorously protested their belief in the ideals of 1917 and the achievements of the Soviet state: 'I regard Communism as the only goal that can be put forward by the modern mind', Sinyavsky argued; 'the West has been unable to put forward anything like it.' In 1960–1, said Daniel,

> I . . . was convinced that the country was on the eve of a restoration of a cult of personality . . . seeing all this happening and remembering the horrors of the purges and the violations of legality under Stalin, I concluded — and I am a pessimist by nature — that the terrible days of Stalin's cult could come back. . . . I feel [he went on] that every member of a society is responsible for what happens in it . . . Nobody has ever publicly stated who was to blame for these crimes, and I will never believe that three men — Stalin, Beria

and Ryumin — could alone do such terrible things to the
whole country. But nobody has yet replied to the question
as to who is guilty.

This was striking at the heart of bureaucratic authority, as
indeed were the implications in Sinyavsky's novels that the
bureaucrats were mere parasites and not genuine Marxists. In
effect, Sinyavsky and Daniel were tried for daring to suggest
that creative literature must be free and critical: 'The viewpoint
of the Prosecution', argued Sinyavsky, 'is that literature is a
form of propaganda, and that there are only two kinds of
propaganda: pro-Soviet or anti-Soviet. If literature is simply
un-Soviet, it means that it is anti-Soviet. I cannot accept this.'[19]
Sinyavsky was sentenced to seven years and Daniel to five
years hard labour.

The trial produced an unprecedented range of criticism from
the Soviet intelligentsia, Western Communists and intellectuals.
A demonstration in Pushkin Square in December 1965 of two
hundred Moscow students protesting against the trial led to the
arrest and subsequent trials of Alexander Ginsberg, Yuri
Galanskov and Vladimer Bukovsky. As for the 'old guard', the
verdict represented confirmation of the basic tenets of socialist
realism. These trials and the subsequent attacks on eminent
Soviet scientists, historians and literary critics further attest to a
consolidation of repression by the Soviet bureaucracy.[20]

It is from within this extreme situation that Solzhenitsyn has
defined his uncompromising attitude to the Soviet regime.
During the late 1960s he increasingly identified himself with the
oppositionists, defending Grigorenko, Zhores Medvedev and
other persecuted writers and thinkers. It is clear now that,
unlike other writers associated with Khrushchev's liberalisation
policies, such as Yevtushenko, Solzhenitsyn's fiction was far
more hostile to some of the basic tenets of socialist realism.
Yevtushenko, for example, helped to build the Khrushchev image
and in that sense did not run counter to Party policy. The same
may be said of other liberal writers — Ehrenburg and
Dudintsev — whose work functioned as valuable criticism from
within the system itself. Literature here was defined in more
or less the same utilitarian terms as in the worst forms of
socialist realism — the difference being that the writer is *really*
on the side of progress and freedom as defined by the 'liberal'

Khrushchev or Party. But Solzhenitsyn, like Sinyavsky, in on the side of an unfettered, creative imagination, of a literature free of any political commitment or dogmatic theories on the nature of historical development. A writer's duty, Solzhenitsyn maintained, is to each individual not solely to society: 'An individual's life is not always the same as society's. The collective does not always assist the individual. Each person has an abundance of problems which the collective cannot resolve.'[21]

That is the point. And, with the weakening of Khrushchev's position and support of Solzhenitsyn, the dogmatic critics quickly reversed the favourable notices for *One Day*.

At his trial, Sinyavsky had suddenly been asked by the Public Prosecutor: 'Who is your positive hero? Who expresses your point of view in the story?' So it was with Solzhenitsyn. Critics now discovered that the main characters in Solzhenitsyn's fiction were not *typical* of Soviet society, rather they were deviant and eccentric aberrations. Reviewing 'Matryona's House', a short story set in 1956 which depicts the bureaucratic mismanagement of Soviet agriculture and the greed, selfishness and inhumanity meted out to an old and sick peasant woman, a leading Stalinist critic pointed to Solzhenitsyn's 'fundamental' error:

> The science of joy is an inseparable quality of our literature, an expression of its deepest optimism . . . It seems to me that 'Matryona's House' was written by its author when he was still in a state of mind in which he could not with any depth understand the life of the people, the movement and real perspectives of that life. In the first post-war years, such people as Matryona really did harness the plough to themselves in villages desolated by the Germans. The Soviet peasantry performed a great feat in those circumstances and gave bread to the people, fed the country. This alone must evoke a feeling of reverence and delight. To draw the Soviet village as Bunin's village of our day is historically incorrect. Solzhenitsyn's story convinces one over and over again: without a vision of historical truth, of its essence, there can be no full truth, no matter what the talent.[22]

Increasingly Solzhenitsyn's fiction was said to slur the historically progressive features of Communism: Ivan

Denisovich was now judged to be *untypical* of those prisoners
held in Stalin's camps, for instead of protesting and fighting
injustice he, like Matryona, merely endured. This 'one-sided'
portrait was an insult to Soviet man and all those loyal
Communists, the victims like Ivan Denisovich of Stalinist
'illegalities' but who remained loyal to the Communist ideal.
Solzhenitsyn, like Sinyavsky and other oppositionists, was now
to be charged with anti-Soviet sentiments and purpose. With the
eclipse of Khrushchev, doctrinaire Stalinists acceded to the
control of Soviet letters, especially the writers' organisations.
And Solzhenitsyn was their main target. His play, *The Love-Girl
and the Innocent* (1956) was banned from the stage; his stories
withdrawn from circulation. Thus although Tvardovsky had
accepted *The First Circle*, arranged a contract and paid
Solzhenitsyn an advance, there was never any real chance that
the book would be published. At a meeting of the Central
Committee's department of literature in 1965 Tvardovsky was
warned of Solzhenitsyn's 'anti-Soviet' sentiments and shortly
afterwards the K.G.B. seized copies of both *The First Circle* and
some of his earlier works, including a verse drama composed in
1949—50, *The Feast of the Victors* (in which Stalin is compared
to Hitler), a work Solzhenitsyn has since repudiated. Using this
and the fact that émigré circles in Germany had published,
without the author's knowledge, some of the short stories, the
K.G.B. now began a systematic campaign of vilification.

But like other oppositionists Solzhenitsyn fought back. In his
letters to the Writers Union and addresses to its members,
Solzhenitsyn vigorously defended the cause of liberty against
the bureaucratic deformations of artistic freedom. In his Open
Letter to the Fourth Writers Congress in 1967 (he was banned
from speaking), Solzhenitsyn attacked the undemocratic and
intellectually stultifying system of censorship — 'a survival of
the middle ages' — through which unknown bureaucrats
without any training or knowledge of literature effectively
controlled the thoughts and minds of thousands of creative
writers:

> Literature cannot develop in between the categories
> 'permitted' and 'not permitted', 'about this you may write'
> and 'about this you may not'. Literature that is not the
> breath of contemporary society, that dares not transmit the

pains and fears of that society, that does not warn in time
against threatening moral and social dangers — such literature
does not deserve the name of literature; it is only a facade.
Such literature loses the confidence of its own people, and its
published works are used as wastepaper instead of being read.

Soviet literature, he argued, no longer held any serious claims as
a world literature, and had fallen away disastrously from the
high points of the 1920s. The only hope lay in the total
abolition of all censorship of fiction and the development of an
atmosphere free from fear and repression. His Open Letter
ended:

> I am of course confident that I will fulfil my duty as a writer
> in all circumstances — from the grave even more successfully
> . . . than in my lifetime. No one can bar the road to the truth,
> and to advance its cause I am prepared to accept even death.
> But may it be that repeated lessons will finally teach us not
> to stop the writer's pen during his lifetime.[23]

Solzhenitsyn's spirited defence of the basic freedom of
writing echoes the young Marx who, writing in the 1840s from
within an equally repressive society, had argued that the first
freedom of the press was that it should not be a trade, an
occupation affording a means to another end, for a free press
embodies 'the essence of freedom, an essence that is full of
character, rational and ethical.' The writer must earn a living,
Marx argued, so that he may exist and write, 'but he must not
exist and write in order to make a living.' He who debases his
work to the status of a mere *means* 'deserves, as punishment for
this inner lack of freedom, an external lack of freedom, namely
censorship, or rather its existence is already his punishment.'[24]
The writer's task is to portray artistically the social world, to
render men's struggle within it meaningful in terms of those
values by which men organise and live together. It is not the
task of literature, writes Solzhenitsyn, to conceal but to tell the
real truth:

> Moreover, it is not the task of the writer to defend or criticise
> one or another mode of distributing the social product or to
> defend or criticise one or another form of government
> organisation. The task of the writer is to select more universal
> and eternal questions . . . the secrets of the human heart and

conscience, the confrontations between life and death, the
triumph over spiritual sorrow.

Solzhenitsyn thus attacks the very heart of socialist realism as it
was practised dogmatically under Zhdanov and in its modified
form under Khrushchev. In 1968 the *Literaturnaya Gazeta*, in an
attack on Solzhenitsyn, reasserted the central tenets of socialist
realism. 'Soviet Literature', it proclaimed, 'inspired by the ideas
of Marxism and Leninism, has truthfully reflected the life of the
people and the moral image of the new man', and Soviet
writers, contrary to Solzhenitsyn's strictures, had produced
works of enduring literary merit. For the strength of socialist
realist writers lay in their dedication to Communism and the
Communist Party, a union so necessary for literature that only
the enemies of the Soviet system could dare suggest otherwise.
Literature, it concluded, forms an integral part of the class
struggle and in the Soviet Union a 'new, highly ideological and
highly artistic literature of socialist realism has been established
whose creative potentials are inexhaustible.' This attack was the
prelude to Solzhenitsyn's expulsion from the Writers Union in
November 1969 which followed stormy meetings between
Solzhenitsyn and the local and national bureaucrats. At one
special session of the Ryazan Writers Organisation the now
standard Soviet criticism of Solzhenitsyn had been used to
justify his expulsion: in *One Day* and other stories, notably
'Matryona's House', 'black spots' on the Soviet Union were
unambiguously painted, for no such person as Matryona could
possibly exist in a modern industrial society. 'I was still hoping
that Alexander Isayevich would write things the people needed',
one writer lamented, while another cast doubt on
Solzhenitsyn's integrity suggesting that his membership was
merely a cynically pragmatic move 'to have a writer's ticket'
and indulge his ideological distortions: 'He casts slurs on our
glowing future. He himself has a black side. Only one who is
ideologically hostile to us could depict such an uninspiring
character as Ivan Denisovich'; Alexey Surkov was more
explicit. Why, he asked, does Solzhenitsyn dwell so much on
the gloomy sides of Soviet reality: other Communists had been
illegally condemned to the concentration camps but this had
not affected their Communist world view. For Surkov, *Cancer
Ward* approached fundamental problems not in philosophical

but in direct political terms. And having argued that the modern Soviet reader was too sophisticated to be seduced by Solzhenitsyn's novel, he added that 'the works of Solzhenitsyn are more dangerous to us than those of Pasternak: Pasternak was a man divorced from life, while Solzhenitsyn, with his animated, militant, ideological temperament, is a man of principle.' This is nowhere better shown than in Solzhenitsyn's speech to the Ryazan Writers Union. Should a writer dwell on problems of the past and continually raise historical questions? What is the point of recalling the past? Solzhenitsyn's answer was unequivocal: to remain silent on the moral and social effects of Stalin's crimes would be to corrupt the new generation: 'The time when one has to be ashamed about the nasty things that are being done is not when they are being talked about but when they are being *committed.*'[2][5]

With support from only seven of the seven and a half thousand members of the Writers Union behind him, Solzhenitsyn was expelled, accused of publishing his books abroad (although he had no control over this), and for denigrating the Soviet Union in *The Feast of the Victors*. He was now denied the essential prerequisites of membership, such as health insurance, pension, holidays and grants, indeed the right to live as a writer at all. In 1969 Tvardovsky was forced to resign as editor of *Novy Mir*; physical harrassment of Solzhenitsyn and his friends was stepped up and a policy imprisoning dissenters in special psychiatric prisons for indefinite periods of time accelerated (for instance Grigorenko from 1968 to 1974).

In 1970 to the delight of the dissident intelligentsia, and especially Tvardovsky, Solzhenitsyn was awarded the Nobel Prize for literature, 'for the ethical force with which he has pursued the indispensable traditions of Russian literature'. The Soviet government promptly refused him permission to travel to Stockholm and a further savage attack on the novelist was mounted: *Pravda* described him as 'spiritually an internal émigré'. But Solzhenitsyn remained at liberty as the bureaucracy cracked down on the dissident movement forcing the *Chronicle of Current Events* to cease 'publication'. In 1972 Pyotr Yakir and his fellow Marxist, Viktor Krasin, were arrested and, after careful preparation by the authorities, brought to open court fourteen months later. Both confessed to the ludicrous charges — contacts with anti-Soviet émigré groups which had 'invented' the dissident movement and of fabricating stories of dissidents imprisoned in Soviet psychiatric hospitals — and, as broken men, 'freely' accepted their guilt and punishment. Solzhenitsyn's comment on a trial reminiscent of the show trials of the thirties was characteristically harsh: Yakir and Krasin had conducted themselves 'basely' in co-operating with the K.G.B. and condemning others to arrest and prison. In contrast, Andrey Amalrik, asked to confirm their 'confession', refused, and was promptly sentenced to a further three years. In this situation of mounting represssion the K.G.B. was responsible for the suicide of a woman friend of Solzhenitsyn suspected of owning a copy of his massive study of Soviet labour camps and prisons, *The Gulag Archipelago*. At once he ordered the book to be published abroad. Expecting to be tried for 'treason', the novelist was finally arrested and exiled from the Soviet Union in February 1974.

Three years earlier Solzhenitsyn had completed *August 1914*. In the epilogue to the French edition he wrote:

> This book cannot at the present time be published in our native land except in *samizdat* because of censorship objections unintelligible to normal human reason and which, in addition, demand the word God be unfailingly written without a capital letter. To this indignity I cannot stoop.[26]

Other writers had been silenced and defeated; Solzhenitsyn continues as the major creative talent produced by the Soviet Opposition.

III

The tragic quality of Solzhenitsyn's work, the tragic universe of the novella (*One Day*) and the two major novels (*The First Circle, Cancer Ward*), flows directly from his refusal to 'realistically' accept Soviet society as it is and to temper his criticisms with the spurious optimism of socialist realism. Solzhenitsyn's opposition to Stalinism is profoundly uncompromising. It is not simply a question of realism, of depicting honestly what the artist knows to be the truth, but a refusal to dilute one's own vision of the world and accommodate it to practical political considerations. This is the aspect of Solzhenitsyn's writings which poses intractable problems both for the Stalinist literary bureaucrats as well as more 'reasonable Marxist' critics such as Lukács. Equally important is the fact that Solzhenitsyn is not a Marxist; in *The Gulag Archipelago* he writes that at the time of his arrest he not merely considered himself a Marxist but that to understand the 1917 Revolution 'required nothing beyond Marxism'. The years in prison changed all that: Marxism was repudiated and Solzhenitsyn's personal beliefs approached a religious rather than materialist world view.[27] A religious standpoint, of course, providing that it does not lead to mysticism and thus a rejection of the social world, can be as 'progressive' when expressed in art as a consistent socialist orientation. At the same time, however, the fragmentation of the intellectual opposition to the Soviet regime during the late 1950s and 1960s, when *The First Circle* and *Cancer Ward* were written, means that a fully coherent social and political vision is impossible. Thus while the opposition of Grigorenko and Yakir before 1972 was inspired by Leninism and Marxism, that of the liberal oppositions is fired by a vaguely defined populist ideology in which they link themselves self-consciously with the traditions of the pre-revolutionary intelligentsia. These are the variegated groups, Goldmann's 'collective subject', which connect Solzhenitsyn with the opposition, and his work reflects the tensions and the contradictions within and between them. It is important to grasp that during the 1960s Solzhenitsyn did not reject the Soviet Union, the Soviet State, but like Sinyavsky positively accepted the invaluable social and economic developments made possible by the 1917 Revolution. At his trial Sinyavsky had declared unequivocally that 'if the monarchy or Western democracy were to return, which is one and the same thing, we would start a revolution again', sentiments which undoubtedly enjoy support from the majority of the Soviet opposition.[28] Solzhenitsyn's uncompromising hostility to the Soviet Union and towards socialism is more the product of the last few years as the Soviet government committed itself to increasing repression. Having rejected Marxism (in the late 1940s) Solzhenitsyn developed a strong attachment to the populist tradition; the revolutionary urban proletariat of Stalinist mythology was rejected and he accepted the widespread view that the masses were apathetic, non-revolutionary and corrupted by years of Stalinist

dictatorship. Clearly this distinguishes Solzhenitsyn from the
Marxist wing of the opposition, although here also many of its
leading spokesmen express grave doubts on the revolutionary
potential of the Russian working class and look for reform
through a revitalised Communist Party (i.e. Roy Medvedev). But
all groups share a passionate concern with freedom and are in
total opposition to the prevailing censorship. It is this passion
for freedom which leads the oppositionists to cite the works of
Kant *and* Marx and Lenin as the philosophical sources of their
dissent. Both idealist and materialist elements are combined in
Solzhenitsyn's writing, a fact which has led some critics to argue
that Solzhenitsyn has rejected the Marxist and materialist
position in favour of an ethical socialism grounded in universal
truths while for others he has written a humanist critique of
Stalinism.[29]

For Lukács, however, Solzhenitsyn's work poses more
complex problems. After all, Solzhenitsyn is exploring the great
human problems of a regime which Lukács has spent his life
defending. Solzhenitsyn, Lukács argues, is a writer in the great
Russian realist tradition of Pushkin, Gogol and especially
Tolstoy; his work constitutes the beginning of a critique of the
Stalinist period. 'The world of socialism', Lukács writes, 'stands
on the eve of a renaissance of Marxism . . . to eliminate Stalinist
distortions and point the way forward . . . In literature, socialist
realism faces a similar task.'[30] The reckoning with Stalinism is
long overdue and Solzhenitsyn's task is in this respect a critical
one. Thus on one level Lukács is moved to a fulsome praise for
Solzhenitsyn's novels, arguing that *Cancer Ward* and *The First
Circle* 'represent a new high point in contemporary world
literature', while *One Day* is a significant overture to [the]
process of literary rediscovery of the self in the socialist
present.'[31] Yet for all this Lukács is ambivalent on
Solzhenitsyn's true stature. He notes that Solzhenitsyn does not
fully appreciate that while Stalinism must be subjected to
criticism, nonetheless Stalin was historically necessary given the
particular historical conditions surrounding the birth of Soviet
Russia. To transform a largely backward economy burdened
with a low level of culture and a primitive technology into a
modern society, an efficient bureaucracy dedicated not to
world revolution but to pragmatism and 'socialism in one
country' was bound to dominate the 'utopian' and unrealistic
platform of the Trotskyist Left Opposition. What Lukács calls

the 'heroic rise of socialism' — the struggles of the 1930s, the collectivisation of agriculture, the purges, the Second World War — could only have succeeded through a disciplined, vanguard party; naturally Lukács deplores the 'excesses' (the political frame-ups) which went with it. But now such primitive, barbaric and illegal practices are unnecessary: socialism can increasingly wear a human, not bureaucratic face. Of course vestiges of Stalinism remain within the modern Soviet system and it is Solzhenitsyn who has emerged as the major talent to portray the resulting crisis. For the Soviet Union, Lukács argues, is now in the throes of a transition in which the old and new jostle with one another for supremacy.

It is at this point that Lukács enters serious reservations on Solzhenitsyn's achievement. He argues that Solzhenitsyn has adopted a 'plebeian' and not a 'communist' point of view in his fiction, by which he means that Solzhenitsyn has refused to accept that during the 'heroic' period of socialism innocent people necessarily suffered and that the bureaucracy had to trample on the rights and freedom of the individual. In *The First Circle*, for example, Solzhenitsyn stands with the common people — the peasant Spiridon — refusing to accept Stalinism as historically necessary, arguing that it must be judged critically by what it did to those who consciously opposed it as well as by that greater number of innocent victims caught in its insane operations. Lukács suggests that this plebeian attitude can lead only to an *eccentric* standpoint:

> For eccentricity is a certain attitude on the part of the subject which arises from the specific nature of reality and the potentially of his own social *praxis*. More precisely, it arises from the fact that a character may well be inwardly capable of denying certain forms of the society in which he is forced to live . . . in such a way that his inner integrity (which they threaten) remains intact: however, the conversion of this rejection into a really individual praxis . . . is rendered impossible by society and therefore he must remain enmeshed in a more or less abstractly distorted inwardness. In this process his character acquires crotchety eccentricity.

Solzhenitsyn's main characters are thus rendered socially and politically inert, impotent, since they refuse to compromise their principles with social forces which seek to deny their own values. In other words, Lukács criticises Solzhenitsyn for his failure to accept a 'realistic' assessment of the Stalin era, that during the transition from capitalism to socialism, in periods which leave no scope for any action by critics and reformers, 'such persons must succumb to a certain social and personal alienation'. If Solzhenitsyn is to justify his talent he must therefore accept the inevitability of the Stalinist bureaucracy and thus of alienation, and creatively criticise those 'illegal features' such as the purges and deportations which were obviously deviations from the true course of Soviet development. An obsessive concentration on other aspects, Lukács suggests, will detract from Solzhenitsyn's power. To create characters within a genuine *praxis* he must go beyond a plebeian point of view, for any 'genuine transforming agency must transcend a mere self-conscious and ordinary plebeian existence and consciousness.' In other words, innocent people suffered but for a 'higher purpose' and this must be the writer's theme. Contrasting Solzhenitsyn with writers who accepted the communist standpoint, Lukács concludes that in these writers

> we see the way in which the brutal, bureaucratic manipulation of the Stalin system turned against those who, for all their sectarian prejudices, worked enthusiastically to bring about the socialist evolution, undaunted by the sacrifices demanded of them . . . until their own tragic downfall, they were able to preserve their inner human commitment to the revolution in the midst of the destruction of their own existences[32].

Lukács echoes here the orthodox post-Khrushchevian criticism of the die-hard Stalinists who defined the proper creative task of literature as portraying the ways in which innocent victims of 'socialist illegality' retained their faith in Communist ideals, justice and the Soviet people.

Lukács's analysis, however, irrespective of its clear ideological function, nonetheless highlights the weaknesses of his fundamental approach to literature. He treats Solzhenitsyn as an isolated case, an individual whose work merely reflects peculiar idiosyncrasies and not as a part of a much broader movement involving a whole stratum of intellectuals totally opposed to the Stalinist regime. Thus, while Lukács recognises Solzhenitsyn's stand against Stalinism, he must reject its *total* character arguing that a 'Communist', that is, a politically responsible point of view is criticism from within the system itself. Lukács fails to treat Solzhenitsyn as part of a movement which in general accepts the achievements of Soviet society but rejects the political structure which distorted that progress *and which still remains*. There is no sociological analysis which relates the texts to a specific group and the values of that group. However, Lukács's approach has located the essence of Solzhenitsyn's position. By denying to his overall novelistic universe a Communist point of view, which for Lukács means simply an acceptance of the 'progressive' features of Stalinism, Solzhenitsyn has condemned his leading characters to a tragic view of life, a standpoint which implies a withdrawal from the world and, in Lukács's terms a denial of *praxis*. What Lukács seems to be saying, then, is that Solzhenitsyn's characters are not positive enough; the 'eccentricity' flows from their negative attitudes towards the regime and their refusal to fully grasp historical necessity.

The question of the tragic vision is one which socialist realism must of course deny. But the tragic mode is not anathema to Marxist aesthetics. In discussing Ferdinand Lassalle's play *Franz von Sickingen,* a tragic drama of the civil wars in sixteenth-century Germany, Marx wrote 'I can therefore only express my full approval of making this the central theme of a modern tragedy.' But the problem in Lassalle's drama lay in the conflict between the ambitious dedicated revolutionary, a man with passionate convictions, and the actual historical situation which from the very beginning doomed his activity to failure. Engels described the situation as 'the tragic collision between the historically necessary postulate and the practical impossibility of its realisation.' Sickingen died, wrote Marx, because 'as a knight' he represented the dying feudal class incapable of allying itself with the peasantry, an alliance which would have fulfilled his morally praiseworthy but historically doomed task. The fact that Sickingen 'begins the uprising under the mask of a war of the knights only means that he begins it as a knight. To begin otherwise, he had to appeal directly and at the very outset to the cities and peasants, that is to those very classes the development of which is equivalent to a negation of knighthood.' Marx's approval of Lassalle's drama was clearly based on the tragic collision between the need to act within an

historical situation in which 'knightly' action must be doomed
to failure.[33]

Trotsky follows Marx's brief discussion. In an important,
although neglected, passage at the end of *Literature and
Revolution* he argues that tragedy constitutes 'a great and
monumental form of literature' embracing 'the heroic tenacity
of strivings, of limitless aims, of conflicts and sufferings'.
Classical tragedy had worked with the idea of *fate*, which
thus limited man's own actions in deciding his destiny; in
contrast modern tragedy places *man* and man's values in the
forefront. Tragedy arises now through the conflict between the
individual and the collectivity, between man's ideals and desire
to change the world and the available means to such ends: 'Our
age is an age of great aims. This is what stamps it. But the
grandeur of these aims lies in man's effort to free himself from
mystic and from every other intellectual vagueness and in his
effort to reconstruct society and himself in accord with his own
plan.' A tragic dialectic, Trotsky argues, necessarily subsists
between the individual and socialist society precisely because a
revolutionary period is one characterised by constant struggle,
of vigilance against class enemies, bureaucratism, conservatism.
This gigantic task of the total reconstruction of society will
involve tragic figures and actions and Trotsky's conclusion that
socialist art will revive tragedy without God clearly implies that
socialist society, because it is not yet Communism but merely a
transitional society, must involve conflict and contradiction.
Out of this will come a revitalised drama and novel.[34]

In contrast socialist realism opposes all tragedy through its
dogmatic commitment to positive heroes dedicated to a glorious
Communist future, the living embodiments of social optimism.
The point is the elimination of all conflict between the
individual and the collectivity, or the resolution of such conflict
in a 'higher purpose'. The dialectical relationship between the
individual and society simply disappears. Life as it should be is
fused with life as it is and the function of art defined in strictly
utilitarian terms to inspire men to change society and augment
social progress. When, in the 1920s, Fedin and Olesha wrote
sympathetically on the tragic position of the pre-revolutionary
intelligentsia living in a society which had changed so
dramatically that adjustment seemed impossible, Stalinist
literary theory quickly moved to eliminate such ideological

heresy. The theme of the 'superfluous man', the conflict between a problematic hero and society, disappeared from Soviet fiction.[35] A Soviet dictionary of literary terms defines with startling clarity the official attitude to tragedy:

> In Soviet literature tragedy, unlike the tragedy of the past, has quite a different affirmative meaning. The hero of such a tragedy fights not for his personal destiny, divorced from the destiny of the people, but for the general cause of the people. If necessary, he sacrifices (knowingly) his life on behalf of this victory. . . . Tragedy in Soviet literature arouses a feeling of pride for the man who has accomplished a great deed for the peoples' happiness; it calls for continued struggles against the things which brought about the hero's death.[36]

Thus even when socialist realism produces tragedy — as with the sublimely entitled *Optimistic Tragedy* — the ending must always be a happy one, in some way embody a 'superior purpose' so that the death of the heroine is a triumph for Communism Sinyavsky has written:

> Most subjects of Soviet literature . . . develop in one direction . . . well known in advance. This direction may exhibit variations in accordance with time, place, conditions, etc. but it is invariable in its course and its destiny to remind the reader once more of the triumph of communism [37]

The moral structure of Soviet fiction is thus determined by an 'ultimate end', known in advance, which inevitably triumphs over the individual. 'Lost illusions, broken hopes, unfulfilled dreams', the stuff of tragedy, clearly conflict with the basic ideology of socialist realism; a novel must be optimistic and geared to a known and certain future, as well as basically 'educational'.

In the novels of Solzhenitsyn, Lydia Chukovskaya and Andrey Sinyavsky the tragic mode is revived, not in Trotsky's terms, but in total opposition to the Stalinist bureaucracy. These novels of opposition against the norms of socialist realism, against 'the higher purpose', bring real, living man once more into Russian literature. In a period dominated by the most appalling horrors, in which millions died through famine, forced exile, and 'socialist illegalities', the sheer magnitude of events might seem to defy the creative imagination. In her two short

novels Lydia Chukovskaya shows the tragedy of an innocent
woman who, although remaining loyal to Communist ideals and
the Soviet Union is driven into isolation, loneliness and
necessary silence by the events of the thirties and forties. In
Going Under, set during the 1949 purges, the widow of one of
the many innocent victims of Stalin's purges is writing what she
calls 'a monument to her dead husband, knowing it will never
be published'. Therefore why write? 'I wanted to find
brothers — if not now, then in the future. All living things seek
brotherhood and I sought mine. I had been writing a book to
find brothers, even if only there in the unknown distance.' At a
rest home for writers she meets Biliban, a survivor of the labour
camps who is turning his experiences into an acceptable and
publishable fiction. She reads his book and knows he has lied:
'Why did you not have the decency to remain silent? Merely
remain silent? After all no-one demanded this from you . . . Do
you mean to say . . . out of respect for those . . . whom you
buried in the earth . . . you couldn't earn your bread and butter
in some other way?' Afterwards she feels ashamed for Biliban is
sick and short of money: 'Forgive me! I didn't have the right to
demand the truth from you. I'm healthy and yet I keep silent. I
was never beaten at night in the investigator's room. And when
they beat you I kept silent. What right have I then to judge you
now?'[38]

The Deserted House, written in 1940, describes how Olga
Petrovna, a widow employed as senior typist in a Leningrad
publishing house, is caught up in the purges of 1936—7. A
passive, non-political supporter of the Soviet regime she prefers
light novels to political news. Her only son, Kolya, more
politically conscious and militant, has accepted that society
must rid itself of 'unreliable elements'. Shortly after the Kirov
murder some friends of Olga Petrovna's are arrested, then the
head of the publishing house, and finally her son. Pathetically
she tries to see him but fails. In the crazed atmosphere of terror
she speaks out against the sacking of other innocent workers
and is sacked herself. A close friend commits suicide and finally
she hears that Kolya has been found guilty of terrorism and
exiled for ten years. She can do nothing: when Kolya smuggles
out a letter to her explaining that he confessed because of
torture he tells her not to complain for to do so would worsen

his position. And she must destroy the letter.[39] There is nothing left, only silence.

Sinyavsky's *The Trial Begins* contrasts sharply with the restrained and disciplined realism of Chukovskaya. Sinyavsky himself has described his approach to literature as broadly surrealistic, in which truth emerges through the absurd and the fantastic, 'a phantasmagoric art with hypotheses instead of a Purpose, an art in which the grotesque will replace realistic descriptions of ordinary life.[40] In *The Trial Begins* the feverish, poisoned and confused atmosphere of the 1949 purges is brilliantly rendered through this concept of 'fantastic realism', by a bewildering juxtaposing of scenes and characters from the 'real' tangible world of terrified bureaucrats and their victims, with the 'unreal' world of dreams, delusions and hallucinations. The novel ends with the author, having failed to portray his 'positive heroes . . . in all the fullness of their many-sided working lives', arrested and serving time in the same labour camp as the novel's victims.[41]

In contrast to Sinyavsky's modernism — his ironic use of self-conscious literary devices, and the interior monologue to communicate a sense of incoherence and fragmentation — Solzhenitsyn's fiction lies firmly within the classical realist tradition. The tragic conflict between the individual and the highly centralised totalitarian state is rendered not through the 'alienation devices' of a Sinyavsky but by a sober, objective narrative which portrays man, although locked in a vast prison network, as a free and moral agent. Nadezhda Mandelstam has perceptively remarked that 'only freedom is truly tragic', for it is only the free man who wrestles with moral questions:

> The free man must have knowledge, foresight and understanding if he is not to lose his way; he must forever be on his guard and never lose contact with reality — even though it may seem to the common run of guardians of the established order that he has his head in the clouds. To preserve his freedom he must suppress his instinct for survival. Freedom does not just fall into your lap; you have to pay for it.[42]

The First Circle and *Cancer Ward* portray a profoundly tragic universe in which man stubbornly resists the appalling pressures upon him and finds in the end that only in opposition can life possess meaning.* Solzhenitsyn's fiction, in sharp contrast to that of Pasternak, is characterised by a confrontation with, not a withdrawal from the world.

In his study of the tragic vision, Lucien Goldmann has argued that because of the limited number of possible answers to the 'great human problems created by man's relationship with his fellows and with the universe' there will be 'successive rebirths' of the same ideas in philosophy, art, literature; the same vision, he suggests 'can assume different aspects' at different times. For Goldmann the tragic vision develops only during a period of 'deep crisis' between man and the world; it does not imply withdrawal only that the world is seen as problematical for the realisation of certain fundamental values. 'What characterises tragedy and provides its real perspective', Goldmann writes, 'is a primacy accorded to ethics, and to an ethical system which does not admit degrees of difference.'[43] The tragic vision is thus a question of all or nothing, springing from the refusal to compromise universal values; the tragic mind does not conceive of 'degrees, transitions or approximations'; it makes no distinction, to use Lukács's expression, between a 'Communist' and a 'plebeian' point of view. The tragic mode, moreover, aspires to a general, not a specific view of the world, whether it deals with the events of one day, one year or an entire epoch. Goldmann's analysis, of course, is with the drama: but the tragic vision expressed through the novel form emerges precisely in a society with a strict political regimentation of theatre and total bureaucratisation of creative writers. As was argued in Chapter 4, elements of the tragic vision emerged in the prose of the twenties expressed through the image of a 'superfluous man'; it is within prose that the Russian writer creates tragedy, as he searches for the meaning of his epoch and poses questions

*Interviewed in 1973 on the fate of the Dissidence movement, Solzhenitsyn summed up the essence of this tragic vision: 'Now this series of self-sacrificing decisions on the part of isolated individuals is a beacon for our future. One is always struck by this psychological peculiarity of the human being: to be apprehensive of even the slightest disturbances on the periphery of his existence during times of prosperity and ease, to try to know nothing about the sufferings of others or his own sufferings still to come, and to make concessions all round, even in important, spiritual and central matters, just so long as the good life can continue. And then suddenly, approaching the ultimate frontier, when man is already destitute, naked and deprived of everything that seems to make life worth living, he finds in himself the strength to resist at the final step, giving up life itself but not his principles!' *Index*, no. 4 (1973) p. 45.

unthought of or suppressed by a bureaucratised and servile intelligentsia.

In contrast to Solzhenitsyn, Sholokhov, as we have seen, has always been willing to accommodate his literature to the requirements of the moment, to compromise and include fictional war-time exploits of Stalin in his novels, denigrate Trotsky's role in the Civil War and generally to follow the Party line. But for the tragic writer his 'all or nothing attitude' is a demand for values impossible to realise in the existing social world, 'authentic, genuinely human values' in opposition to the dominant, pragmatic values imposed on society by the state. All values are linked with human action, with practice. But tragedy implies that the world cannot be changed and 'authentic values' realised. Goldmann writes:

> To refuse the world while remaining within it means refusing to choose and refusing to be satisfied with any of the possibilities it offers; it means making a clear, an unrestricted judgment, of their inadequacy and limitations, and setting up against them a demand for real and unambiguous values . . .[44]

The tragic mind realises the importance of human action: if the individual simply held his values, never attempting to act upon them, desiring them abstractly as good things in themselves, he would constitute a romantic rather than tragic figure. 'Tragic man', writes Goldmann, 'never gives up hope', and he accepts the world so that he might live his genuine values. It is in this sense that the tragic vision is both realistic and idealistic, confronting the world as it is, refusing to indulge in mythical and romantic fantasies so that the individual's own absolute values can be lived. One such value is truth; in all circumstances this value must be lived even if the world denies it. But the individual must choose and once made he must live that choice.

The tragic vision, then, emerges at a time of profound crisis for the Soviet regime, a society plagued by a lagging economic growth and recurrent agricultural crises. Unable and unwilling to restore the total terrorism of the Stalin era, the bureaucratic élite was forced initially to allow the development of dissent and freedom of thought. But while dissenting groups of intellectuals seized this opportunity they remained fragmented and unsure of the policies and action necessary to change Soviet society. The Oppositionists' belief in democracy, freedom and truth are values which appear unrealisable in practical terms, ideals with no real hope of fulfilment. It is these values which find expression in the literary works of Solzhenitsyn, Chukovskaya and Sinyavsky. But it is Solzhenitsyn who expresses the essence of this tragic vision more profoundly than any other Soviet writer. The revival of the tragic mode within the novel form, then, is bound up with the growth of an oppositional intelligentsia which challenged the dominant values of Soviet society not in the name of revolutionary Marxism but of humanist individualism. The relation between Solzhenitsyn's 'problematical heroes' and the lack of proletarian hegemony in Soviet society will be the subject of the next chapter.

9 Solzhenitsyn: The Novels

Since the publication of *One Day* in 1962 Solzhenitsyn's name has become synonymous with opposition to Stalinism. Solzenhitsyn's is not simply an individual protest against totalitarianism but forms an organic part of a much broader movement of social dissent. For many years now he has enjoyed close personal ties with all kinds of oppositionists from the liberal Tvardovsky to the Marxist Medvedev brothers. Unlike the latter, Solzhenitsyn's understanding and interpretation of Russian history and society is resolutely non-Marxist. He places great emphasis, for example, on the autonomous role and authority of ethics, a view which Marxists would clearly reject. Solzhenitsyn belongs to that part of the opposition which conjoins political with religious dissent. A deeply religious man, Solzhenitsyn's extra-literary pronouncements frequently emphasise the ethical element in social life and especially its religious content. It is the novelist's voice when Ivan Denisovich Shukhov observes that the Russians had 'forgotten which hand to cross themselves with'. Combined with this stress on the importance of ethics is an overriding concern, not with the urban working class, but with the Russian peasant, with his suffering and the moral goodness associated with the lack of property.

Thus in his recent 'Lenten Letter' of protest to the Patriarch of All Russia' (1972) Solzhenitsyn accused Patriarch Pimen of sacrificing the Church's interests for the sake of concessions and good relations with the Soviet government. Here Solzhenitsyn has argued that the 'fate' of Russia rests with the 'FORCE OF RIGHTEOUSNESS', with 'the radiant ethical atmosphere of Christianity in which for a millenium our morals were grounded'. The Church must stand against the atheist bureaucrats; its leaders must learn to sacrifice their own material interests.[1] The words recall Solzhenitsyn's portrayal of the selfless, peasant widow Matryona who, cheated out of a

pension by bureaucrats and cynically used by her selfish
relatives, lives a life of suffering without 'gadgets and
possessions', with 'no earthly goods . . . but a dirty white goat, a
lame cat and a row of fig plants', the 'one righteous person
without whom . . . no city can stand.'[2]

This concern with morals is closely bound up with
Solzhenitsyn's conception of literature itself. He differs from
Western writers in following the traditional Russian emphasis on
the civic responsibility of the writer, his moral duty to society
and the individual, arguing that the function of literature is to
discover truth and teach man by the force of example. His
Nobel Prize speech was dedicated to the proposition that only
art and literature which flows from *sincerity* is genuine, 'utterly
irrefutable' and capable of conquering 'even the resisting heart'.
The writer's duty in a world riven with different ideological
systems and conflicting moral codes is to help man comprehend
his own nature and the truth of life:

> Art is capable of the following miracle: it can overcome
> man's characteristic weakness of learning only from his own
> experience, so that the experience of others is wasted on him.
> From man to man, augmenting his brief span on earth, art
> can convey the whole burden of another's long life
> experience, with its cares, colours and flavour, can re-create
> in the flesh the experiences of other men and enable us to
> assimilate them as our own.[3]

For Solzhenitsyn the tragic vision is compounded from these
various elements and given its profoundest expression in the
two autobiographical novels, *The First Circle* and *Cancer Ward*.
This chapter will concentrate on these two novels as
exemplifying what he himself in his Nobel Prize speech has
called 'a world vision'.

I

In his essay on Solzhenitsyn, the American critic Edmund
Wilson has deplored what he calls Solzhenitsyn's 'masochistic
point of view', his solitary theme of 'passive' endurance, of
mere survival, arguing that Anglo Saxon heroes, in similar
circumstances, must have shown greater powers of resistance.
Solzhenitsyn's concern with the virtues of endurance, he
believes, is closely tied up with traditional Russian religious

teaching of 'obedience and resignation to inevitable misfortune', a view which comes close to Lukács's argument that Solzhenitsyn's characters are not sufficiently *positive*, unwilling to fight on, against terrible odds, for the 'just' cause, for the future.[4] Solzhenitsyn's refusal to sacrifice his characters in the interests of the Party, his implied view that the progress made by the Soviet Union in the past fifty years was in spite of not because of Stalinism, determines both the sharp edge of criticism within the novels and their 'endurance' quality. *One Day, The First Circle, Cancer Ward* and many of Solzhenitsyn's stories are set in prison and labour camps and have as their 'heroes' men unjustly and illegally sentenced for 'political' crimes under the infamous Article 58 of the Soviet Criminal Code. Supporters of the Soviet state, bewildered by events they can barely understand, they retain their humanity in prison regimes which afford not the slightest hope apart from mere survival.

One Day, more than the other novels, clearly approaches this position. The first published Soviet novel to deal with Soviet Labour camps, it makes clear that under the Stalin regime virtually anyone was suspect and liable to join the millions of prisoners serving sentences they had little hope of ever completing. Shukhov knows what happens to prisoners who assert their democratic rights: in the camp is Buinovsky, a former naval officer and loyal Communist, who protests at the cruel treatment meted out to the prisoners in the freezing dawn. Buinovsky has been in the camp three months when he asserts to the guard Commander that he has neither the right to strip men in the cold nor does he 'know Article Nine of the Criminal Code'. The guards, he ends, are 'not behaving like communists.'[5] His reward is swift: ten days in the cells which in the frozen climate means simply death.* For Shukhov there are no heroics: 'Better to growl and submit. If you were stubborn they broke you.' It is a passive attitude forced on him by the situation, one which distinguishes Shukhov from Communist intellectuals who survived Stalin's camps or those imprisoned since Stalin's death. Anatoly Marchenko's *My Testimony*, written in 1967, deals with conditions and life in the same camp in which *One Day* is

---

*As with many of Solzhenitsyn's fictional characters, Buinovsky was based on a real person. In real life he survived, meeting Solzhenitsyn accidentally again in 1962.

set some fifteen years afterwards. Illegality and savage
repression are still evident, although with the death of Stalin it
seems possible to assert a degree of intellectual independence:
Marchenko openly calls his captors anti-Leninist and, in an
argument with camp officials on the superiority of Soviet over
capitalist democracy, cites Lenin's remark that the existence of
industrial strikes implies some measure of freedom and
democracy. You have slandered Lenin, he is told: to which he
replies by showing them the exact quote in a volume of the
Collected Works: 'Marchenko, you must have misinterpreted
Lenin. With your views you interpret him in your own special
way, and that's bad. You won't last very long outside.'[6] In
1951 no such latitude was possible, and it is not surprising that
Shukhov is concerned almost exclusively with food, warmth,
sleep and simple survival. Eating the small portions of bad food
has itself become an art more important to him than questions
of Soviet Communism:

> First he only drank the liquid, drank and drank. As it went
> down, filling his whole body with warmth, all his guts began
> to flutter inside him . . . And now Shukhov complained about
> nothing: neither about the length of his stretch, nor about
> the length of the day . . . This was all he thought about now:
> we'll survive. We'll stick it out, God grant, till it's over.

Shukhov's day is actually a good one, 'almost a happy day', in
which he has escaped detention, scrounged an extra bowl of
soup and been given some extra tobacco.[7]
    Shukhov's day is seen from his point of view: his experiences
are rendered in his own peasant language and Solzhenitsyn
employs a direct, objective and restrained realism observing the
different aspects of camp life in meticulous detail. The
matter-of-fact tone and the emphasis on details of a rather
uneventful day clearly restrict the story's potential scope to a
mere narrative of mundane events. Larger questions are rarely
posed. Discussing this aspect of *One Day*, Lukács has drawn a
distinction between the novel and the novella, arguing that
while the novel strives to depict historical totality, the novella,
because it lacks such breadth of vision is more often a prelude
to precisely such mastery and scope. He suggests that *One Day*
never concretely depicts the historical past, apart from brief
references to the trumped up 'crimes' of the prisoners, or a

definite future, concentrating instead everything into the events of the moment, the day, so that 'everything which could and should become the task of the great novels and dramas of the future is consciously eliminated.'[8] Lukács's point seems valid: *One Day* does not express the mature vision of the later novels, and, by focusing on the character of Shukhov (and this is also true of Matryona and indeed Chukovskaya's heroine in *The Deserted House*), the tragic conflict between the individual and the collectivity is realised only on a very narrow plane. All forms of totalitarianism strike at the concept of the individual striving to eliminate every form of conflict between the individual and society. Tragedy here flows from a refusal to submit to the requirements of such systems, and the concentration and labour camp constitutes the highest expression of the totalitarian desire to destroy the individual. Never for one moment are the prisoners allowed to forget they have no rights, their labour highly organised as virtual slave labour with each member of a group forced to co-operate out of necessity to maintain specific work norms. Yet Shukhov, contrary to critics such as Edmund Wilson, does resist — through his labour. He discovers a positive joy in his work: 'Real jail', he reflects, 'was when you were kept back from work', and he works with 'zest' on building the wall ('his wall') of a power station:

> At the spot he was working on, the wall had previously been laid by some mason who was either incompetent or had scamped the job. But now Shukhov tackled the wall as if it was his own handiwork. There, he saw, was a cavity that couldn't be levelled up in one row: he'd have to do it in three, adding a little more mortar each time. And here the outer wall bellied a bit — it would take two rows to straighten that.[9]

The work is forced labour — in Marx's terms, alienation — but Shukhov, instead of accepting his own slavery, transcends it. For by investing his work with a sense of creativity, which every form of regimentation must effectively destroy, Shukhov retains his individuality. He is too deeply involved in his work, 'he worried about anything he could make use of, about every scrap of work he could do — nothing must be wasted without good reason.' And when the day's work is ended

> . . . Shukhov — and if the guards had put the dogs on him it
> would have made no difference — ran to the back and looked
> about. Not bad. Then he ran and gave the wall a good look
> over, to the left, to the right. His eye was as accurate as a
> spirit level. Straight and even. His hands were as young as
> ever.[10]

When the other gangs have finished their work and at the risk of
arriving back at camp late, Shukhov rejects the idea of wasting
good mortar; eight years in the camps had not changed his
nature.

But although Shukhov's responses are not wholly passive,
Solzhenitsyn's approach does not raise the important question—
why? Discussing his intentions for the novel, Solzhenitsyn was
quite clear:

> . . . I have always felt that to write about the fate of Russia
> was the most fascinating and important task to be performed.
> Of all the drama that Russia lived through, the fate of Ivan
> Denisovich was the greatest tragedy. I also wanted to expose
> the false image of prison camps. While still in the camp I
> made up my mind to describe one day of prison life. Tolstoy
> once said that a novel can deal with either centuries of
> European history or a day in one man's life . . .[11]

Thus, although the camp represents a microcosm of Soviet
society with its anti-democratic hierarchical structures of power
and authority and the prisoners a broad cross-section of Stalin's
Russia, the story never raises itself to a full statement on why
innocent peasants, film producers, naval officers, government
bureaucrats, Baptists, etc. have had their lives physically
shattered. Thus the intellectuals in the camp are portrayed as
somehow irrelevant given the viewpoint of the story. Shukhov
overhears two conversations, both on the ideological elements
of the Soviet film director Sergei Eisenstein, which, given the
setting, seem ascetically perverse. To Tsezar, the film producer,
Ivan the Terrible is 'a work of genius', while to prisoner X123 it
is 'a vile political idea — the justification of personal tyranny'.
Geniuses, X123 goes on, 'don't adjust their interpretations to
suit the taste of tyrants!' And when later Tsezar defends
Eisenstein's artistic intentions in Battleship Potemkin,[12]
Shukhov has no interest in such esoteric problems or in those

larger questions which come to preoccupy the main characters
of Solzhenitsyn's next two novels. His tragedy is that of the
ordinary Russian, of countless innocent victims sacrificed, not
for a 'future good' but for a bleak and repressive present. It is
said that Khrushchev liked *One Day* because its peasant 'hero'
transcends his dehumanising and crippling enslavement through
his positive attitude to work, but the more significant point is
that given the viewpoint of Shukhov — a simple man concerned
almost exclusively with the physical side of life — Solzhenitsyn's
story could never pose those awkward, *historical* questions
which dominate *The First Circle* and *Cancer Ward*.

II

Between 1955 and 1967 Solzhenitsyn completed the three
major fictions that take as their point of departure the Stalin
era. For the characters which populate *One Day, The First
Circle* (1955—64), and *Cancer Ward* (1963—7) the October
Revolution has been the single, most important event in shaping
their past and present experiences. The majority have lived all
their lives under the Soviet regime and it is in this sense that
Solzhenitsyn is a Soviet and not simply a Russian writer: *One
Day, The First Circle* and *Cancer Ward* form a single whole
distinct from both his more recent and much publicised
religious and political views and his current multi-volumed
study of pre- and early-Soviet society. Interpretation of the
novels, therefore, must be guided by a genetic and historically
specific approach and not analysed in terms either of his greater
involvement in the dissident movement during the late sixties or
his current role as Defender of the Christian Faith, the Russian
People and the Russian Nation.

During the writing of *The First Circle* Solzhenitsyn had few
contacts with dissident intellectuals. The Opposition which
developed during the sixties had its roots in the immediate
post-Stalin years: various liberal groups, highly critical yet
hopeful of Soviet society, existed in the late 1950s, reflecting
the mood of sections of the progressive intelligentsia, and it is
this, somewhat diffuse, dissident 'movement' which finds
expression in Solzhenitsyn's fiction. In the 1970s Solzhenitsyn
repudiates Soviet society, socialism and Marxism. But in 1955,
like other liberal thinkers, he accepted the Soviet system and
looked for improvement from *within* it. Thus both *The First*

Circle and *Cancer Ward* are in no sense anti-Soviet novels; on the contrary from the internal evidence available there seems to be a strong case for arguing that they were written for publication in the Soviet Union (not for the desk) as part of the debunking de-mythologising of Stalin and Stalinism and the critique of bureaucracy set in train by Khrushchev. This is a point of some importance for one of the striking aspects of Solzhenitsyn's fiction is its close relation with traditional — or 'critical' — realism. Solzhenitsyn is neither a 'modernist' nor a 'socialist realist' but a writer who, in the second half of the twentieth century, has revived a literary form thought outmoded, even extinct by Western novelists. It is in this sense that *One Day* approximates to classical realism in its refusal to classify characters as 'good' or 'bad', or strive for the all-embracing monistic vision of socialist realism. The literature of a totalitarian society, *in general*, will eliminate ambiguity and diversity, transforming fiction into ideology. Solzhenitsyn's novels thus restate the basic tenets of classical realism through a tragic conflict between the individual and the collectivity and his concept of literature's role in exposing injustice and evil, awakening and giving man moral guidance. Unlike Kafka, Musil, Hesse or the practitioners of the *nouveau roman*, Solzhenitsyn's is an optimistic view of man and the world, of the human spirit triumphing over the most terrible deprivations and ultimately over death itself, an affirmation of the possibility of human community.

The action of *The First Circle* takes place in December 1949 in the special Moscow prison called Mavrino. A technical and research institute, Mavrino houses some of the leading Soviet scientists, prisoners engaged in high-level secret work. In Soviet slang Mavrino is a *sharashka*, a prison institution hidden by a respectable facade. But Mavrino is more than a prison — it is the first circle of hell where the prisoners are precariously poised on the brink of the lower depths — the concentration camps of Siberia. Stalin is about to launch a new purge; already Gumulka has been arrested in Poland, Rajk tortured and murdered in Hungary. The Mavrino research institute, which works on telephonic communication, has been earmarked to play an important role in Stalin's plans and the dramatic structure of the novel is built around the choices which the leading characters are forced to make, either to help in research and thus co-operate with the M.V.D. (the Ministry of Internal Affairs) or refuse and risk transfer to a harsher regime.

The novel introduces both fictional and historical characters — Stalin, his minister of State Security, Viktor Abakumov, and his personal secretary, Lieutenant-General Alexander Poskryobyshev Yakonov, a colonel in the M.V.D., has the job of inventing a secret telephone coding device, the need for which has now become imperative: a high-ranking Soviet diplomat, Innokenty Volodin, hearing of the imminent arrest of his family doctor, Professor Dobroumov, for the violation of state secrets (exchanging scientific knowledge with Western scientists) decides to warn Dobroumov, although aware that socialist phones are tapped and his voice could be identified. To contact Dobroumov will endanger the whole of his career, yet he knows that he must act, for 'if you always look over your shoulder, how can you still remain a human being?'[13] He makes the call, but only to Dobroumov's wife, and in desperation leaves the warning message which, when he hears the 'soft click' on the line knows has been intercepted. Although Volodin has disguised his voice the authorities quickly reduce the list of suspects to six or seven, and the M.V.D. demand from the Mavrino scientists 'proof' of the guilty man. The science of 'voice prints' has been born.

The hero of the novel is Gleb Nerzhin, a thirty-one year-old mathematician with some knowledge of linguistics. He has spent two years at Mavrino working with Lev Rubin, a philologist who specialises in Germanic languages:

> For two years they had sat back to back twelve hours a day. Very soon they had discovered that they had both served on the Northwestern and the Byelorussian fronts during the war, and that both had been arrested at the front, in the same month . . . under the same Paragraph 10, which was *universally applicable*, that is, it was applied without regard to education, property qualification or material situation. And both had got ten years — like everybody else. (p. 35)

Much of the novel is built around the clash of views, values and general philosophy between these two intellectuals. Nerzhin* is

---

*Nerzhin is Solzhenitsyn — in terms of age, wartime experiences, ideology. And like his fictional counterpart Solzhenitsyn destroyed the manuscripts he had been writing secretly for four years.

portrayed as a courageous, honest man with an overriding
passion for the truth; above all, he is genuinely seeking to
understand the historical roots of Stalinism, the social forces
which led to what he calls the defeat of Leninism. He is
implacably hostile to the 'great leader' and the servile
functionaries without whom the Stalinist system would have
been impossible. Although ostensibly engaged on phonetics,
Nerzhin is secretly writing a history of the Soviet Union, a work
which has become his major intellectual activity at Mavrino.
Composed in tiny handwriting, 'those little sheets of paper were
a kind of coming of age for him — the first fruits of his thirty
years.' (p. 59) As a boy, growing up during the purge years of
the 1930s, Nerzhin had refused to believe in Stalin's 'wise
leadership' and the charges brought against the Old Bolsheviks.
At the age of thirteen he knew the names of the Party Leaders,
Commanders of the Red Army, Soviet Ambassadors, had
studied the speeches at Party congresses, the memoirs of the
Old Bolsheviks and the different histories of the Communist
Party. In December 1934, reading of the Kirov murder, 'he
suddenly felt, in a flash, that the murderer was none other than
Stalin — because only Stalin stood to gain by it. In the midst of
the jostling crowd of grown-ups, who did not understand this
simple truth, he felt desperately lonely.' (p. 245) The crude,
judicial murders, the false confessions of the old revolutionaries
branded as fascist and imperialist agents, while praised by
hordes of sycophantic writers, did not fool the young Nerzhin:

> Throughout his youth Gleb Nerzhin had heard the furious
> clangour of the silent tocsin, and he had vowed that he would
> get at the truth and make sense of all this. Strolling in the
> Moscow streets at night, when it would have been more
> normal to have been thinking about girls, Gleb dreamed of
> the day when it would all be clear to him and perhaps he
> might see what it was like behind those high walls where all
> the victims, to a man, had slandered themselves before going
> to their death. (p. 246)

And now, in Mavrino, at the expense of his career, freedom,
family life, his wish is granted. 'Once the mind is possessed by a
single great passion, everything else is ruthlessly excluded —
there is no room for it . . . ' (p. 246) The task which
professional historians had prudently ignored in favour of more

distant history, was now his life's work.[14] At one moment he reflects on the value of his five years in prison where he has known people more closely than he ever did in the outside world; their reflections had probably 'saved him from countless youthful mistakes, from countless false steps.' (p. 306)

In sharp contrast to Nerzhin, Lev Rubin refuses to accept that Stalin's regime constituted a distortion of Leninism and Marxism. Thus although arrested for his opposition to the post-war Stalinist policy of vengeance against *all* Germans he yet remains, like so many other Communist inmates of the camps and prisons, a supporter of Stalin. For Rubin is that most tragic figure, a sincere Stalinist, a man who has dedicated his life to high social ideals, to Marxism and the international working-class movement, but who remains imprisoned within the bureaucratic distortion of Marxism by which the most savage and inhuman cruelties are vindicated posthumously by appeals to a distant future. He ramains staunchly convinced that socialism will triumph over bureaucratic 'excesses'. Rubin's Marxism, which justifies totalitarianism as historical necessity, is in essence a form of fatalism, a belief that *in the end* 'progressive forces' within the historical situation, irrespective of their 'temporary malfunctioning', must work towards the ultimate goal of Communism without any kind of human intervention, of *praxis*. Thus the prison officers and warders are merely the instruments for 'implementing a law which in itself was absolutely right, just and progressive'. Prisoners who criticise them merely reflect their own prejudices and are 'blind to the great law by which everything took its inevitable course.' (p. 496) Rubin, in short, has a progressive attitude towards his own slavery.

Rubin works on the telephonic prints decoder not from compulsion but out of conviction: thus while he expresses admiration for Volodin's bravery in warning Dobroumov, objectively he was 'working against the forces of progress'. For Rubin, the state is both omnipotent and omniscient: if ludicrous claims are made for the Russian origins of all major scientific discoveries, then those thinking differently are 'objectively standing in the way of progress and must be swept aside.' (p. 236) While Nerzhin rejects Stalin as a philistine, Rubin invests him with the qualities of Robespierre and Napoleon 'rolled into one', a 'really wise' leader who 'sees far beyond what we can possibly see' (p. 51). Rubin's is the 'realistic', Communist point of view, the propagandistic concept of truth, by which the wretched victims of Stalinism exonerated the system that enslaved them illegally. The novel makes clear that the cost has been too great. Thus although Rubin is unwilling or unable to genuinely understand the historical basis of Stalin's rule he feels that moral standards have actually declined 'and that people were losing their sense of values', that an ethical vacuum has been created inside the heart of Communism. Rubin's solution is to establish a system of Civic Temples and a permanent priesthood of selfless revolutionaries to inspire devotion and loyalty from an enraptured People, proposals to be smuggled out of Mavrino and presented to the Party Central Committee. The solution to totalitarian politics is merely 'moral' totalitarianism (the building of architecturally dominant Temples to inspire feelings of grandeur in the People, and an elaborate system of rituals binding them to the State), in which the masses are regarded as mere children — passive objects to be manipulated and developed as willing agents of a paternalistic state. Solzhenitsyn's portrayal of the Stalinist mind is here highly pertinent and acute. For while Rubin regards himself as a Marxist his failure to understand Stalinism from a Marxist standpoint leads him to propose moral solutions to economic and political problems, to advocate the kind of utopianism from which Marx had clearly distinguished Marxism one hundred years before. Rubin's espousal of an autonomous ethic (a theme which recurs in *Cancer Ward*) as the solution to a sterile — although from his point of view, historically necessary — materialism, flows concretely from his inability to understand that bureaucracy represents a check and denial of revolutionary *praxis*, existing not to advance revolutionary consciousness but to emasculate and retard it. The lack of moral involvement and the widely expressed cynicism of many young Russians towards the Soviet system, a theme well documented in the literature of the early sixties, is at bottom the result of a profoundly anti-democratic bureaucratic structure which stifles initiative and creative energy. Rubin's understanding is thus diametrically opposed to that of Nerzhin: to impose upon the people 'ethical' chains is to reject, not advance, the ideals of 1917.

Solzhenitsyn depicts the other prisoners in Mavrino in terms of their sympathy with these two extreme, although sincerely felt, positions. Thus when the scientist, Bobynin, is asked by Abakumov to inform on the progress of the decoding schedule behind the backs of the other bureaucrats he treats the request with absolute contempt. To command people against their will, Bobynin asserts, is possible only if they have something to lose. He has nothing: both his wife and child were killed in the war, his parents are dead, and he owns nothing apart from a handkerchief; his denims and underwear are government issue:

> You took my freedom away a long time ago and you can't give it back to me because you havn't got it yourself . . . You can tell You-know-who-up-there — that you only have power over people so long as you don't take *everything* away from them. But when you've robbed a man of *everything* he's no longer in your power — he's free again. (pp. 106—7)

When the physicist Gerasimovich is asked to invent an infra-red camera for M.V.D. agents capable of taking photographs at night, he refuses, although knowing that by this act he condemns both himself and a wife who cannot survive without him: in anguish but with scorn he tells his captors, 'No, it's not in my line! . . . putting people in prison is not my line! . . . I'm not a fisher of men. There are more than enough of us in prison as it is . . .' (p. 607) And there is Ilya Khorobrov who, refusing to work more than the twelve hours required by the Soviet Constitution, is transferred to the labour camps.

In contrast, Solzhenitsyn portrays those who are willing to buy themselves freedom: Ruska Doronin, a cynical although likeable double informer, playing off the prisoners and the prison bureaucrats; Sologdin, who, denounced by his wife to the Secret police and enduring the Vorkuta camps, has created a coding device which he coolly plans to use as a means for his release. Sologdin realises that the bureaucrats need both their prisoners and their ideas if they themselves are to survive. Thus knowing that Abakumov must satisfy Stalin's demand for a decoder, Sologdin destroys the plans of his invention. Yakanov is dumbfounded and furious. You have committed suicide, he tells Sologdin. But Sologdin is fully conscious of his actions: to give Yakanov the final plans is to hand over the one thing he knows may bring him freedom. Thus he agrees to reconstruct them only when Yakanov guarantees a signed ministerial

statement that the invention is Sologdin's. Sologdin is the
Soviet individualist: 'You were taking a great risk, my dear sir.
This could have ended very differently' says Yakanov, and
Sologdin replies that no, he has grasped the general
situation — *'and your own situation too . . .* Fortune doesn't
often smile on us, but when it does one must grasp it with both
hands.' (pp. 557—8, italics added)

In *One Day*, the point of view was Shukhov's. *The First Circle*
has no such single focus* and the novel depicts both the prison
bureaucracy and the relations outside the prison based on
Volodin: his father-in-law the Public Prosecutor Major-General
Makarygin and his daughters, especially the youngest, Clara,
who works in Mavrino and is critical of her father's extravagent
mode of life; the opportunist novelist, Galakhov, married to
Dinera Makarygin, economically and socially successful but
creatively barren; and an Old Bolshevik, Radovic, a survivor of
the purges who remains a querulous dissenting voice in the
Makarygin home. Here, among these free intellectuals, the same
problems and questions on art, philosophy and politics which
exercise the minds of the prisoners in Mavrino play a decisive
role in the shaping of the novel's structure. For Solzhenitsyn
explicitly contrasts the apparent freedom of those outside
prison with the forced confinement of those within it and
asks — who is really free?

Thus Galakhov, having spent his life in compromise with the
Stalinist bureaucracy, is less free to write than the imprisoned
Nerzhin, whose secret history of Stalinism is clearly the
expression of an 'inner need', an inner freedom which no prison
system can effectively destroy.[15] Solzhenitsyn's emphasis on
the crucial factor of sincerity is unambiguous: Galakhov has
willingly prostituted art in the interests of material rewards and
a spurious fame, consciously tailored his literary output to the
dictates of Stalinist orthodoxy, of socialist realism. During the
long scene at the Prosecutor's house, Galakhov, reflecting on a
projected play 'based on a conspiracy between the imperialist
powers and the Soviet diplomats' efforts to keep the peace',

*Solzhenitsyn has described his novels as polyphonic, each character becoming the
main one as the action involves him. The novels have no single hero, then, but dozens
of heroes. This is truer of *The First Circle* than of *Cancer Ward* in which Kostoglotov
approaches the classic problematic hero, but in both novels the basic constituent of
classical realism — Goldmann's category of 'individual biography' — provides
ultimate shape to the novels' structure.

experiences profound unease at attempting to write on themes
of which he has little first-hand knowledge: 'with every year he
felt more and more that life abroad, or in some remote
historical period, or even a fantasy about people on the moon,
would be easier to tackle than the reality of Soviet life, so
complex and so full of pitfalls for a writer.' (pp. 434—5) He has
become a 'safe' writer, the sense of creativity blunted by years
of conformity and censorship, so that at the age of thirty-seven
with his books published in vast quantities, 'he couldn't think
what to write about', plays, stories, novels 'died in front of his
eyes'. When his tormented brother-in-law Volodin asks him,
'What ideas have you produced to comfort our tormented age?'
he strikes at the heart of Galakhov's insincerity, for the act of
writing demands the kind of responsibility and integrity which
Galakhov has never given. Truth suffers, and Volodin asks,
clearly speaking for Solzhenitsyn, 'Aren't writers supposed to
teach, to guide? . . . Isn't that what was always thought? And
for a country to have a great writer . . . is like having another
government. That's why no regime has ever loved great writers,
only minor ones.' (p. 436)

Galakhov knows, of course, that to live in the Soviet Union
under Stalin a writer must sacrifice truth to the higher reality of
Party dogma. But the matter was never that simple: Olesha and
Babel turned to the genre of silence while others wrote for their
desk drawers in hope for a distant generation. A creative writer
does not have to write anything at all other than through
choice. Galakhov's 'unhappy consciousness', his consciously
understood lack of inner freedom, is at once the fate of an
entire generation of able Soviet writers and artists for whom
creativity became a mere means to a comfortable and privileged
life.

Solzhenitsyn's portrait of Galakhov represents a sharp
criticism of those writers who legitimised the Stalinist system
through their uncritical portrait of the 1930s and the war years,
and suggests that their lack of creative freedom is indissolubly
bound up with their social function as 'engineers of the soul',
literary ideologists whose fiction functioned mainly as a form of
social control.[16] Galakhov is seen and portrayed as *feeling* a
failure, a willing prisoner of the Soviet bureaucracy. This acute
sense of failure, the inability to rise above the clearly defined
problems posed by Stalinism, is brought out more poignantly in

the character of Radovic, a veteran of the Civil War and a
prominent figure in the early years of the Comintern. Radovic,
who 'had survived the purges only because during the most
critical times he was never out of hospital', is an orthodox
Marxist, but one who has now become 'a complete failure'.
Able to eat only through a tube, forbidden by his doctors to
smoke, Radovic is both physically and politically worn out. He,
whose philosophy is that of *praxis*, merely exists 'by keeping
quiet', and controlling his temper. During the party he goes to
Makarygin's library (the Prosecutor prudently reads only
detective novels) where he picks up one of a flood of Stalinist
hack works on Tito in which the Yugoslavian Communist
leader, like Trotsky in the thirties, is attacked viciously as a
fascist imperialist agent. Radovic understands clearly enough
that Tito's only crime was his political independence from the
Kremlin, his refusal to accept Stalin's authority in Yugoslavia,
and that the current political trials in Eastern Europe, the
apparent confessions of the accused, are 'frame-ups'. For
Radovic knows of the beatings, the starvation, the sheer
brutality which forces men to accuse themselves of the most
absurd crimes. He knows all this: and remains silent.

   Radovic is fully alive, also, to the profoundly non-socialist
principles which underpin the Soviet social structure. Socialised
property has not brought with it egalitarian socialist norms and
socialist principles of freedom, but rather a repressive and
unequal society dominated by a privileged layer of bureaucrats.
Thus when Clara Makarygin attacks her father for living at the
expense of others, for his chauffeur-driven car, expensive
Moscow flat, extravagant style of life, Radovic echoes her
criticisms of inequality — but he does so theoretically,
abstractly. When Makarygin justifies his high salary as the result
of 'accumulated labour' Radovic appeals to his 'Communist
conscience' — 'What about those double salary packets you get
every so often? You get paid eight thousand a month or so,
don't you? And the charwoman gets two hundred and
fifty!' — the Prosecutor can only think that Radovic has even
'lost touch with reality', has become 'an anarchist'. In this, one
of Solzhenitsyn's most forceful scenes, the old and politically
impotent Communist talks of the 'need to purge ourselves
of . . . bourgeois corruption', of the need 'to go back to Lenin',
yet when Makarygin asks if Soviet Communism has

degenerated, has endured its Thermidor,[17] Radovic can only
reply through the slogans of the early 1920s: 'The capitalist
world is torn by conflicts that are infinitely worse. And as all
the members of the Comintern foretold, I too firmly believe
that we shall soon witness an armed clash over world markets
between England and the United States!' (pp. 448—9) In *Cancer
Ward* a similar figure from the past, a survivor of the years of
revolution, Shulubin, exercises a far more significant role in the
novel's structure than does Radovic in *The First Circle*, and
goes much further in condemning the silent compromise with
Stalinism. But for both their character is forged from a lack of
inner strength and a sense of hopelessness in the face of
totalitarianism.

Yet this sense of hopelessness is absent in Nerzhin. For him
all the important questions are bound up with the revolution,
the meaning of life itself, happiness, ethics and love — all
revolve around the fundamental problem of Stalinism. In his
secret history Nerzhin, who has dedicated his life to
understanding the betrayals of 1917, is searching out the
fundamental meaning of the Stalin era; he is not satisfied with a
merely pessimistic and pragmatic compromise like Radovic. But
Solzhenitsyn does not depict Nerzhin as a Marxist revolutionary
in the traditions of Trotsky and the Left Opposition, for
example, but rather as an austere, ascetic intellectual who
actually welcomes imprisonment, not as did the pre-1917
Marxists as a 'school of revolutionary theory' to issue in
revolutionary class struggle, but rather as an intellectual
sanctuary, the sole bastion of free enquiry remaining in the
Soviet Union: 'Thank God for prison! It has given me the
chance to think things out.' (p. 48) It is this extreme ascetism
which divides Rubin from Nerzhin on the one hand and
Nerzhin from the Marxist revolutionary tradition on the other.
For Nerzhin is portrayed as an intellectual dissident without
any connection with revolutionary groups — Stalinism had
wiped out all effective revolutionary opposition — and his quest
for an understanding of the Stalin era becomes, not as Lukács
terms it, 'eccentric', but necessarily individualistic. His refusal
to compromise in this context means total isolation with no
hope of changing Soviet society. It means also the breakdown
of Nerzhin's marriage. Outside Mavrino there are none of those
revolutionary groups which in the twenties sustained the wives

of imprisoned oppositionists: they were fighting under the banner of revolutionary Marxism against bureaucratic nationalism and the struggle had meaning well beyond their own personal problems. The total elimination of the Left and Right Opposition during the 1920s and 1930s with the consequent distortions of their political programmes, the rewriting of Soviet history, presents an intractable problem for those intellectuals who grew to maturity in the purge and war years and became critical of Stalin's regime *without* the truthful historical material by which to judge and understand Soviet development. The political struggles of the 1920s which eventuated in Stalinist dictatorship and the future course of Soviet society is precisely the major structure missing in Solzhenitsyn's novel and therefore from Nerzhin's secret history. Any novel which takes as its theme the fate of those opposed to Stalinism cannot ignore the one consistent political tendency to have fought Stalinism from the beginning in the 1920s. This structure is missing from the novel — apart from the character of Adamson who, depicted as an ex-Left Oppositionist plays no really significant role — precisely because Solzhenitsyn, linking Stalinism with Marxism and Leninism, sees no alternative to it from within Marxism itself. To be sure, Nerzhin judges Soviet society in terms of its rejection of socialist norms but he does so non-historically so that his standpoint becomes one of individualistic criticism. Nerzhin (and Kostoglotov) must therefore remain a problematic hero existing on the periphery of society, unable even to live a 'normal life' within the civil institutions. And it is the failure to link Nerzhin's opposition to Stalinism in the forties with the explicitly Marxist opposition of the twenties which results in the disjunction between ideas and action. The tragic vision, while embodying 'absolute values', is tragic precisely because there seems no way of creating through these values a new social world. For if the values are purely critical, if they lack a rich historical content, then *praxis* is wholly eliminated. In the discussions between Nerzhin and Rubin which form the bulk of *The First Circle* their respective understanding of revolution, their attitudes towards the role of the working class and the Communist Party, the question of means and ends, of dialectics, morality, personal realationships, all flow from the novel's overall tragic universe and the structure of values within it. Thus

although Nerzhin and Rubin do not compromise their
fundamental beliefs, the beliefs themselves are diametrically
opposed. Nerzhin's asceticism contrasts sharply with Rubin's
sense of *deprivation* and Nerzhin refuses to co-operate with the
prison authorities in full knowledge of the consequences: he
angrily rejects the offer of a pardon and a Moscow flat:

> Pardoned? . . . What makes you think I want a favour from
> them? You think I want to be told I've worked so well that
> all is forgiven and I can go? . . . You're putting it the wrong
> way round. Let them admit first that it's not right to put
> people in prison for their way of thinking — and then *we* will
> see whether we can forgive *them*.' (p. 60)

Nerzhin rejects precisely those values which sustain the lives of
Prosecutor Makarygin, Galakhov and the prison bureaucrats:
'What was the point of living out the whole of your life? Did
one live just for the sake of living, just for the sake of one's
bodily comfort? Comfort, indeed! What was the point of living
if comfort was all that mattered?'

He realises that his decision was not merely an incident 'but a
turning point in his life', that for him there was no other choice.
In a world which seems dominated by a constant transvaluation
of all values and dogmatic political ideology, sound and truthful
beliefs are essential. When Ruska Doronin argues that history is
a meaningless force, that within it there is neither truth nor
error, Nerzhin quietly reprimands such futile scepticism: 'It's
not a guide to action, and people can't just stand off, so they
must have a set of positive beliefs to show them the way . . . it
can never give a man the feeling that he's got firm ground under
his feet'! And Nerzhin's humanist values are clearly the basis for
his philosophy of life. But these values are *ascetically*
humanistic: Nerzhin maintains that the happiness which comes
from 'easy victories, from the total fulfilment of desire, from
success, from feeling completely gorged — *that* is suffering!'
Whereas Rubin 'realistically' assesses 'life as it is', Nerzhin
argues that no one really understands what they strive for, that
man exhausts himself 'in the senseless pursuit of material
things', that he dies without realising spiritual wealth: 'When
Tolstoy wished to be in prison, his reasoning was that of a truly
perceptive person in a healthy state of mind.' (p. 50) The
essence of Nerzhin's asceticism lies here: the rejection of the

world as it is, a world which denies those values by which man should live. This is endurance not for its own sake but born of the kind of integrity which refuses compromise. In Solzhenitsyn's portrait of Stalin's Russia the question of ethics overrides all other questions; for Solzhenitsyn it is fundamental to his world vision. But, of course, for the fictional Nerzhin ethics are divorced from revolutionary ideology, becoming unattainable ideals standing outside and beyond man; Nerzhin's values, indeed, are absolute ones, closer to the spirit of Kant's idealism than to Marx's materialism, universal ethical premises by which man should live. Such a conception of ethics clearly approaches a religious standpoint forming perhaps the most significant structure within the novel, shaping both the relations between the prisoners and those between men and women. The Stalin regime, therefore, is judged not historically but critically for its failure to generate genuine social ideals that would override the pragmatic, egoistic values which Solzhenitsyn identifies with contemporary Soviet society.

Counterpointed to Nerzhin is the rich, socially successful diplomat Volodin. Solzhenitsyn's portrait of Volodin, like that of the Stalinist Rubin, is suble, multi-faceted, for Volodin is no simple 'time server' (such as Makarygin and Galakhov), but has a deeply troubled conscience, not over his socially privileged position which he has enjoyed to the full, but rather over more fundamental questions of justice and truth. Recently he has read his mother's diary and the section headed, 'Ethical Considerations', where he learns that 'the most precious thing in the world' is 'the consciousness of not participating in injustice. Injustice is stronger than you are, it always was, and it always will be, but let it not be committed through you.' (p. 418) The 'old fashioned' ethical imperatives, 'Truth, Goodness and Beauty', 'Good and Evil' — absolute values — strike at Volodin's very being, for in this diary of an old bourgeois Russian who rejected every facet of the Revolution he discovers that something is missing from his life. He gradually rejects his philosophy of hedonism, 'that we only live once', and matures to an awareness 'that a crippled conscience is as irretrievable as a lost life.' (p. 421) At the Makarygin party the Prosecutor banteringly accuses him of Epicureanism (which Radovic approves since 'Epicurus was all right, he was a materialist; Karl Marx wrote a dissertation about him') but Volodin answers that contrary to popular opinion Epicurus saw in 'insatiable desire' the chief impediment to human happiness. (pp. 432–3)

Volodin and Nerzhin, from radically different perspectives, have reached the same conclusion. Volodin's tragedy is that he has realised too late that to assert sincerity and human decency in Soviet Russia constitutes sufficient grounds for imprisonment and possibly death. Later in the novel, arrested through Rubin's identification of the voice prints, Volodin understands that even his disappearance and death will not have the slightest effect on the conduct of his friends and relatives. Disowned, disgraced, Volodin's isolation and hopelessness is complete.

Nerzhin, by contrast, after five years of prison has concluded that human suffering is the pursuit of material things, an attitude which is closely connected with his feelings that Stalinism, through betraying the Russian people, can be defeated only by a superior moral purpose, one based on the 'People' and not imposed dictatorially from above. Nerzhin's populist conception is extremely important, not because it indicates what Lukács calls a 'plebeian attitude' but for Solzhenitsyn's understanding (through the novels) that socialism can be achieved only *with* the masses not *against* them, that Stalinist bureaucracy and ideology, while glorifying Communism through an artificial cult of the proletariat, actually functions to repress, control and work against the interests of the working class. Nerzhin totally rejects an intellectualist, élitist conception of the people:

> One belonged to the People neither by virtue of speaking the same language as everybody else nor by being among the select few stamped with the hallmark of genius. You were not born into the People, nor did you become part of it through work or education.
>
> It was only character that mattered, and this was something that everybody had to forge for himself, by constant effort over the years.
>
> Only thus could one make oneself into a human being and hence be regarded as a tiny part of one's people. (p. 470)

Such a statement is clearly inconsistent with Nerzhin's avowed Leninism. The contradiction is resolved, however, if Solzhenitsyn's portrait of Nerzhin identifies Marxism with Stalinism. As we have seen, the one significant structure missing in the novel is that of the Left Opposition, and the impression is thus conveyed that there was never any *Marxist* alternative to Stalinism. In *The Gulag Archipelago* Solzhenitsyn leaves no doubt that for him Leninism leads inevitably to Stalinism, but in *The First Circle* and *Cancer Ward* the link is not so clear. Nonetheless, it is there: and in his short stories as well as the novels, Solzhenitsyn explicitly rejects the urban working classes to dwell, not simply on the Russian peasant, but on those vestiges of pre-industrial Russia, the customs and the rituals that have survived fifty years of Soviet power and which live on in the consciousness and actions of the People. Perhaps this is the key to Solzhenitsyn's vision. For here is a writer living within a society in which the civil institutions are weak, totally subordinate to the dominant political institutions and thus incapable of maintaining and sustaining that independence of outlook and spirit so essential for the life of a creative writer. As a privileged servant of the state the Soviet writer exists *above* and not *within* society, responding not to the values generated by and through the civil institutions, but to the bureaucratically imposed values of the ruling caste. When a nation's literature becomes ideology the values which sustain it are those of the state with orthodoxy tightly guarded by a vast, bureaucratic editorial apparatus. Nadezhda Mandelstam remarks that 'the orders fulfilled by writers did not come to them from the community, which had been all but done away with; they were passed down from unimaginable heights in the form of suggestions and recommendations of a most general nature, eventually reaching those for whom they were intended via an army of editors.'[18] As the major novelist of the post-Stalin period Solzhenitsyn's fiction reflects the tragedy of a socialist state which represses and dominates the social class in whose name it rules. It is in all these senses that Nerzhin's 'populism', his relationship with the simple peasant Spiridon Yegorov, a Mavrino prisoner and odd-job man whose life is the antithesis of a class-conscious proletarian, can be understood. During the Revolution Spiridon had refused to fight for either the Reds or the Whites, had desired only peace; but he had been recruited to fight on both sides. After the defeat of the Whites he formed part of the army which crushed the Kronstadt rebellion. During the N.E.P. period he became an 'intensive cultivator', supported by government funds to farm lands and improve cultivation only to be attacked in 1929 as a dangerous kulak. Yet instead of exile, Spiridon was made 'a commissar for collectivisation'. Unable to prevent the peasants from slaughtering their livestock he was given ten years for 'economic counter-revolution'. Released from prison, Spiridon enjoys a short time with his wife and children before the German invasion. Without any problems of conscience he willingly co-operates but when the Nazis burn down the village as an act of reprisal against the local partisans, Spiridon changes sides. When the Germans retreat taking the peasants with them, Spiridon, looking for his family, goes with them. Interred in a German concentration camp he is finally released and sent back to Russia but imprisoned immediately for 'co-operating' with the Germans. During thirty years Spiridon has lost his land, his family and is now almost blind. Through this character, Solzhenitsyn has telescoped the experiences of the three decades which followed 1917: the confusions of the immediate revolutionary period, the hopes engendered by socialism and finally destroyed by the internecine warfare within the Communist Party and the consolidation of the bureaucratic state.

From a dogmatic Marxist point of view Spiridon clearly reflects the most backward stratum of the Russian working class. Marx had written scathingly of the peasant with his petty-bourgeois illusions while other Marxists have been unequivocal in denying the peasant any independent role in the forging of revolution. At best the peasant supports the politically independent revolutionary role of the industrial proletariat and there is no doubt that Rubin's judgement that only the proletariat 'was consistently revolutionary in its outlook' represents orthodox Marxism. Both Rubin and Sologdin regard Nerzhin's relationship with Spiridon as populism, 'going to the people' in search of the 'great truth' which the Marxist analysis of society into classes has seemingly failed to give. For Rubin 'the people' remains an idealist abstraction unless divided into distinct social strata; Sologdin simply regards them as drab and incapable of building the great society which must always be the task of a privileged élite.

The essence of Stalinism lies in its profound mistrust of the working class; the Soviet bureaucracy functions to emasculate revolutionary theory and prevent the emergence of an independent political consciousness. As was argued in Chapter 4

the Soviet bureaucracy's social base was broadened quite
deliberately during the late 1920s to attract bourgeois and
careerist elements, political appointees owing allegiance to the
apparatus and its head. This privileged social stratum, swollen to
gigantic proportions by the needs of a centralised economy,
secret police forces and labour camp administration would have
little sympathy for revolutionary theory, internationalism and
the participation of the masses in socialist democracy. It is
against the dogmatic, Stalinist ideology which has legitimised
bureaucratic rule that Nerzhin's relationship with Spiridon must
be understood. In rejecting the Marxist concept of a
revolutionary proletariat, Nerzhin turns to the antithesis of
everything that the Stalinist system stands for: when he asks
him what life means Spiridon answers, 'wolf hounds are right
and cannibals are wrong' (p. 486), a reply which puzzles
Nerzhin. Spiridon seems to suggest that while it is not man's
nature to learn to kill other men, for other animals killing is
right because it conforms with their nature. Socialism, far from
encouraging actions 'proper and worthy of human nature'
(Marx) has seemingly turned man against himself. The tragic
dimensions of Solzhenitsyn's universe are nowhere better
expressed than in Nerzhin's intellectual search for the truth of
Soviet history and his rejection of the very springs of that
development: the *praxis* of the revolutionary proletariat. And it
could not be otherwise: there was, indeed, no way of translating
socialist values into practice in the era of Stalinist
totalitarianism.

III

On one level, *The First Circle* can be read as a damning criticism
of bureaucratic domination. The role of bureaucracy in the life
of modern society has attracted increasing attention from
sociologists since Max Weber's pioneering studies some sixty
years ago. For Weber, the bureaucratisation of social life formed
the dominant characteristic of capitalist economic development,
'the parcelling out of the human soul', a process which leads to
great tension between the democratic trends associated with
bourgeois society and the anti-democratic ethos of bureaucratic
organisation. In Weber's analysis bureaucracy becomes the
major source of authority: organisation is the locus of power in
modern society compounded of hierarchical structures involving

an administrative staff of permanent, salaried officials. A modern state, he argued, requires 'stable, strict, intensive, and calculable administration' and the choice lies simply 'between bureaucracy and dilletantism'. Socialist society would be no exception to Weber's pessimistic prognosis: 'The future belongs to bureaucracy', he once wrote, 'where once the modern trained official rules, his power is virtually indestructible, because the whole organisation of the most basic provisions of life is fashioned to suit his performance.' In Weber's view, therefore, a socialist revolution would prepare the groundwork for total bureaucratic domination. Writing of the 1905 Russian Revolution, and with Marxist theory in mind, he suggested the result of socialist practice as 'a new bondage', and that 'all the economic weather signs point in the direction of diminishing freedom.'[19]

Solzhenitsyn's portrait of the Soviet bureaucracy in *The First Circle* hardly supports Weber's theory. The bureaucracy functions openly through fear and terror; the officials are appointed not through technical competence but rather for their ideological servility. At the apex of the pyramid stands Joseph Stalin, and below the 'little Stalins' in the secret police, judiciary and Party, mediocrities servile to their superiors and bullying to their subordinates. Stalin's bureaucracy, far from solving the basic problems of Soviet industrialisation — low productivity of labour, agricultural stagnation, technological backwardness — or embodying norms of efficiency and stable administration hinges on oppression, ignorance and fear. Bureaucracy, which has penetrated into every corner of Soviet society, is depicted by Solzhenitsyn as a dehumanising force in which man is turned into an object to be manipulated at will. In the labour camps the bureaucratic organisation of work is shown to be both inefficient and corrupting, while in *The First Circle*, among intellectuals, work is transformed from the expression of creativity into a means to their freedom. Here the sense of alienation is acute. Work is devoted to the potential decoding of messages, but from Stalin down to Yakanov relationships are bureaucratically organised with little hope of genuine communication. Solzhenitsyn's achievement is not that he shows how men retain their humanity within the most inhuman, degrading situations, but rather his portrait of the nexus of fear which links major and minor bureaucrats, free men and prisoners indissolubly together. The prison bureaucrats *rely* on the 'goodwill' of the prisoners for their very survival: thus Yakanov, with bitter memories of his six years in prison during the 1930s, must somehow produce the telephone scrambler for Stalin if he is to survive as the oppressor of others. At the top of his 'profession', wielding absolute power, enjoying a high salary and an 'affluent' life-style, Yakanov remains terrified. For his existence depends not on the technical competence of his bureaucratic role but on the whims of one man, Joseph Stalin. Solzhenitsyn's masterly portrait of Stalin is the centre of gravity of the whole novel: the fate of so many of the novel's characters hinges on this ageing dictator.

As we have already seen, Nerzhin has rejected Stalin's pretensions to greatness, his writings dismissed as simply 'crude and stupid', compounded of 'errors', and 'distortions'. For Rubin, however, Stalin is the 'cleverest' man in the world, beyond all criticism, and he angrily tells Nerzhin not to meddle 'in matters outside [his] competence'. But in the important discussion on dialectics with the cynical Sologdin (in Chapter 60) Rubin the 'Marxist' is easily confused by Sologdin's scepticism and echoes the platitudes and dogma of Stalin's writings. Stalin himself is shown as possessing the most primitive understanding of Marxist dialectics. He is working on a study of linguistics and Solzhenitsyn brings out with remarkable clarity its fundamentally non-dialectical character. Stalin's pamphlet, 'Marxism and Linguistics', the product of his 'mature years', is in fact a complete negation of Marxism, yet like all Stalin's writings quickly became essential reading for the Communist Party faithful, printed in vast quantities and translated into virtually every language. The pamphlet purports to show that language, rather than constituting part of either the 'base' or 'superstructure' of society, is independent of both; it is, furthermore, not class based but national in character, wholly free of class influence. What Stalin's pamphlet makes clear is that the discussion of language forms part of a much broader revision of Marxist theory in which the concepts of contradiction, conflict and qualitative change no longer apply:

It should be said in general for the benefit of comrades who have an infatuation for such explosions that the law of transition from an old quality to a new by means of an explosion is inapplicable not only to the history of languages: It is not always applicable to some other social phenomena of a basal or superstructural character. It is compulsory for a society divided into hostile classes. But it is not compulsory for a society which has no hostile classes.

Stalin is simply rejecting the Marxist theory of society in favour of a largely *consensus* model in which nationalism, the family, Party and the cult of the Proletariat function as integrating forces. The pamphlet represents the summation of Stalin's *anti-Marxism* his profoundly conservative ideology. Inside Mavrino are scholars whose knowledge and understanding exceed Stalin's simple and limited intelligence. He dwells on his own mediocrity: 'If only Kant or Spinoza were still alive, or anyone of that calibre, even if they were bourgeois . . . Should he ring up Beria, perhaps? Useless. Beria knew nothing about philosophy.' (p. 124) In sharp contrast are the Old Bolshevik scholars whose books now line Stalin's study, 'upstarts with no roots in the country and nothing constructive to offer' (p. 145), the majority murdered on Stalin's orders yet through their work a painful reminder of his own inadequacies.[20]

The essence of Solzhenitsyn's depiction of Stalin lies in the contrast he draws between Stalin and Lenin on basic political issues. Unlike Lenin, Stalin is shown to hold the masses in great mistrust; they must be ruled by an iron hand. When *Pravda* greets his birthday with columns of sycophantic praise, other pages report pilfering, sabotage, corruption, and Stalin reflects that there is 'still a lot wrong with the people'. Solzhenitsyn captures Stalin's snobbery in the dictator's reflection that a book attacking Tito was by an author 'with an aristocratic name' (p. 114). As for socialist egalitarianism, Stalin congratulates himself on realistically rejecting Lenin's remark that with socialism 'cooks should be able to run the country', in favour of functional inequality:

A cook is a cook and his job is to get the dinner ready, whereas telling other people what to do is a highly skilled business . . . done by specially trained personnel . . . toughened by years of experience, while in turn the control of this personnel could be entrusted to one pair of hands — the practised hands of the Leader. (p. 121).

Stalin can neither trust the masses, nor intellectuals, bureaucrats
or soldiers. Only one man had he trusted — Hitler. Here was
someone cast in his own likeness, for Stalin 'had learned to be
wariest of people who were indifferent to worldly goods'
(p. 132). Even when warned by Churchill, Stalin had refused to
believe in Hitler's projected attack on Russia. After that it was
clearly difficult to trust anyone again.

Solzhenitsyn lays bare the profoundly anti-democratic,
unprincipled, élitest, chauvinistic character of Stalinism. He
draws particular attention to the religious element. Brought up
in a church school the influence remained to the end of Stalin's
life, especially in the quasi-religious mode of expressing
'Marxist' ideas; now, frequently photographed with the
Patriarch of the Russian Church, 'he had been gratified at being
mentioned in the church's prayers as the "Leader Elect of
God", and this was why he had maintained the cathedral and
monastry at Zagorsk from Kremlin funds' (p. 114). This is a
portrait not of a man in 'a tired, overworked mood' (Lukács),
but of the essence, striking at the heart of Stalin and Stalinism,
of bureaucratic domination.

IV

It has been argued so far that *The First Circle* forms a coherent
expression of the disparate and contradictory ideas and values
of the post-Stalin dissident intelligentsia. As was suggested in
Chapter 8, the immediate post-Stalin years were a time for
evaluating the past: Khrushchev's revelations had raised hopes
among the liberal intelligentsia and generated the kind of
questions which only honest research could answer. Historians
such as Roy Medvedev gained partial access to previously
forbidden archives; many spheres of Soviet life and culture were
opened to investigation and critical comment for the first time.
Much of this work, of course, formed part of a legitimate
debunking of the Stalin myth and to this end some of the
results were officially published — although with the eclipse of
Khrushchev the greater percentage found publication either in
samizat or abroad. Solzhenitsyn, then, was writing during a
period of serious crisis for the Stalinist system. His unique
experiences, combined with his rejection of Marxism, posed
questions essentially historical in nature: what was the meaning
of the past thirty years, the suffering and the terror? There were

few honest historians ready to supply the answers. Millions of innocent Russians, condemned by a now discredited political criminal, could so easily disappear from history and literature, forgotten as the 'victims of socialist illegality', 'black spots' on the march to Communist society. Nerzhin's 'secret history' fulfils this need in fictional form, but during the late 1950s it became obvious that the task of grasping the full implications of the past must fall, not to a bureaucratically controlled history, but to literature. Thus although the time-span in the novels is relatively short, Solzhenitsyn evokes a vivid historical dimension through the rich and varied experiences of his many fictional characters, experiences given added depth and richness through his 'polyphonic' method of composition.

As Solzhenitsyn's novels are profoundly historical so, too, are they overwhelmingly autobiographical. It is doubtful if Solzhenitsyn has 'invented' a single character, event or experience. Literary forms, of course, are not given, but flow from a complex relation between the writer's material and the task he sets himself. Superficially Solzhenitsyn appears to revive the nineteenth-century realist mode, but he departs from this in two important ways. His realism is pre-eminently *factual* and thus specifically historical; there are few contrivances of plot or character and the endings are neither apocalyptic nor do they tie the fictional threads neatly together but remain 'open' and deliberately ambiguous. And secondly, his 'problematic heroes', the means whereby an entire historical epoch is recovered, have totally rejected society. They thus exist as 'marginal' or 'superfluous' men, their normal lives broken from the beginning, forced to live apart rather than in society. These are the two significant formal structures of Solzhenitsyn's fiction which together with the substantive structures, reappear in his second major novel.

Cancer Ward is set two years after Stalin's death in a provincial cancer clinic far from Moscow. It is a period of the first 'thaw' when some political prisoners were freed and the draconian censorship of literature slightly relaxed. In short 'a troubled period' (Lukács), when Stalin's heirs were struggling to come to terms with his legacy. The novel's dramatic structure reflects this crisis through the sharp ideological conflicts which occur between the different members of the cancer hospital. *The First Circle* had shown Solzhenitsyn as pre-eminently a novelist of ideas conveyed not abstractly but historically. The richness and substantiality of character within the novel flows directly from this groundwork of ideas; and equally, the richly realised human relationships, the shades and subtleties of character are built upon the conflict of ideas and values. In *Cancer Ward* Solzhenitsyn probes more deeply into relations of love and sex than in *The First Circle*, where the relations of men and women are rather the tragic affirmation of fundamental values than of physical consummation. Given the setting it could hardly be otherwise: although drawn with great feeling and sympathy, the relations of Nadya and Nerzhin, Datomie Makarygin and Volodin, Clara Makarygin and Doronin seem reserved and cool, lacking in that substantiality of character with which Solzhenitsyn invests the Mavrino prisoners, both captors and bureaucrats.

In *Cancer Ward* Solzhenitsyn has dramatised more starkly than in *The First Circle* two extreme positions (Stalinist and Oppositionist), and the novel's two main characters, Rusanov and Kostoglotov, embody these two positions in a wholly uncompromising way. Oleg Kostoglotov is the book's 'problematic hero' who, like Solzhenitsyn, experienced the rigours of Stalin's labour camps to be condemned to perpetual exile in Kazakhstan. Kostoglotov is not, as Nerzhin, an intellectual in the obvious sense but he shares the same hatred of injustice and tyranny and remains implacably hostile to the Stalinist regime. In the army Kostoglotov had objected to the differential treatment of officers and men, especially their segregation during meal times and the various privileges officers enjoyed. Kostoglotov has a plebeian hostility to privilege far more sharply expressed than Nerzhin.

In contrast is the character of Rusanov, the K.G.B. agent, a petty and cowardly bureaucrat whose police career was launched during the purge years with the denunciation of a close friend as a counter-revolutionary. In *The First Circle*, Solzhenitsyn had created an intelligent and sincere Stalinist, Rubin, but here he sketches a wholly repulsive Stalinist bureaucrat, a man who for twenty years has worked in 'personal records administration' (euphemism for secret police), who dreams of reintroducing public executions as a deterrent against speculators and who looks back with nostalgia to the thirties, when 'the social atmosphere was . . . cleansed', as the 'clever-dick' intellectuals were 'shut up' while men of 'principle' walked with 'dignity'.[21] Rusanov is a bureaucrat in the same mould as Drozdov (*Not by Bread Alone*) and the Public Prosecutor Globov (*The Trial Begins*), one of Solzhenitsyn's finest creations embodying every major feature of Stalinist ideology. A self-confessed representative of the working class and advocate of socialism, Rusanov is shown as a bigoted nationalist (a cancer victim, Federau, cannot be a member of the Communist Party because he is a German living in Russia), stupidly dogmatic ('there are questions on which a definite opinion has been established and they are no longer open to discussion' [p. 150]) and contemptuous of the working class ('Gradually with the years, he and Kapitolina Matveyevna developed an aversion to teeming human beings, to jostling crowds, finding it increasingly unbearable to travel on public transport, wary of those like the badly dressed who clearly lacked "a proper sense of responsibility".' [pp. 212–13]). Here is the typical anti-democratic, élitist mentality, a microcosm of the entire bureaucratic structure. Like his beloved chief, Rusanov has his own isolated office guarded by a double set of doors through which the victims are discreetly ushered.

Rusanov's mentality is that of those brought to power by Stalin and sustained through totalitarian politics as a deeply conservative stratum in Soviet society. Status rather than class conscious, Rusanov exhibits all the characteristics of 'commodity fetishism', an overriding passion for things and objects. After forty, he believes a man's flat provides a precise index of his value to society and, in conversation with the naive, admiring peasant, Federau, Rusanov dwells at length on the details of the exact price of his furniture, the quality of the floor and wall tiles, the structure of the bathroom with its shower and towel rail, not 'mere trifles' but sheer necessities of daily life, for 'a man's life had to be good and pleasant to give him the right kind of consciousness.' (p. 402) When his wife visits him they talk only of 'things', his prospects for the 'personal' pensions granted to high officials (his one remaining major ambition) and the changes to their flat while he is in hospital, the painting of his room, new pipes in the bathroom, etc. Between them and their daughter, Aviette, exists an indissoluble bond of status anxiety, commodity consciousness and concern with money as the visible sign of social achievement. For Aviette, 'a complete revolution' in the Soviet way of life is not only more fridges and washing machines but 'lobbies made out of plate glass . . . just like the Americans' and glass lampshades. Rusanov refuses, *on principle* to tip workers who repair or decorate his flat, for, paid a proper salary (with bonuses) he has never asked for the extra payments demanded by 'unscrupulous workers' and 'money grubbers' (pp. 196—7).

Rusanov's fear and hatred of the working class reflects his bureaucratic, parasitical function in the system of terror and administration of people which he sees as necessary and just. He lives his life apart from the masses whom he judges as ignorant, dirty and politically gullible. It is thus essential that the news is subtly camouflaged. For him literature is journalism, the newspapers his bible, written in code which only an initiated and privileged minority can fully comprehend. Although his life has been devoted to sending thousands of innocent victims to their deaths in the labour camps, Rusanov prefers not to discuss death: 'We musn't even remind anyone of it.' (p. 132) His values are conventional and bureaucratic, opposed to the ideals of revolutionary socialism and the forging of genuine human relations. For him human reciprocity rests on a hierarchy of scarce ability, status and wealth in which inequality functions as the essential spur for effort, efficiency and initiative. When Rusanov attempts to impose these rigid bureaucratic norms on the unstructured community of cancer patients he meets with a profound shock.

At the start of the novel Rusanov and Kostoglotov develop an immediate dislike of each other. When the bureaucrat demands that the electric light be extinguished, Kostoglotov tells him that there are others in the ward. Rusanov is furious: 'Why should you take it upon yourself to decide for everyone? There are different sorts of patients here and distinctions have to be made . . .' Distinctions there will be, replies Kostoglotov, 'They'll write you an obituary: Party member since the year dot. As for us, they'll just carry us out feet first.' (pp. 29—30) This early exchange sets the pattern for the later, more abrasive discussions on Soviet history, philosophy and culture; it is a conflict between two entirely opposed worlds, Rusanov as the defender of privilege and Kostoglotov with his pristine, 'plebeian' hatred of inequality. When Rusanov defends a corrupt government official, an embezzler, as an example of

bourgeois survivals in the Soviet Union, Kostoglotov explodes:
for him it is a simple matter of human greed — greedy people
existed before the Revolution, they will exist after it. He rejects
the crude Stalinist dogma which elevated every example of
selfish social activity to the status of 'cultural survival',
anachronisms from a bygone age. To justify any course of
activity in terms of 'social origins' is not Marxism, he retorts,
but 'racism'. When Kostoglotov shouts at Rusanov, 'Why do
you keep cackling on about social origins like a witch doctor?
You know what they used to say in the twenties? "Show us
your calluses! Why are your hands so white and puffy?" Now
that *was* Marxism!' (p. 436), he speaks with the authentic voice
of the working masses and expresses a profound opposition to
the bureaucratic stratum which formally acts in their name. Of
course, Kostoglotov's attack on Rusanov is not a Marxist
criticism, neither does it have Nerzhin's intellectual rigour, but
it remains implacably hostile to parasitic privilege.
Kostoglotov's assertion of a 'pure form' of proletarianism (while
sociologically false) is directed against a bureaucracy which
from its inception was founded upon and recruited from the
middle classes. When someone points out that 'socialism
provides for differentiation in the wage-structure', Kostoglotov
angrily dismisses such an argument: 'You think that while we're
working towards communism the privileges some have over
others ought to be increased, do you? You mean that to
become equal we must first become unequal, is that right? You
call that dialectics, do you?' (p. 438)

It is now that Shulubin, the old Bolshevik whose life had
been warped by his willingness to compromise, raises the
question of Lenin's 'April Theses', quoting the section which
demands that a socialist economy reward its officials with a
salary 'no higher than the average pay of a good worker'.
Rusanov is appalled: 'Imagine paying the health service director
and the floor-scrubber the same rate! Couldn't he think of
anything cleverer than that? There was absolutely nothing to be
said.' (pp. 439—40)

Kostoglotov remains adamant: Shulubin's interjection merely
provides intellectual substance to his pristine sense of equality.
He refuses to accept the argument advanced by another patient
that criticism of the Soviet state must be tempered by the fact
that it has existed a mere forty years. Kostoglotov retorts, 'I'll

always be younger than this society. What do you expect me to do, keep silent all my life?' (p. 438)

Kostoglotov is repeatedly told that he must be reasonable, that he should not expect too much from the present difficult situation, that things will improve and socialism be vindicated. But he is not prepared to be reasonable: a later conversation with Shulubin shows how this all or nothing attitude is central to his character. Unlike Kostoglotov, Shulubin always knew how to be reasonable, he understood the virtues of silence during the 1930s. Like others he realised that the purge trials were phony and aimed solely at consolidating Stalin's authority within the bureaucratic state. But in the interests of self-preservation he stifled all criticism. The intellectual, Shulubin, contrasts sharply with Kostoglotov in their different responses to totalitarian politics. We wanted to live, says Shulubin, 'we all applauded as one man' Stalin's anti-socialist blood bath: 'I kept silent for twenty-five years . . . First I kept silent for my wife's sake, then for my children's sake, then for the sake of my own sinful body.' (p. 469) Only the possibility of death has loosened his tongue; yet even in the hospital he talks openly only to Kostoglotov. An honest scientist, a lecturer in the Moscow agricultural academy, Shulubin suffered the fate of so many thousands of Soviet intellectuals who, confessing their 'mistakes', withdrew from the harsh world of politics into the realm of harmless scholarship, 'the study of pure biology'. One of the small percentage to survive the purge years, Shulubin was steadily demoted until the final humiliation when, as a provincial librarian, he obeyed the Party command to destroy 'dangerous books' — genetics, left-wing aesthetics, ethics, cybernetics.

The Stalinist degeneration of the 1917 Revolution, its high ideals, is expressed with great force in Solzhenitsyn's portrait of the pitiable Shulubin. Critics and writers such as Lukács and Ehrenburg share the same moral universe as Shulubin (and Radovic) as time-serving intellectuals, their function to legitimise totalitarianism and through their published work justify the necessity for 'iron government' and the annihilation of the Bolshevik Party and revolutionary socialism. Shulubin's conversations with Kostoglotov which pose such awkward questions must have been one of the main reasons for the Soviet ban on *Cancer Ward*, for the defenders of the Stalin regime did not disappear with the death of Stalin.

Shulubin's life is in ruins, empty, without meaning. His children are indifferent to his fate. He recalls 1917 when, scorning danger to his life, he was 'happy to give [it] for world revolution'. Now he asks: what happened to those glorious ideals, how was it that genuine revolutionary *praxis* turned into abject surrender and compromise? It is clear that Shulubin does not understand what happened, only that it did and that he compromised. In his discussions with Kostoglotov the question of ethical socialism is raised precisely as a condemnation not an understanding of Stalinism. The Old Bolshevik Shulubin cites not Marx, Lenin or Trotsky as his intellectual mentors but the religious mystic — philosopher Vladimir Soloviev, the populist nineteenth-century socialist Mikhailovsky and the anarchist Prince Peter Kropotkin. All three thinkers were implacably anti-Marxist: the link between them is the belief that a good society is one based, not on the socialisation of production but on universal ethical premises. This turning to idealistic ethics and the rejection of a Marxist explanation for Stalinism is common to *The First Circle* and *Cancer Ward*: whether ethical socialism, as distinct from the scientific socialism of Marx and Engels, represents Solzhenitsyn's own point of view is irrelevant, for the point is rather its function within the novels, the fact that the arguments are refuted *only* by bureaucrats (Rusanov) and dogmatists (Rubin). Ethical socialism and the notion of an autonomous ethic in general act as significant structures within Solzhenitsyn's fiction in the clear absence of a Marxist analysis of Stalinism; and more crucially, its universal moral ideals become the medium through which the Stalinist distortion of socialism is criticised. It is in this double sense that this structure has to be understood.

It is clear, too, that Shulubin's charge that Kostoglotov himself must have compromised with Stalinism, his character and ideals corrupted but for his 'good fortune', is false: for Kostoglotov's character, like Nerzhin's, is the antithesis of the compromising Shulubin. In the army, Solzhenitsyn writes, Kostoglotov 'was devoted to democracy' (p. 240), with a fierce commitment to egalitarian and humanistic ideals. At one point Kostoglotov says, 'suspect everything', a critical sentiment which induces Rusanov to cry, 'But that's nothing to do with our way of life.' The bureaucratic Rusanov, of course, exists because of hierarchical authority and he thus opposes Kostoglotov's apparent scepticism: but Kostoglotov's

questioning of authority springs from his plebeian opposition to
the *given*, received opinion, the 'idols of the market place'. He
repeatedly argues that if he knows what is happening to him
then he may act, even though the situation may well be
hopeless.

Kostoglotov's relations with the nurse Zoya and the hospital
doctor Vera, reflect these values. He has formed an easy-going
relationship with the 'cuddly' Zoya, whose world is in no sense
problematical, her values straightforwardly conventional. While
she likes Kostoglotov she rather doubts her suitability for exile
'in perpetuity'. His desire for her is largely physical, and his
basic aim, to make love in the doctors' room, is constantly
frustrated by Zoya's refusal, so their relationship remains both
generally and sexually unsatisfactory. The basis of this failure
lies in the conflict of values which characterises their
relationship from the beginning. It is clear, for example, that
Zoya, given her values and political socialisation, cannot
genuinely comprehend Kostoglotov's experiences. She knows he
has been exiled, but her greatest fear is not for the supposed
political illegality of his actions but rather that he was 'a real
criminal', a member of 'a gang'. When Kostoglotov tells her that
he was arrested simply for criticising 'him' (Stalin) she is
relieved 'that he'd never lured anyone into dark backstreets and
murdered him.' In this brief exchange Solzhenitsyn confronts
two diametrically opposed values, of conformism and rebellion.
Totalitarianism of any kind rests ultimately in some form of
general consent: the attitude which accepts authority as
legitimate simply because it is there will condone repressive acts
on the grounds that the authorities 'had sound grounds for
action'. Zoya asks Kostoglotov: 'What did you do? Why
criticise? Why be dissatisfied?' It is an attitude which practically
supports the Rusanov's of the world, a passive acquiescence in
bureaucratic rule, one antithetical to Kostoglotov's values and
his life. Thus when Zoya, reacting to Kostoglotov's admiring
attentions, begins singing songs from a popular film which
romanticises the lives of professional criminals in the labour
camps, Kostoglotov angrily rejects her naive assertion that his
life was no different from theirs: 'I hate them . . . they're
predators, parasites, they live off other people.' (p. 189)

Finally, when Kostoglotov has grown tired of Zoya's 'playing
at love', their relationship ends with no regrets on either side.

But Kostoglotov's feelings for Vera are wholly different; their relationship is far deeper and potentially more permanent because it is not solely physical. In their discussion on marriage the question of life's purpose is again posed, a question which dominates the whole novel. What is the basis of relations between men and women? Vera and Kostoglotov agree that it does not lie in sexual efficiency, and criticising 'a scientific' manual on sexual happiness Kostoglotov argues against a materialism which reduces all human experience to questions of percentages and categories, a dehumanised science of life which 'destroys everything human on earth. If you give in to it, if you accept it and everything it entails . . .' (pp. 361–2) Here, in Kostoglotov's affirmation of humanism, lies one of the most significant structures in *Cancer Ward*, a humanism opposed to mere 'objective science', that a science which is not informed and guided by the values of a genuine human community must end by treating humans as objects. This explains why Kostoglotov, 'a progressive thinker' compared with Rusanov, believes in the curative power of folk medicine and why the geologist Vadim, heartily pro-Stalinist and a believer in 'science as such', is portrayed as lacking in humanity. Thus when Shulubin asks Vadim, why study science, and he replies because it is interesting, Shulubin retorts that the making of money, acquiring business is also 'interesting' and in that sense 'science becomes no different from the ordinary run of selfish, thoroughly unethical occupations' (p. 408). At once Vadim asserts that the function of science is to create 'material' not 'ethical' values. Counterposed here are the values of 'bureaucratic efficiency' (in practice, bureaucratic inefficiency) and social utility as defined by the ruling élite, and the genuine values of human community. The question of ethical socialism arises within the context of a bureaucratic deformation of revolution which denies the very basis of socialism, the participation of the masses in socialist economy and their positive role in shaping and formulating policy. For bureaucracy can exist only as a socially administrative stratum elevated above the masses, a hierarchy of permanent officials owing allegiance to the 'machine' and the 'boss'. Bureaucracy substitutes itself for mass action vigorously imposing its norms on a population which must accept a passive role.

The conflict between the values of bureaucracy and human

community are especially brought out in the important discussion on sincerity in literature. Aviette, Rusanov's daughter, is asked if she thinks that sincerity is essential for the creation of good literature. Like a sound Stalinist she replies that sincerity 'can't be the chief criterion for judging a book' since the writer might well express, quite sincerely, 'alien' attitudes that could become socially dangerous and militate against a 'truthful presentation of life'. Truth, Aviette asserts, is not equivalent to the negative aspects of Soviet society; truth does not have to be 'harsh', but on the contrary, is 'radiant, uplifting, optimistic'. Literature must avoid too much gloom, for the ordinary person wants life 'decorated and embellished' (p. 310). Of course, Solzhenitsyn's portrait is a caricature, but Aviette's defence of socialist realism was real enough in the world of Stalin, Zhdanov and the bureaucratisation of literature. It is far easier to describe the existing situation, she argues, than to depict the future, for truth *is* not what is but what *must be* — the writer's duty is not to dwell on present shortcomings but the 'wonderful tomorrow' (pp. 311—12).

But for the inmates of the cancer ward the wonderful tomorrow is death or permanent disability. When Kostoglotov leaves to begin his exile he thinks of Vera. He does not see her: he knows he has nothing to offer. This tragic resolution flows, not simply from his cancer, but from his uncompromising opposition to the Soviet bureaucracy, his values which have effectively isolated him from the kind of human community in which genuine lasting human relationships are possible. The cancer may not have killed him but it seems to have destroyed him. The disease has brought Kostoglotov from exile to a community of free men in the cancer hospital but, as in *The First Circle*, the women are not part of that community. Kostoglotov and Vera can enjoy only a spiritual kinship in which feelings must remain abstract and the relationship unconsummated.

Unlike the 'critical' novels of Dudintsev and Ehrenburg, Solzhenitsyn's tragic affirmations provide coherence to the whole text. The failure of thought to eventuate in action — indeed, to even contemplate action — dominates both novels to the extent that the man—woman relation is never adequately realised. Perhaps in this lies Solzhenitsyn's major weakness as a novelist for he fails to portray genuine human passion and the women rarely rise as characters in their own right above the men. Nerzhin, for example, is depicted as more progressive in his attitudes than Rubin or Sologdin but his relationship with Nadya must remain austere.[22] It is in this important sense that comparisons with Tolstoy seem inappropriate. The absence within the novels of an identifiable community outside the prisons and hospitals means isolation for those individuals who resolutely affirm the inviolability of their values. Such integrity must necessarily lead, in the absence of potential action, to a heightened subjectivity, the affirmation of self at the expense of community. Solzhenitsyn's heroes are ultimately defeated by history, by living at a time when there seems no hope for those fundamental changes in Soviet society so necessary for the realisation of their values.

V

Since the defeat of the Left Opposition in the 1920s and the physical elimination of all forms of opposition to Stalin's totalitarian regime in the thirties, a coherent political alternative to Stalinism has never developed in the Soviet Union. The 1917 October Revolution created the foundations of the first workers' state, the socialised property relations which have survived the barbarities and bureaucratic deformation of the Stalin era. At no point in Soviet history has the working class formed the dominant class as Marx and Lenin envisaged, and since the late twenties a bureaucratic caste has substituted itself for the dictatorship of the proletariat. The resulting lack of hegemony has produced a socially conformist, state-controlled literature. During the twenties the absence of hegemony in a society which was not yet dominated by a privileged bureaucracy found its expression in the revival within the novel form of the 'superfluous man', the problematic hero in conflict with the new, emerging socialist society. Once society was subjugated by bureaucracy the novel eliminated virtually all problematic elements — the first person narrative, for example, favoured by 'superfluous men' disappears as a distinctive literary mode in socialist realism. Solzhenitsyn presents the 'superfluous man' theme some thirty years later but with one significant difference. Whereas Olesha, Fedin and Leonov portrayed their heroes as pre-revolutionary intellectuals unhappy with Bolshevism and unable to adjust to socialism,

Solzhenitsyn's heroes are Soviet through and through. Born
after 1917 they accept the workers' state, they revere Lenin and
his ideals, but reject bureaucratic domination. Here surely lies
the significance of Solzhenitsyn's novels, that they break
through the limits prescribed by the totalitarian system to assail
it from *without*. Solzhenitsyn's vision, expressed through an
autobiographical, factual realism, vividly captures the tragic
consequences of the October Revolution through the lives of his
many characters. Solzhenitsyn's fiction has been decisively
shaped by 1917: revolution is its theme. But he is not, of
course, a revolutionary writer, in any sense, rather a profoundly
conservative one for whom the novel chronicles the unresolved
and tragic conflict between the individual and society. His heroes
are very different from those of nineteenth-century realism who,
through compromise, luck, effort were integrated into society.
For Solzhenitsyn's heroes no such integration is possible: to
affirm freedom is to live in isolation. The tragic vision demands
an uncompromising standpoint: there is no hope for the kind of
praxis which can lead out of the stagnation, corruption and
horror of the Stalinist system. It is in this sense that
Goldmann's argument that the tragic vision is unhistorical has
relevance: 'Refusal, in the radical and absolute form which it
assumes in tragic thought, has only one dimension in time: the
present.'[23] But it is precisely within the novel form that the
tragic vision expresses itself historically (and here the difference
with drama is obvious), for the genuine novelist has no duty to
grasp the future, only the *present as history*.

In the absence of such hope Solzhenitsyn has turned to the
historical novel and fate of modern Russia. This unfinished
work cannot be judged here, but in turning away from
contemporary Russia he leaves unanswered the questions posed
by Nerzhin and Kostoglotov. What is to be done? To reject
Marxism, Lenin and socialism and advocate the restoration of
capitalism in the Soviet Union as Solzhenitsyn suggests in *The
Gulag Archipelago* is no answer to the novels. In his review of
The Gulag Archipelago Roy Medvedev writes that

> it is not only the most honest and courageous men of their
> time who become revolutionaries. A revolution especially
> during its ascent, attracts people who are resentful, vain,
> ambitious, self-seeking, men of cold hearts and unclean

hands, as well as many stupid and obtuse fanatics capable of anything. But this is no reason to condemn every revolution and every revolutionary.[24]

It is the strength of Solzhenitsyn that his two great novels have affirmed this undoubted truth.

Conclusion: *Praxis* and the Novel Form

It has been the central argument of this book that the author as creator lives within his work through values and *praxis*, and that a sociological theory of the novel form requires the author's presence. In the work of Lukács and Goldmann and modern structuralism, semiology and positivism, the writer has disappeared, his fiction the result of impersonal socio-economic forces or its significance made dependent entirely on internal linguistic and literary criteria. In contrast Part Two of this study has attempted to show how the writer transmutes his specific and social values into significant literary structures through his *praxis* as a member of certain social groups; the writer achieves in his work a coherent expression of the everyday, taken-for-granted experiences of the group or groups.

This relation is not mechanical. The novel form is partly autonomous and not reducible entirely to economic, political, and social structure. It is not simply that the novel strives to capture the plenitude of human experience, its ambiguity and openness, but actually depicts man's struggle to assimilate the social, historical and natural world to his human purposes. This is *praxis* within the novel form itself which, mediated through nineteenth-century realism and individualistic philosophy, took the form of a problematic hero asserting his ambitions, will or values within a knowable, human and profoundly *historical* world.* But towards the end of the nineteenth century this sense of *praxis* within the novel becomes highly problematical. The rise of working-class movements and socialist ideology pose a challenge to bourgeois hegemony, but the challenge is hollow. In a period when proletarian hegemony has yet to penetrate society, the realist novel, however sincere the author, is rarely

---

*The great strength of the realist novel lay in its grasp of the present as history, society as a constantly evolving totality and man as both product and producer of *his* world striving to assert his freedom and autonomy.

able to grasp the significance of working-class politics and socialism; conflict is resolved by a return to stasis, reconciliation or death. As for the search for a 'democratic art' through which to render working-class life and struggle this yields a non-problematic and deterministic literary structure.

All these problems are brought out in those novels portraying revolutionary movements as well as those informed by revolutionary ideas or the threat of revolution. In George Eliot and Mrs Gaskell the problematical becomes non-problematical and their novels end with class conflict and potential revolution resolved through altruistic ideology and fortuitous death. When the realist novel becomes 'future oriented', politically committed (Chernyshevsky, Turgenev, London, Gorky), realism degenerates into propagandistic ideology, experience is again rendered non-problematical. This closed form similarly informs the reified world of Gissing and Zamyatin, and the defeated, revolutionary world of Serge and Koestler. At issue here is the loss of the historical dimension, the sense of both society as history and man as an active semi-autonomous agent. When the traditions of nineteenth-century realism are carried over, uncritically, into future oriented fiction (especially socialist realism) the result is a closed, deterministic, unfree literary structure; history and *praxis* are simultaneously eliminated.

Solzhenitsyn's fiction is in sharp contrast, remaining open and generous to the ambiguity and diverse richness of human experience, refusing to reconcile the problematic hero with a society which strives to deny his freedom and autonomy. Solzhenitsyn provides no final events to close his novels, no tying up of loose ends, nothing is fixed at the end: there is a future, but it remains deeply *problematiçal.* In general the closed form seems coeval with bourgeois hegemony (Balzac, Dickens, Mrs Gaskell, George Eliot), and the open with its decline or absence of hegemony (Flaubert's *Sentimental Education*, the 'superfluous man' fiction of Turgenev, Dostoevsky, Fedin, Olesha and, of course, Bely, Solzhenitsyn, Sinyavsky).[1] Modernism is precisely this awareness by the novelist that while experience necessitates a pattern and structure within fiction (so that it becomes art) it cannot be contained totally, but remains elusive, ambiguous and expansive. It is in these senses that Solzhenitsyn is a *modern* novelist, building on the strengths of nineteenth-century realism within a profoundly problematic universe. Solzhenitsyn's novels recapture the dialectical tension between freedom and determinism lost in the ahistorical, ideologically committed fiction of Gorky, London, Zamyatin, Serge and Koestler. The tragic vision finds expression within the novel form through an open structure which situates man as both an historically determined and yet free agent. The paradox is obvious: revolutionary writers portray revolutionary aspirations and revolutionary practice through a conservative form and content; the revolutionary dynamic of realism and modernism is captured by the conservative Solzhenitsyn. It bears repeating that literature is not ideology or weapon in the class struggle. Of course, some novels, by their powerful presentation of capitalist inequalities and practices, help to win converts to the socialist movement, but this documentary function is not what is meant by *praxis* within the novel. *Praxis* refers to the dialectical quality of fiction, the complex structure which affirms man's freedom within a social — historical nexus that seems to deny him that freedom.

This book has stressed the *historical* dimension of the novel, and the way in which the modern novel loses the sense of the present as history. The point here is not that *all* fiction should be historical in this sense, only that those novels which have revolution as their theme cannot eliminate the profoundly historical nature of revolutionary practice and ideas as they develop from a particular economic and political situation. Revolutionary ideas and practice have meaning only in terms of history, of the past, the present and the future. Revolutions are not episodes but violent transformations of power from one class to another. The novel of revolutionary ideas and organisation, of success and failure, must be judged, therefore, in terms of history.

The present as history, openness, a balance between freedom and determinism, problematic hero and community, all these seem necessary constituents of novels which portray revolution and working-class politics. As has been argued the failure of overtly socialist and revolutionary novels to fuse these various elements into a coherent structure is partly the consequence of a lack of working-class hegemony in capitalist and socialist societies. The individual is sacrificed to historical laws, trends and the future. Like Gorky's *Mother*, Paul Nizan's *Antoine Bloyé* (1933) is that rare novel which combines Marxism with

literature. A loyal member of the French Communist Party
until the Nazi-Soviet pact (1939), who died at Dunkirk in 1940,
Nizan attempted to portray the empty sterile life of a railway
engineer born into the working class, from his birth in the
1860s to his death in the 1920s. As with Gissing, Nizan portrays
a social world which is oppressive and alien, the passive hero
merely the product of an external environment, his existence
faithfully mirroring the curve of capitalist development, a life
measured by the only traces left at its end — the pay slips. It is a
life in which 'nothing happens' and 'nothing more can happen',
during which 'the years mounted up, one on top of another,
and the cumulation had gone on in silence, unobserved.'[2]
Bloyé's 'solid, modest bourgeois life' is empty, his work serving
to hide his own inactivity, his lack of substance. Nizan's 'hero'
is the 'superfluous' man, non-problematical and unfree, the
pawn of vast and impersonal capitalist forces:

> Far from him, even before he was born in offices, at
> shareholders' meetings, in the parliament, in learned bodies,
> factory owners had for thirty years past been voicing their
> demands. Industry required new human material. It felt a
> growing need for men able to read a blueprint, to supervise
> the making of a part, to carry out orders issued from above,
> to think up those modest projects and inventions of detail
> that foster industrial progress and increase production.[3]

This is Nizan, the author, interposing between the reader and
the fictional world, explicitly stating the novel's political
message. Thus Bloyé's reflection during a demonstration of
striking railway workers that 'these unimportant men possessed
the strength, the friendship, and the hope that he was
denied . . . The truth of life was on the side of the men who
returned to their poor houses, on the side of the men who had
not "made good" '[4] emphasises the unfree, ideological structure
of this fictional form. Capitalism crushes true individuality and
man becomes part of a vast and anonymous urban mass, lonely,
isolated and alienated. Man is transformed into an object within
an increasingly collectivist capitalist society.

Antoine Bloyé (which is a finely wrought elegy on capitalist
alienation), together with the novels of Jack London, Zamyatin,
Serge and Koestler analysed in earlier chapters, seem to support
those arguments with which this book began, that the death of

the novel is identified with the decline of a liberal, capitalist free-market economy and the development of collectivist, capitalist economies and ideologies. Of course, there is much that is true in these suggestions, especially when applied to totalitarian societies such as the Soviet Union, but perhaps the more important point is not the omnipotence of capitalist economy for the specific evolution of culture but rather the absence of proletarian hegemony in societies where bourgeois domination is no longer stable but increasingly dependent on the support of working-class political parties and organisations (Social Democratic parties, Communist parties, trade unions). If there is a crisis in the novel then it must be traced not to collectivism but to the problematic nature of bourgeois hegemony and the failure of proletarian revolution in Russia and Europe. Collectivist economic and political trends exist in both capitalist and socialist societies, generating conformist norms and practices as well as a deep sense of alienation and pessimism. But collectivism in itself cannot be held responsible for a crisis in modern fiction: a collectivist, socialist economy based on the democratic participation of the broad mass of the people, the right to recall political representatives, a genuine workers' control of industry, a multiplicity of socialist political parties, free and independent trade unions, together with a democratic control of police, army and bureaucracy would produce within the institutions of civil society a variegated, open and truly human culture. The culture of a collectivist economy would, of course, not be free of conflict or tragedy, but it would be a culture in which man may pursue those purposes and ends which have given shape and meaning to the novel form. In its origins and development the novel was never simply a literary form of a specific social class; it neither corresponded to an actual class consciousness nor resonated dominant class values. For at the heart of the novel form lies man's *praxis*, his never-ending, restless quest to realise his humanity and purposes, the affirmation of his ultimate freedom.

Notes

(Place of publication is London unless otherwise specified)

CHAPTER 1

1. George Steiner, *Language and Silence* (1967) p. 104.
2. W. J. Harvey, *Character and the Novel* (1965) p. 24. And for a similar thesis, L. Trilling, *The Liberal Imagination* (1954) and George Orwell, 'Inside the Whale', *Collected Essays* (1961).
3. I. Watt, *The Rise of the Novel* (1963) p. 33.
4. Ibid., p. 87.
5. Ibid., p. 68.
6. Ibid., p. 23.
7. Ibid., p. 49.
8. A. Hauser, *A Social History of Art* (1962) III, pp. 53—63.
9. Madame de Staël, *De La Litterature* (1800).
10. G. W. F. Hegel, *Lectures on Fine Arts* (1920) IV, pp. 26—73, 123—71.
11. N. A. Dobrolyubov, *Selected Philosophical Essays* (Moscow, 1956) pp. 394—8.
12. G. V. Plekhanov, *Art and Social Life* (1953) p. 164.
13. K. Marx, *Capital* (Moscow, 1958) I, pp. 177—8.
14. K. Marx, *Grundrisse*, ed. D. McLellan (1973) pp. 164—6.
15. K. Marx, *Economic and Philosophical Manuscripts*, ed. T. B. Bottomore (1963) pp. 190—4.
16. Marx and Engels, *Literature and Art* (New York, 1947) pp. 37—40, 69—70. Cf. M. Lifshitz, *The Philosophy of Art of Karl Marx* (1973) pp. 70—1.
17. In *Readings in Russian Poetics*, ed. L. Matejka and K. Pomorska (Cambridge, Mass., 1971) pp. 60—3.
18. F. R. Leavis, 'Reply to F. W. Bateson', *Scrutiny* (1953).
19. F. R. Leavis, 'Under Which King, Bezonian', *Scrutiny*, I (1932).
20. Steiner, *Language and Silence*, pp. 368—70.
21. G. Lukács, *Studies in European Realism* (New York, 1964) ch. VI.
22. G. Lukács, *Essays on Thomas Mann* (1964).
23. Lukács, *Studies*, p. 141.
24. Ibid., p. 135.
25. Lukács, 'Dostoevsky', in *Dostoevsky* ed. R. Wellek (New Jersey, 1962).
26. Lukács, *Essays on Thomas Mann*, p. 57.
27. L. Trotsky, *On Literature and Art* (New York, 1970) p. 70.
28. C. Caudwell, *Illusion and Reality* (New York, 1967) p. 207.
29. E. Fischer, *The Necessity of Art* (1963) p. 111.

30. N. Frye, *The Critical Path: An Essay on the Social Context of Literary Criticism* (New York, 1972).
31. L. Goldmann, *Pour une Sociologie du Roman* (Paris, 1964).
32. L. Goldmann, *Marxisme et Sciences Humaines* (Paris, 1970) pp. 130—50; *The Hidden God*, ch. 1.
33. G. Lukács, *The Theory of the Novel* (1971) pp. 56—67.
34. Ibid., p. 89.
35. Goldmann, *Pour une Sociologie du Roman*, pp. 19—57.

CHAPTER 2
1. R. Williams, 'Base and Superstructure', *New Left Review*, 82 (1973) p. 8. Cf. F. Jameson, *Marxism and Form* (Princeton, N.J., 1971) ch. 5.
2. A. Gramsci, *Prison Notebooks* (1971) pp. 3—14, 77—84. See also J. Merrington, 'Theory and Practice in Gramsci's Marxism', in *The Socialist Register*, ed. J. Saville and R. Miliband (1968) pp. 161—2.
3. See the evidence in R. Williams, *The Long Revolution* (1965) ch. 5.
4. K. Marx, *Theories of Surplus Value* (1969) vol. 1, p. 285.
5. L. Trotsky, *Literature and Revolution* (New York, 1957) pp. 125—6.
6. Marx and Engels, *Literature and Art*, p. 18.
7. H. Levin, *The Gates of Horn* (New York, 1963) pp. 37—8.
8. Quoted in R. Giraud, *The Unheroic Hero* (New Jersey, 1957) p. 21.
9. Stendhal, *Le Rouge et le Noir* (1830).
10. Balzac, *Lost Illusions*, trans. H. J. Hunt (1971) pp. 647—8.
11. Quoted in Giraud, *The Unheroic Hero*, pp. 67—8.
12. Quoted in C. Grana, *Bohemian versus Bourgeois: French Society and the French Man of Letters in the Nineteenth Century* (New York, 1967) p. 101.
13. R. Williams, *Culture and Society* (1963) pp. 99—120; P. J. Keating, *The Working Classes in Victorian Fiction* (1971) ch. 9.
14. K. Tillotson, *Novels of the Eighteen-Forties* (Oxford, 1962) pp. 206—7.
15. Elizabeth Gaskell, *Mary Barton* (1970) pp. 162, 219—20 and the whole of ch. 15.
16. Ibid., pp. 241—2.
17. Ibid., pp. 435—42.
18. George Eliot, *Felix Holt, The Radical* (1965) p. 69.
19. Ibid., pp. 276—7.
20. Tragic heroes respectively of *Rudin* (1855), *On the Eve* (1859) and *Fathers and Sons* (1861).

CHAPTER 3
1. For the concept of realism developed in this chapter I have drawn on Erich Auerbach's exemplary *Mimesis: The Representation of Reality in Western Literature* (New York, 1957). See also F. W. J. Hemmings (ed.), *The Age of Realism* (1974).
2. A. Hauser, *A Social History of Art*, vol. III, p. 44.
3. Goldmann, *Pour une Sociologie du Roman*, pp. 52—3.
4. Lukács, *Studies in European Realism*, p. 119.

5. Ibid., p. 6.
6. Lukács, *Writer and Critic* (1970) p. 6.
7. Lukács, *Studies*, pp. 147—8.
8. Alain Robbe-Grillet, *Towards a New Novel* (1965) pp. 66—7.
9. Marx, *Early Writings*, p. 202.
10. K. Marx and F. Engels, *The Holy Family* (Moscow, 1956) p. 125.
11. K. Marx and F. Engels, *Selected Works* (Moscow, 1962) vol. II, p. 53.
12. L. Trotsky, *The Revolution Betrayed* (1936).
13. Marx and Engels, *Selected Works*, vol. I, p. 253.
14. Ibid., pp. 363—4
15. Marx, *Capital*, vol. III, pp. 773—4.
16. Marx, *Early Writings*, pp. 30—1.
17. Cited by H. Levin, *The Gates of Horn*, p. 33.
18. Marx, *Early Writings*, pp. 25—6.
19. Marx wrote that the 'true secret' of the Commune was as a 'working-class government, the product of the struggle of the producing against the appropriating class, the political form at last discovered under which to work out the economic emancipation of labour.' Marx and Engels, *Selected Works*, vol. I, p. 522.
20. Cited in K. Kumar (ed.), *Revolution* (1971) pp. 136—8.
21. Marx, *Grundrisse*, ed. McLellan, pp. 54—7.
22. K. Marx and F. Engels, *The German Ideology* (Moscow, 1965) pp. 430—2.
23. Trotsky, *On Literature and Art*, pp. 67—8.
24. Cf. Auerbach, *Mimesis*, pp. 398—9.
25. Quoted in L. Nochlin, *Realism* (1971) pp. 23, 41.
26. Ibid., p. 34.
27. The meaning of realism in art and literature as a distinctive approach only crystallised during the 1850s especially with the publication in 1857 of Champfleury's essays *Le Réalisme* and the review *Réalisme* (1856—7). Realism was defined as the truthful representation of the objective, contemporary world involving meticulous observation and careful analysis. Champfleury, a minor novelist, argued that the essence of realism was 'sincerity in art'. Linda Nochlin, in her admirable survey of realism in art, remarks that by the middle of the nineteenth century 'sincerity became a Realist battle-cry.' (*Realism*, p. 36.)
28. In *Documents of Modern Literary Realism*, ed. G. Becker (Princeton, N. J., 1963) pp. 245—6, 442.
29. Quoted in F. M. Borras, *Maxim Gorky* (Oxford, 1967) p. 109.
30. M. Gorky, *Mother* (New York, 1966) p. 351.
31. M. Mihajlov, *Russian Themes* (1968) p. 264
32. Quoted in J. West, *Russian Symbolism* (1970) p. 154.
33. Ibid., p. 114.
34. Quoted in Borras, *Maxim Gorky*, p. 48.
35. West, *Russian Symbolism*, pp. 179—80.
36. F. D. Reeve, *The Russian Novel* (1967) p. 341; M. Slonim, *From Chekhov to the Revolution* (New York, 1962) p. 192.
37. A. Bely, *Petersburg* (1960).

38. B. Brecht, 'Against Georg Lukács', *New Left Review*, 84 (1974) pp. 50—3. Cf. W. Benjamin, 'The Author as Producer', *New Left Review*, 62 (1970). See also A. Swingewood, 'Marxism and Literary Theory', *Literature and History* (Oct 1975).

CHAPTER 4

1. V. I. Lenin, *On Literature and Art* (Moscow, 1970) p. 250; S. Fitzpatrick, *The Commissariat of Enlightenment: Soviet Organisation of Education and the Arts under Lunacharsky* (Cambridge, 1970) p. 126.
2. G. Lukács, *The Meaning of Contemporary Realism* (1963) pp. 33—4; *Studies in European Realism*, pp. 168—70.
3. G. Plekhanov, *Art and Social Life*, pp. 180—95.
4. The film director, Sergei Yetkevitch, 'Teenage Artists of the Revolution', in *Cinema in Revolution* (1973) pp. 13—14.
5. Quoted in J. Ruhle, *Literature and Revolution* (1969) p. 6.
6. These quotes can be found in a recently published collection of articles, *Socialist Realism in Literature and Art* (Moscow, 1971) pp. 41—7, 153—5.
7. R. W. Mathewson, *The Positive Hero in Russian Literature* (New York, 1958) p. 202.
8. Lenin, *On Literature and Art*. For a different view see C. V. James, *Soviet Russian Realism* (1973).
9. R. A. Maguire, *Red Virgin Soil: Soviet Literature in the 1920s* (Princeton, N. J., 1968) pp. 8, 15—16, 444.
10. Quoted in James, *Soviet Russian Realism*, p. 52.
11. Lenin, *On Literature and Art*, pp. 28—34, 48—62.
12. Quoted in J. Freeman, *Voices of October* (New York, 1930), p. 29.
13. M. Gorky, *Untimely Thoughts* (New York, 1968) p. 85.
14. Quoted in Freeman, *Voices of October*, p. 30.
15. Quoted in H. Borland, *Soviet Literary Theory and Practice during the First Five Year Plan* (New York, 1950) pp. 2—3; Freeman, *Voices of October*, p. 33.
16. R. Fuelop-Mullar, *The Mind and Face of Bolshevism* (New York, 1961).
17. Maguire, *Red Virgin Soil*, p. 157.
18. For this astonishing document see B. D. Wolfe, *The Bridge and the Abyss: The Troubled Friendship of Maxim Gorky and Lenin* (1967) p. 144.
19. Fuelop-Mullar, *Mind and Face of Bolshevism*, pp. 55, 100, 179—84. See also B. Schwarz, *Music and Musical life in Soviet Russia, 1917—70* (1972) pp. 11—31.
20. Quoted in E. J. Brown, *The Proletarian Episode in Russian Literature* (New York, 1953) p. 14.
21. Ibid., p. 15.
22. Freeman, *Voices of October*, p. 45.
23. Lenin, pp. 46, 141, 155.
24. Fitzpatrick, *Commissariat of Enlightenment*, p. 101.
25. Lenin, *On Literature and Art*, p. 178. Similar remarks can be found in Lenin's interpretation of a book published in 1921 by A. Averchenko,

a White émigré, *Twelve Knives in the Revolution's Back*. Lenin argued that irrespective of Averchenko's anti-Bolshevik ideology, 'some of the stories deserve reprinting . . . Ability has to be supported.' Objective truth, Lenin suggested, emerges in spite of the author's hatred of Communism.

26. L. Trotsky, *The New Course* (Ann Arbor, 1965) pp. 15, 21–2, 45–53.
27. Trotsky, *On Art and Literature*, pp. 79–80.
28. Trotsky, *Literature and Revolution*, p. 14.
29. Quoted in Brown, *Proletarian Episode*, p. 23.
30. Trotsky, *On Art and Literature*, pp. 76–7. The reference to subconscious processes, which probably springs from Trotsky's admiration for Freud, is echoed in Voronsky's writings also and clearly posed a threat to the Proletkult and later the Stalinist ideal of a one-dimensional, party-minded, future-oriented literature. For the unconscious must defy even totalitarian organisation.
31. Maguire, *Red Virgin Soil*, pp. 161–3.
32. Quoted in ibid., p. 230.
33. Freeman, p. 43.
34. Ibid., *Voices of October*, p. 45.
35. Maguire, *Red Virgin Soil*, pp. 189–91.
36. Ibid., p. 218.
37. Ibid., p. 80.
38. Brown, *Proletarian Episode*, p. 39.
39. Ibid., p. 40. Cf. James, *Soviet Russian Realism*, pp. 64–5.
40. Maguire, *Red Virgin Soil*, p. 175.
41. These two quotes from Brown, *Proletarian Episode*, pp. 88, 91.
42. Borland, *Soviet Literary Theory*, p. 23.
43. Ibid., p. 60.
44. Ibid., p. 14.
45. Ibid., p. 139.
46. Ibid., p. 123.
47. Brown, *Proletarian Episode*, p. 154.
48. Quoted in M. Hayward and L. Labedz (eds), *Literature and Revolution in Soviet Russia 1917–62* (1963) pp. 56–7.
49. Brown, *Proletarian Episode*, p. 201.
50. Borland, *Soviet Literary Theory*, pp. 124–5.
51. Brown, *Proletarian Episode*, p. 202; Borland, *Soviet Literary Theory*, ch. 5.
52. Brown, *Proletarian Episode*, pp. 213–14.
53. K. Loks, a Marxist critic writing in 1923. Quoted by R. Maguire, 'Literary Conflicts in the 1920s', in *Survey* (winter 1972) p. 107.
54. K. Fedin, *Cities and Years* (New York, 1962); L. Leonov, *The Thief* (New York, 1931); Y. Olesha, *Envy*, in *The Wayward Comrade and the Commissars* (New York, 1962).
55. M. Parkhomenko and A. Myasnikov (eds), *Socialist Realism in Art and Literature*, pp. 41–52. See also B. Thomson, *The Premature Revolution, Russian Literature and Society, 1917–1946* (1972) pp. 186–205.

56. Parkhomenko and Myasnikov (eds), *Socialist Realism*, pp. 55—7.
57. N. Bukharin, 'Poetry, Poetics and the Problem of Poetry in the U.S.S.R.', in H. G. Scott (ed.), *Problems of Soviet Literature* (1935) especially pp. 199—210.
58. Scott, *Problems of Soviet Literature.*
59. Brown, *Proletarian Episode*, p. 226.

Part Two, Introduction
  1. G. Flaubert, *Sentimental Education*, trans. R. Baldick (1964) pp. 293, 240.
  2. K. Mochulsky, *Dostoevsky* (Princeton, N. J., 1967) pp. 115—29.
  3. Flaubert, *Sentimental Education*, p. 365.
  4. I. Howe, *Politics and the Novel,* (New York, 1957).
  5. I. Turgenev, *Fathers and Sons* trans. H. Stevens (New York, 1960) p. 239.
  6. N. G. Chernyshevsky, *What is to be Done*, trans. by B. R. Tucker (New York, 1961). Cf. R. W. Mathewson, *The Positive Hero in Russian Literature* (New York, 1958) ch. 5.
  7. I. Turgenev, *Virgin Soil*, trans. R. S. Townsend. (1972) p. 236.
  8. F. M. Dostoevsky, *The Devils*, trans. D. Magarshack (1953) p. 421.
  9. Ibid., p. 525.
 10. Cf. L. Trilling, 'The Princess Casamassima', in *The Liberal Imagination* (1955), pp. 61—74.

CHAPTER 5
  1. For references and further discussion, see my *Marx and Modern Social Theory* (1975) ch. 7.
  2. G. Orwell, 'George Gissing', *Collected Essays, Journalism and Letters* (1968) IV, pp. 485—93.
  3. Quoted in J. Korg, *George Gissing* (1965) p. 65.
  4. G. Gissing, *The Nether World* (1889) pp. 129—30, 274, 164—5, 74.
  5. G. Gissing, *Workers in the Dawn* (1880) III, pp. 250—1.
  6. Ibid., I, pp. 324—6.
  7. Gissing, *The Nether World*, pp. 57—8.
  8. G. Gissing, *Demos: A Story of English Socialism* (1892) pp. 138, 412—13, 453.
  9. Ibid., p. 405.
 10. J. Goode, 'George Gissing's *The Nether World*', in Howard, Lucas and Goode (eds), *Tradition and Tolerance in Nineteenth-Century Fiction* (1968) p. 240.
 11. K. Marx, *Capital* I, pp. 737, 299.
 12. Cited in J. Baines, *Joseph Conrad: A Critical Biography* (1971) p. 242.
 13. Cited in A. Fleischman, *Conrad's Politics* (Baltimore, 1967) p. 23.
 14. J. Conrad, *The Secret Agent* (1963).
 15. J. Conrad, 'Autocracy and War', in *Notes on Life and Letters* (1921) pp. 106—7.
 16. J. Conrad, *Nostromo* (1963) pp. 81, 101, 128.
 17. In his penetrating essay on Conrad, Irving Howe has drawn attention

to the similarities between Trotsky's theory oof permanent revolution and the political history of Costaguana: for Trotsky, undeveloped societies, dominated by foreign capital, can achieve democracy only by telescoping the bourgeois and proletarian revolutions. *Politics and the Novel*, pp. 101–2.

18. Quoted in Baines, *Joseph Conrad*, p. 243. Cunninghame Graham's relationship with Conrad is explored with great detail in both Fleischmann and Baines. In my view Fleishmann exaggerates Graham's influence on Conrad's changing political attitudes.

19. Conrad, *The Secret Agent*, pp. 43–4, 72–3, 83, 249. Similar sentiments inform his short story, 'An Anarchist' (1908).

20. Quoted in Baines, *Joseph Conrad*, p. 401. Cf. Ian Watt (ed.), *The Secret Agent: A Casebook* (1973) pp. 230–49.

21. *The Secret Agent*, pp. 62–3.

22. J. Conrad, *Under Western Eyes* (1964) pp. 140, 182.

23. Ibid., pp. 117–18. Cf. Irving Howe's comments on this passage, *Politics and the Novel* pp. 89–90. For a different view see A. Guerard, *Conrad the Novelist* (Cambridge, Mass., 1958) p. 246; D. Daiches, *The Novel and the Modern World* (Chicago, 1965) pp. 57–62; F. R. Leavis, *The Great Tradition* (1962) pp. 241–4.

24. Conrad, *Nostromo*, p. 429.

CHAPTER 6

1. H. G. Wells, *The Sleeper Awakes* (1968) pp. 71, 145–6 especially. M. Hillegras, *The Future as Nightmare* (New York, 1967) has attempted to show that virtually every feature of post-Wellsian utopias (Zamyatin, Huxley, Orwell) — topography, science, and plot derive from Wells.

2. G. Orwell, *Collected Essays, Journalism and Letters* (1970) vol. 2, pp. 45–9, 172; vol. 4, pp. 41–7

3. Jack London, *The Iron Heel* (1945). Everhard forms 'fighting groups' — terrorists which the novel tends to glorify — to maintain the struggle, an action which is inconsistent with London's (and Everhard's) avowed Marxism. London's sympathy with the Russian Social Revolutionary Party, who advocated the use of terrorism to achieve political ends, is doubtless the explanation for this apparent contradiction within the novel.

4. See on this P. Gay, *Edward Bernstein and the Dilemma of Democratic Socialism* (New York, 1952).

5. London, *The Iron Heel*, pp. 187–8.

6. Ibid., pp. 112–13.

7. Trotsky, *On Literature and Art*, pp. 223–4.

8. R. Dahrendorf, 'Out of Utopia: Toward a Re-Orientation of Sociological Analysis', *American Journal of Sociology* (Sep 1958).

9. Jack London, *Revolution and Other Essays* (1910). Most of these essays were written in the years 1904–7 when London's involvement in the American Socialist movement was at its height.

10. Quoted in P. Foner, *Jack London — American Rebel* (New York, 1947) p. 96.

11. G. Woodcock, 'Utopias in Negative', *Sewanee Review*, vol. 64 (1956).
12. London, *Revolution and Other Essays*, chs 20—2.
13. Ibid., pp. 215—16.
14. Quoted in A. M. Shane, *The Life and Works of Evgenie Zamyatin* (New York, 1968) p. 145.
15. Ibid., p. 19.
16. E. Zamyatin, *A Soviet Heretic: Essays by Evgenie Zamyatin*, trans. and ed. Mirra Ginsburg (New York, 1970) pp. 50—1.
17. Shane, *Evgenie Zamyatin*, p. 40.
18. The complete text of Zamyatin's letter is in Zamyatin, *A Soviet Heretic*.
19. 'Literature, Revolution and Entropy', in Zamyatin, *A Soviet Heretic*.
20. Quoted in Shane, *Evgenie Zamyatin*, p. 48.
21. Zamyatin, *A Soviet Heretic*, pp. 34—50.
22. Shane, *Evgenie Zamyatin*, pp. 27, 56—8.
23. Thomson, *Premature Revolution*, p. 18; Orwell, *Collected Essays*, vol. 4, p. 99.
24. E. Zamyatin, *The Dragon and Other Stories* (New York, 1966).
25. E. Zamyatin, *We* (1972) p. 37. All further references are to this edition and are indicated by parentheses in the text.
26. See for example, R. L. Jackson, *The Underground Man in Russian Literature* (The Hague, 1958) pp. 151—4.
27. For example, P. Parrinder, 'Imagining the Future: Zamyatin and Wells', *Science Fiction Studies*, vol. 1, no. 1 (1973). In the twenties Stalinist critics were quick to point out the superficial similarities of the two theories.
28. On this point see R. Russell, 'Literature and Revolution in Zamyatin's *My*', *Slavonic and East European Review* (Jan 1973).
29. E. Zamyatin's 'Herbert Wells', in *A Soviet Heretic*. He also admired Wells politically, describing him as a humanist socialist whose 'banner is not covered with blood'.
30. K. Marx, *Grundrisse*, ed. D. McLellan (1973) p. 166.

CHAPTER 7

The first part of this chapter has drawn on R. V. Daniels, *The Conscience of the Revolution* (New York, 1960) and E. H. Carr, *A History of Soviet Russia*, vols 2—6 (1950—64).

1. These quotations are taken from D. Caute, *The Fellow Travellers* (1973) pp. 181, 174, 121—4, 166. See also I. Deutscher, *The Prophet Armed: Trotsky 1929—40* (Oxford, 1963) pp. 367—70.
2. Quoted in J. Ruhle, *Literature and Revolution* (1969) p. 152.
3. Quoted in S. F. Cohen, *Bukharin and the Bolshevik Revolution* (1974) p. 65. Cf. Trotsky, *History of the Russian Revolution* (Ann Arbor, 1960) III, pp. 378—418.
4. Quoted in M. Lewin, *Lenin's Last Struggle* (1969) p. 4.
5. Alexandra Kollantai, 'The Workers Opposition', Solidarity pamphlet no. 7 (n.d.).
6. V. I. Lenin, 'On Cooperatives'; 'How We Should Reorganize the Workers' and Peasants' Inspection'; 'Better Fewer, But Better' (1923).
7. Daniels, *Conscience of the Revolution*, pp. 148—9.

8. L. Trotsky, *Writings, 1938–9* (New York, 1969) pp. 130–1.
9. Bukharin, quoted in Cohen, *Bukharin*, p. 187.
10. Ibid., p. 286.
11. Ibid., pp. 310–15.
12. Quoted in R. Conquest, *The Great Terror* (1968) p. 134.
13. Ibid., pp. 497–8, 515, 526, 271–2; Joseph Berger, *Shipwreck of a Generation* (1971) p. 23.
14. L. Trotsky, *Writings, 1937–8* (New York, 1969) p. 141.
15. Deutscher, *The Prophet Armed*, pp. 411–19.
16. V. Serge, *Memoirs of a Revolutionary* (Oxford, 1963) pp. xv–xvi.
17. L. Trotsky, *The Revolution Betrayed* (1967) pp. 105, 87–9; cf. Berger, *Shipwreck of a Generation*, pp. 80–1, 90.
18. Quoted in I. Deutscher, *The Prophet Unarmed: Trotsky 1921–9* (Oxford, 1959) p. 139.
19. L. Trotsky, *Writings 1932–3* (New York, 1972) p. 243.
20. A. Koestler, *The Invisible Writing* (1954) ch. IX.
21. Serge, *Memoirs of a Revolutionary*, p. 364.
22. Ibid., p. 261.
23. V. Serge, *The Case of Comrade Tulayev* (1968) pp. 85, 88, 92–4.
24. Ibid., p. 217.
25. Ibid., p. 288.
26. Ibid., p. 243.
27. Serge, *Memoirs of a Revolutionary*, pp. 348–50, 377–9.
28. Ibid., p. 265. Cf. R. Greeman, 'Victor Serge and Revolution', *Tri-Quarterly*, no. 8. (1967) and 'Literary and Revolutionary Realism in Victor Serge', in *Literature and Revolution*, ed. J. Ehrmann (Boston, 1970).
29. A. Koestler, *Darkness at Noon* (1970) pp. 40–1. After he had left the Party Koestler wrote, 'Both morally and logically the Party was infallible: morally because its aims were right, that is, in accord with the Dialectic of History, and these aims justified all means; logically because the Party was the vanguard of the proletariat, and the proletariat the embodiment of the active principle in History.' R. Crossman (ed.), *The God that Failed* (1950) p. 43.
30. Koestler, *Darkness at Noon*, p. 52.
31. Ibid., p. 82.
32. Ibid., p. 137.
33. B. Nicolaevsky, *Power and the Soviet Elite* (1965) p. 25.
34. Conquest, *The Great Terror*, p. 190. For Koestler's paraphrase, see *Darkness at Noon*, pp. 199–200.
35. *Darkness at Noon*, p. 153.
36. Conquest, *The Great Terror*, p. 528.
37. The text was first made public in 1961 by Bukharin's widow and is reprinted in full in R. Medvedev, *Let History Judge* (1972) pp. 183–4. See also Cohen, *Bukharin*, pp. 370–1.

CHAPTER 8

1. I. Ehrenburg, *Men, Years – Life*, vol. 6, p. 43; Ruhle, *Literature and Revolution*, p. 100.

2. Hugh McLean, 'How Writers Rise from the Dead', *Problems of Communism* (Mar—Apr 1970). Some writers have never resurfaced (Zamyatin, Trotsky, Bukharin) since their work poses too great a threat to the Stalinist system.

3. See *Samizdat: Voices of the Soviet Opposition*, ed. G. Saunders, (New York, 1974).

4. A. Amalrik, *Will the Soviet Union Survive until 1984* (1970) pp. 7—13. General Pyotr Grogorenko had been sacked from his post at the Frunze Military Academy in 1961 for criticising the privileges of Party leaders and discrimination against Jews in the Soviet Army. Since then he has defended the rights of the Crimean Tartars, spoken out against the trial of Daniel and Sinyavsky and opposed the 1968 Russian invasion of Czechoslovakia. Like many other oppositionists he was sent to the Serbsky Institute of Psychiatry and diagnosed as insane. He was released in 1974. In 1969 Yakir addressed an open letter to the Party journal, *Kommunist*, criticising Stalin's military policy in the Second World War, the purges which eliminated 80 per cent of the top officers, technicians and scholars, and concluding that 'Stalin was the greatest criminal' the Soviet Union has ever known. He demanded a posthumous trial. During the 1960s Yakir and Grigorenko were devoted communists and their criticisms of the Soviet bureaucracy contrast sharply with the liberal views expressed by Andrey Sakharov whose *Progress, Co-existence and Intellectual Freedom* (1969) argues that 'both capitalism and socialism are capable of long-term development, borrowing positive elements from each other, and actually coming closer to each other in a number of essential aspects.' (p. 67) Neither the Yakir letter not the Sakharov memorandum have been published in the Soviet Union.

5. Both R. Medvedev, *Let History Judge* and Z. Medvedev, *The Rise and Fall of T. D. Lysenko* (New York, 1968) were inspired by Khrushchev's de-Stalinisation policies; the archives were opened for the first time since Stalin's assumption of power although of course complete access to materials never applied. Like Solzhenitsyn the authors hoped their work would be published. See also R. Medvedev, *De la Démocratie Socialiste* (Paris, 1972) esp. pp. 320—7.

6. R. Medvedev, *Let History Judge*, p. 541.

7. Ehrenburg, *Men, Years — Life*, vol. 4, pp. 302ff; vol. 6, pp. 306—7. Ehrenburg quotes Pasternak's response to the purges — 'If only someone would tell Stalin about it', and Meyerhold — 'They conceal it from Stalin' (vol. 4, pp. 196—7) and writes that he knew differently. He realised that the trial and death of Bukharin was a frame-up and that the orders must have come from Stalin, but argues that criticism must have weakened the Soviet Union. Silence therefore became a necessary 'curse'.

8. Z. Medvedev, *Ten Years After 'One Day in the Life of Ivan Denisovich'* (1973); P. Benno, 'The Political Aspect', in M. Hayward and B. Crowley (eds), *Soviet Literature in the Sixties* (1965). See also A. Rothberg, *The Heirs of Stalin: Dissidence and the Soviet Regime, 1953—1970* (New York, 1972).

9. R. Rubin, 'Highlights of the 1962—1963 Thaw', in Hayward and Crowley (eds), *Soviet Literature*.

10. Rothberg, *Heirs of Stalin*, p. 62. Cf. J. Berger, *Art and Revolution: Ernst Neizvestny and the Role of the Artist in the U.S.S.R.* (1969) pp. 80—6.

11. See Rothberg, *Heirs of Stalin*, ch. 2; P. Johnson (ed.), *Khrushchev and The Arts* (M.I.T. Press, 1965).

12. Dudintsev's novel, while critical of the Soviet bureaucracy, is seriously flawed by the spuriously happy ending which takes place in 1951 when Stalin was still alive. The same criticism applies to Ehrenburg's sequel to *The Thaw, The Spring*, which in many important respects diluted the criticisms made in the first novel. In both writers the tragic vision is clearly absent.

13. A. Werth, *Russia: Hopes and Fears* (1969) p. 290.

14. M. Hayward, 'Conflict and Change in Soviet Literature' in M. Hayward and L. Labedz (eds), *Literature and Revolution in Soviet Russia* (Oxford, 1963) pp. 214—17.

15. Rothberg, *Heirs of Stalin*, p. 399.

16. For example Yuri Bondarev's *Silence*, first published in *Novy Mir* in 1962, which dealt with the aftermath of the Second World War, the corruption and illegalities practised against innocent Communists. The period 1946—50 is portrayed as an era of arbitrary rule, of lawlessness. After the publication of Solzhenitsyn's *One Day* and Bondarev's novel, publishing houses were flooded with manuscripts dealing with previously forbidden themes. Khrushchev warned indeed that such 'dangerous themes' would have to be stopped.

17. Quoted in Werth, *Russia*, pp. 305—6.

18. Rothberg, *Heirs of Stalin*, pp. 144—7, 161—2, 268—75.

19. The documents of the trial have been translated and edited by L. Labedz and M. Hayward, *On Trial* (1968). Quotes from pp. 192, 181, 266. Sinyavsky left Russia in 1973 and is now living in France. Daniel has remained in the Soviet Union.

20. There can be no doubt that the oppositional intelligentsia have been increasingly harried and persecuted by the KGB since 1966 in a concerted effort to eliminate dissidence. The political use of psychiatry, defining dissidence as 'schizophrenia', is now an acceptable substitute for prison. See R. and Z. Medvedev, *A Question of Madness* (1971).

21. Quoted in D. Burg and G. Feiffer, *Solzhenitsyn* (1972) p. 290.

22. Rubin, 'Highlights of the . . . Thaw', pp. 94—5.

23. L. Labedz (ed.), *Solzhenitsyn, A Documentary Record* (1970) pp. 68—9.

24. Marx and Engels, *On Art and Literature*, p. 55.

25. Labedz, (ed.), *Solzhenitsyn*, pp. 133—41. See also pp. 92—3, 156. Zhores Medvedev, *Ten Years After 'One Day in the Life of Ivan Denisovich'*, writes that the Ryazan Regional Party committee had been carefully rehearsed before the expulsion meeting to make certain that the 'right' decision was taken.

26. Quoted in Rothberg, *Heirs of Stalin*, p. 358.

27. *The Gulag Archipelago* (1974) p. 213. See also his Nobel Prize Speech

and the short prose poem, 'The Easter Procession', which shows
Solzhenitsyn's deep belief in the Christian religion.

28. Labedz and Hayward (eds), *On Trial*, p. 205.
29. L. Feuer, 'The Intelligentsia in Opposition', *Problems of Communism*
    (Jan/Feb 1970) pp. 10—11; E. Fischer, *Art against Ideology* (1969)
    p. 30.
30. G. Lukács, *Solzhenitsyn* (1970) p. 15.
31. Ibid., pp. 33, 13.
32. Ibid., pp. 61, 86.
33. Marx and Engels, *On Art and Literature*, pp. 41—9.
34. Trotsky, *Literature and Revolution*, pp. 240—4.
35. Mathewson, *The Positive Hero*, pp. 91—101, 231.
36. Quoted in ibid., pp. 333—4.
37. A. Sinyavsky, *On Socialist Realism* (New York, 1965) p. 43.
38. L. Chukovskaya, *Going Under* (1972) pp. 38, 129—30, 134.
39. L. Chukovskaya, *The Deserted House* (1967).
40. Labedz and Hayward (eds), *On Trial*, p. 24.
41. A. Sinyavsky, *The Trial Begins* (London, 1960) p. 123.
42. N. Mandelstam, *Hope Abandoned* (1974) p. 278.
43. Goldmann, *The Hidden God*, p. 320.
44. Ibid., p. 57.

CHAPTER 9

1. The letter was published in the *Sunday Telegraph*, 9 April 1972.
2. A. Solzhenitsyn, 'Matryona's House' in *Stories and Prose Poems*
   (1971) p. 54.
3. Nobel Prize Speech, *Index* (London, 1972).
4. E. Wilson, *A Window on Russia* (1973) pp. 276—7.
5. A. Solzhenitsyn, *One Day in the Life of Ivan Denisovich* (1963) p. 43.
6. A. Marchenko, *My Testimony* (1969) p. 368.
7. *One Day*, pp. 161—2, 178, 183.
8. G. Lukács, *Solzhenitsyn* (1971) p. 15.
9. *One Day*, p. 106.
10. Ibid., p. 123.
11. L. Labedz (ed.), *Solzhenitsyn: A Documentary Record* (1970) p. 7.
12. *One Day*, pp. 94—5, 131.
13. A. Solzhenitsyn, *The First Circle*, trans. Michael Guybon (1970). All
    further references are to this edition and are indicated in the text by
    parentheses.
14. Contemporary history has always been a dangerous practice even for
    the most ardent Stalinist historian: unpersons and unevents dominate
    the field, enemies are suddenly friend, friends become enemies. Roy
    Medvedev's *Let History Judge* (1972) is the first serious attempt by a
    Soviet scholar to go beyond the crude falsifications of Stalinist
    historiography.
15. During the Stalin era many gifted writers quite consciously distorted
    their work, to harmonise it with the current orthodoxy. Alexander
    Fadayev was one such writer. When challenged by Ehrenburg about
    the rewriting of his Second World War novel *The Young Guard* he

replied, 'Of course, even if I do succeed, the novel won't be the
same. . . . Times are hard and Stalin knows better than you or I.'
Ehrenburg, *Men, Years — Life*, vol. 6, p. 160. On hearing Khrushchev's
denunciation of Stalin at the twentieth Party congress he went home
and shot himself.

16. Cf. H. Swayze, *Political Control of Literature in the U.S.S.R.,
1946–59* (New York, 1962).

17. Trotsky frequently used the analogy of the French counter-revolution
and fall of Robespierre on 9th Thermidor of Year II (27 July 1794,
hence the Thermidorians) with the Stalinist assumption of power.
When he makes this comment Makarygin also notes that 'We've heard
that kind of nonsense long ago: only those who did the talking are
dead.' *The First Circle*, p. 449.

18. N. Mandelstam, *Hope Abandoned* (1974) p. 409. See also the
evidence of the bureaucratic break-up in 1970 of the editorial board
of *Novy Mir* in Medvedev, *Ten Years After 'Ivan Denisovich'*
pp. 119–27.

19. See Weber's discussion of bureaucracy in *From Max Weber*, ed. Gerth
and Mills (1961) pp. 196–244.

20. A biography of Stalin had been published in the 1940s and must
remain as one of the most astonishing documents in a century
dominated by the deliberate and systematic distortion of truth.
Described variously as a 'sage' and 'genius', a 'lucid and profound'
thinker, 'an incomparable master' of Marxism, the book ends with
Stalin as God: 'His advice is a guide to action in all fields of Socialist
construction. His work is extraordinary for its variety; his energy truly
amazing. The range of questions which engage his attention is
immense, embracing the most complex problems of Marxist-Leninist
theory and school textbooks; problems of Soviet foreign policy and
the municipal affairs of the proletarian capital; the development of
the Great Northern Sea Route and the reclamation of the Colchian
marshes; the advancement of Soviet literature and art and the editing
of the model rules for collective farms; and, lastly, the solution of
most intricate problems in the theory and practice of war.' *Joseph
Stalin, A Short Biography* (Moscow, 1949) pp. 202–3. Earlier the
authors had written that 'Stalin never allowed his work to be marred
by the slightest hint of vanity, conceit or self-adulation' (p. 89).

21. A. Solzhenitsyn, *Cancer Ward* (1971) pp. 162, 207. All further
references are to this edition and are indicated in the text by
parentheses.

22. *The First Circle*, ch. 53.

23. Goldmann, *The Hidden God*, p. 34.

24. R. Medvedev, 'On Gulag Archipelago', *New Left Review*, no. 85
(1974).

Conclusion

1. These formulations are too schematic: in reality Dickens, Flaubert,
and Turgenev for example provide examples of both open and closed
forms but the *tendency* is towards one type or another. Cf.

A. Friedman, *The Turn of the Novel* (New York, 1970) pp. 15—37
and from a different point of view, F. Kermode, *The Sense of an
Ending* (1968).

2. P. Nizan, *Antoine Bloyé* (1973) pp. 139, 203.
3. Ibid., p. 57.
4. Ibid., p. 167.

Index